**FREE PRESS
PAPERBACKS**

Other Books by William Damon

Some Do Care: Contemporary Lives of Moral Commitment
(with Anne Colby)

The Moral Child

Self-Understanding in Childhood and Adolescence
(with Daniel Hart)

Child Development Today and Tomorrow

Social and Personality Development:
Infancy through Adolescence

Social and Personality Development:
Essays on the Growth of the Child

The Social World of the Child

Greater Expectations

Overcoming the Culture of Indulgence in Our Homes and Schools

William Damon

FREE PRESS PAPERBACKS

New York   London   Toronto   Sydney   Singapore

FREE PRESS PAPERBACKS
A Division of Simon & Schuster Inc.
1230 Avenue of the Americas
New York, NY 10020

First Free Press Paperbacks Edition 1996

FREE PRESS PAPERBACKS and colophon are trademarks
of Simon & Schuster Inc.

Manufactured in the United States of America

10 9 8 7 6 5 4 3 2

Library of Congress Cataloging-in-Publication Data

Damon, William
   Greater expectations: overcoming the culture of indulgence in our homes
and schools / William Damon.—1st Free Press Paperbacks ed.
     p.   cm.—(A Free Press Paperbacks book)
   Originally published: New York: Free Press © 1995
   Includes bibliographical references and index.
   ISBN 0-684-82505-8
   1. Child rearing—Moral and ethical aspects. 2. Moral development. 3. Moral education.
   I. Title.
HQ769.D225   1995
649'.7—dc20
                                                      94–31735
                                                       CIP

For Anne

They are hopeful. . . Their lives are filled with expectation. . . They are more brave than persons of other ages. . . They are high-minded. . . And they choose to do what is noble rather than what is expedient. . .

Such, then is the character of the young.

—Aristotle

Life is a daring adventure or it is nothing.

—Helen Keller

Contents

Preface

In my professional life, my primary goal has been to understand children's development from the dispassionate viewpoint of a scientist. Although I respect any effort to create good social policy for youth, I have been uncomfortable with the strident advocacy and facile ideological positioning of recent times. I have seen too many profound questions of child development reduced to gibberish by the distortions of political debate. As world history has taught us over and over again, politics and science are not a good mix. When ideological bias takes over, truth generally suffers.

Yet increasingly while observing today's young people, I find myself unable to maintain a dispassionate attitude. My concerns can no longer be contained within the boundaries of scientific objectivity, however highly I esteem such a perspective. I cannot watch with objective detachment while our society steadily becomes a less wholesome climate for raising children.

For some time now I have tried to keep my concerns confined to a quiet level of moderation. It has disturbed me whenever I have discerned an apocalyptic tone creeping into my talks and writings about today's youth. The tone rubs against the grain of how I think and how I work, and I have resisted it. But lately, reluctantly, I have begun to believe that our times demand it.

At this very moment, there is a battle for the future of our society. On one side of the battle, many dedicated people have recognized that there is a serious problem with youth today, and they have mobilized themselves to do something about it. Volunteers from all sectors of society, community leaders, philanthropists, many of our great corporations, are committing their time and resources to young people who are plainly in trouble. At the same time, on the other side, the problems are rapidly getting worse. Every day brings grimmer tidings about violence, criminality, discouragement, and self-destructiveness among today's young people. Both the intensity and the scope of these afflictions are escalating rapidly. Even the gravest incidents now penetrate deep into sectors of society that were once considered invincible in their stability.

The stakes in the battle are the lives and future hopes of our young. It is a battle between the extraordinary efforts that we must launch to save our young and the deteriorating cultural circumstances that continue to place them in ever greater jeopardy. My fear is that, unless we change our direction, the battle will be lost. Valiant though our best efforts may be, they will prove to be inadequate until we attack the source of our cultural deterioration. Otherwise, to switch metaphors, we shall never do more than put some brave fingers into a crumbling dike.

Denying the problem will only contribute to the decline. In some academic and professional circles, it has become fashionable to romanticize the lives of children who are living in the most desperate circumstances. The assumption is that to paint a bleaker picture would be to show disrespect for them and their families. This sort of response makes me so incredulous that I stand in danger of losing my last remaining bit of moderation on the matter. We cannot blind ourselves to the truth out of the fear that some may find it offensive; and it is especially reprehensible to do so when the stakes are so high. Of course one can find children who will do fine in virtually any social environment. In every corner of our society, there are young people who are an inspiration to be around. But this does not mean that all is generally well with youth today. Too many children—the affluent and the poor alike—are drifting through their childhood years without finding the skills, virtues, or sense of purpose that they will need to sustain a fruitful life.

Social commentators have argued about where we may look for the sources of present-day youth problems. Some have placed the source in economic troubles; others have placed it in historical events; and still others have placed the source in demographic shifts and other population changes. All of these forces no doubt have played their parts. Yet I keep returning to the most obvious source of all: the manner in which we raise our young. In all the places that children are raised—the family, the school, the community—one conspicuous change has occurred within the lifetime of everyone reading this book: All the commonly accepted standards for young people's skills and behavior have fallen drastically. Less is expected of the young, and in turn less is received. Either as a cause or as a result, instruction, discipline, the very fostering of competence and character in the young are fast becoming lost arts. Every social analysis that I have seen pales in the light of this one disquieting cultural fact.

My first attempt to write for the public was *The Moral Child*, a fairly straightforward effort to translate scientific findings on children's moral development into a coherent statement that parents, teachers, and concerned citizens might find useful. The attention that the book generated brought me many invitations to speak before parent groups, church groups, teachers, and other people who are in frequent contact with children. I came away from those talks learning much. Most strikingly, I came to appreciate the full seriousness of the youth crisis that has been building for at least the past few decades.

Naturally in my own studies I had seen plenty of children who were having trouble; and my work in recent years had taken me into neighborhoods where "disadvantage" is a euphemism for what young people are up against. But what I had not fully realized was the extent to which a very broad spectrum of our population has sensed that something has gone wrong in the passing of essential standards between the generations. In the very best of conditions, parents are uneasy and vaguely frustrated. In the more severe conditions—and these may be found among pockets of affluence as well as poverty—parents are afraid, and their fear has spread throughout their communities.

One of my points in this book is that the youth crisis that we face in our society is a general one. It is not confined to a particular class, ethnic group, gender, or any other social grouping. I am well aware that this claim runs counter to theories that propose economic causes for every social problem. Yet the affliction that I have observed threatens children of the wealthy as well as children of the poor. It is true, of course, that the danger wears many faces; and in critical ways the faces that it wears in our poorer communities are more menacing. But I am convinced that, at its core, the predicament that has beset today's youth is one problem and not several. Or, a bit more precisely, it is one interconnected *web* of problems that define a common pattern. A term that I use to capture the interconnected web is "demoralization." To use the term for this purpose, I draw on both of the word's two related meanings: a loss of moral standards and a debilitating lack of spirit.

The notion of demoralization places the source of our predicament squarely in that nebulous domain called "culture." Critics of modern culture have shown how the rise of unbridled individualism and egoism have undermined our long-standing sense of moral commitment. Although I indeed do see this as part of the problem, my focus in the present book is not on the misplaced cultural values themselves, nor on their overall societal effects. There has been enough written on those scores already. Rather, my focus in this book is on a specific set of misconceptions about children and the damaging childrearing practices that result from these misconceptions.

Modern cultural sensibilities no doubt have fostered some of these misconceptions; and these same sensibilities also have sheltered the misconceptions from critical examination. In turn, the misconceptions now play a significant role in nourishing certain modern leanings, such as unabashed egoism, by ensuring their transmission across generations. Apart from their links to general cultural sensibilities, the misconceptions have an origin and a life of their own. In fact one of the many ironies that I shall be discussing is that parents who disdain egoistic values, and whose explicit goal is to raise their children with a strong sense of social responsibility, often make parenting choices that lead their children in the opposite direction from the one they intend. I have heard these parents express surprise and dismay when later they notice the presence of the unwanted cultural ethic in their own children's character.

My original working title for this book was "With best intentions," because I believe that there are no villains in this story, only many unintended casualties. The errors that trouble me are not the product of hatefulness or calculated mischief. To the contrary, most adults in our society have a genuine concern for the younger generation. But it is a concern led astray by popular misconceptions about the nature of children and their developmental needs. When led too far astray, as I have seen it on too many occasions, this concern can turn into a misguided attempt to shield children from the formative challenges of responsibility and reality. The consequences for children, for their senses of self, for their spirits of initiative, and for their moral fibre, are serious and lamentable. This is why I was tempted by the associations with my first working title: roads paved with good intentions can indeed lead to unfortunate places.

In the end, though, this seemed a bit too apocalyptic, even for my current mood. I do not believe that our society has gone to hell or that we are necessarily doomed. The battle is by no means over. For one thing, it is important to emphasize that I am referring in this book *only to trends and warning signs*. As I noted above, there still are many young people who are thriving in all respects. There still are many families that are responsive to their children's needs and that hold strong expectations for their children's intellectual and moral growth. There still are schools and teachers that function effectively. There still are communities that provide safe and nurturing environments for young people to grow up in. Many places I go, including in the less affluent areas of our society, I see children and adolescents with the high spirits and noble aspirations that always have marked youth throughout the ages.[1]

As for the others, the waste of human potential is tragic. But all is not lost, either for them or for the society. They can still learn, and so can we. We can win the battle and raise the standard once again. First we must take a keener look around, admit the problem, and recognize it for what it is. Then we must regain our true bearings and start moving again in the right direction.

This may take a something of a revolution in our thinking about young people and what is best for them. It will be a revolution that draws upon some new ideas as well as some ageless intuitions that adults traditionally have had about the younger generations. Much of the revolution will spring from common sense. In fact, so much of the revolution will spring from common sense that I also thought of this as title for the book; but it had been used before.

Acknowledgments

My first debt is to Erwin Glikes, who encouraged this project from the start and helped me find a way to examine the cultural conditions that troubled us both. His support and advice were essential to all the books that I have written for a public readership, from *The Moral Child* to *Some Do Care*. I know that I am not the only scholar/author who will miss Erwin Glikes's keen personal interest, his generous counsel, and his integrity.

Susan Arellano once again has been a splendid editor—prodding and sharp-eyed, yet temperate enough in her feedback so that I could feel my own way and, no doubt, make my own mistakes. If there are passages in the book that don't make sense, most likely this is because I resisted some of her suggestions.

Many people have contributed to the ideas that I have put forth in this book. In thanking them, I must make clear that no one except me should be held responsible for any conclusions that I have drawn. Because of my own personal feelings of concern, I have gone out on a number of limbs that even my closest friends and associates may find unstable in certain places. If they do believe so, they may well be right; but I have deemed it imperative to state my full case.

My approach to education has been shaped during the course of my long-standing working relationships with Howard Gardner and David Perkins, both of whom I continue to learn from all the time. I borrowed many of their ideas for Chapter 9. During the past four years, in an informal networking arrangement, I also have had the fortune to meet regularly with some of this country's most inspired educational researchers. Among those who have influenced my writings through their ideas and methods include Alan Collins, Margarita Azmitia, Michael Cole, Rochel Gelman, Ron Gallimore, Shirley Brice Heath, Milbrey McLaughlin, Lauren Resnick, Barbara Rogoff, and Francisco Villaurel. This networking, and my own educational research on project-based learning, has been supported by grants from the John D. and Catherine T. MacArthur Foundation. The research program has also been supported through grants from the Pew Charitable Trusts and the Spencer Foundation. Bob Schwartz from Pew was enormously helpful in getting the program off the ground, Pete Gerber has been a extraordinarily engaged and insightful program officer on the MacArthur end, and Pat Graham from Spencer has given me invaluable advice on this work as on many other matters. Thanks, too, to Kim Marshall for his support as well as for many informative and thought-provoking conversations. Again, none of these people or foundations are in any way implicated in, or responsible for, the present book's conclusions, which are solely my own responsibility.

My work on Chapter 8 was greatly aided by discussions with Ann McGillicuddy-DiLisi, as well as by some important materials that she sent me. I also have benefited many times from Diana Baumrind's views about parenting in our society. Some unpublished writings that Colwyn Trevarthen gave me, and a collection of papers that Nancy Eisenberg edited for my *New Directions for Child Development* series, helped me better understand the potential of a child's natural endowment, as I discuss in Chapter 6. In my Chapter 10 treatment of community, I draw heavily on writings by Amitai Etzioni and Ernie Cortes, as well as on conversations that I have had with them. The general framework that I present in Chapter 7 borrows from many sources, but I should mention in particular the theoretical writings of my fellow developmentalists Barbara Rogoff and James Youniss. Fritz Oser provided me with invaluable material for my sections on children's spirituality and faith.

Anne Gregory did a fine job organizing the multiple scattered references required for this book, and Pat Balsafiori has provided me with excellent secretarial support during the entire span of the project. As always, Anne Colby has supported my efforts in many ways, including the formulation of character and competence as our main focus of concern.

Part I
The Decline

1
Introduction

Imagine an account of human life in the twenty-first century. The genre is science fiction, perhaps delivered in a futuristic novel or movie. The account is set in any city or town of the populated world. The main characters are all younger than twenty. They are the children and adolescents who inhabit the streets, the homes, and the schools of this typical community of tomorrow.

A Fable of Our Near Future

The scene opens on a bleak deserted neighborhood in the heart of town. It is daytime, just after working hours, and the place has emptied out. The sense of emptiness is not a great change from earlier in the day. From nine to five, some government offices and a few small shops provide a bit of life to the area, but it is a muted, confined life that mostly takes place off the street. Most of the area's stores and the oldtime movie theaters have been boarded up for decades. The remaining businesses, there only to serve the government workers, are barricaded behind steel grates that have been adorned with rolls of barbed wire. After the working day is done, nowhere is there an open eatery, a pharmacy, or newsstand.

Soon it is clear why. Roving bands of youth begin bringing a more vivid life to the neighborhood, though it is a macabre and chilling one.

3

Some of the youths are crammed into cars that creep ominously around corners like big cats on the prowl. Others dart through the alleys or leap across the rooftops. The youngsters move in a quick, guarded pantomime, signaling each other by hand or by eye contact. Before long, taunts, gunshots, and screams punctuate the watchful silence. Then flashes of fire, smoke, the screeching of car motors and wheels, and the wail of police sirens bring the scene to a climax. Stretchers carry away three young corpses. No photographer comes to chronicle the grisly sight: such events have long since lost their news appeal. Next follows an uneasy calm. Then, before anything approaching a decent interval has passed, similar events unfold with a dreary predictability.

The scene now shifts to the outskirts of town. We are in a leafy residential area. But barricades and angry signs have taken away some of the idyllic suburban charm. The signs warn that only neighborhood residents and their announced guests are allowed access to the streets. Private patrols have established checkpoints to enforce the edict.

In any event, there is very little outdoor traffic among young folks in this part of town. Almost all the action takes place inside—if one considers TV gazing, snacking, napping, and an occasional stony-eyed pass at homework to be "action." There is a listless, isolated quality to the activity. Even the phone calls that break up the monotonous silence lack the gossipy glee that one used to associate with teenage telephoning. So lethargic are the movements of the young people that we almost wonder if the scene is being shot in slow motion. Many of these youngster have a pale, flaccid, washed-out look.

Despite the overall pall, in one of the homes a genuine drama does take place. A boy of sixteen, three days away from his next birthday, quietly slips into his father's study and turns on the home computer. With a few taps on the keyboard, he opens the data base file where his dad has catalogued the family's collection of guns. The boys studies the size, type, and location of each gun listed. After some thought, and without bothering to turn off the computer, the boy walks to the hallway, opens a cabinet, and removes a thick single-barrel shotgun. He knows that the gun has been kept loaded for the purposes of instant household protection. Leaving the cabinet door open, the boy takes the shotgun down into the basement. After a ten-minute pause in which he neither leaves a note nor makes any other significant gesture, he ends his life with a shot to his head.

At the suburban high school the following day, there is some consternation at the news of the boy's suicide, but the feelings lean more toward sorrow than surprise. Suicides occur periodically, here and in every other suburb around. In the meantime, there are other happenings at school that demand more urgent talk and vigilance. The most pressing is the epidemic of knifings that is placing both students and teachers at daily risk. The sophisticated metal screening devices at the school entrances have done little to deter students from creating knife-like weapons out of sharp objects and using them against each other and the staff. Once a problem thought to be limited to students from the "tougher" parts of town, the knifings by now have no discernible link to students' social status or group identity. The girls are now as likely to do it as the boys.

A panorama of school life reveals an atmosphere that is in all other ways consistent with the sense of dread that emanates from the frequent knifings. Graffiti have been splattered everywhere, inside as well as out, easily defeating the token, halfhearted efforts of school officials to rub them out. Shaved heads, tatoos, and gaudy jewelry ornament most of the young bodies. The students wear a motley assortment of clothes or quasi-uniforms resembling degenerate war gear. The most popular T-shirts of the day bear a pair of boldface insignia, one written on the front and one on the back: "Sick of it all," and "Nothing to lose."

We move down the corridors into the school's central offices. A counselor is calling a student's home about some apparently excused absences, only to find that the parent's letters have been forged. A young boy is in the principal's office for threatening his teacher with a gun. Three students are separated from their class after hurling racial epithets at a fourth. A girl is complaining that her locker has been broken into and all her belongings stolen. A small group of boys are huddling in a corner, shielding an exchange of money for drug packets. In the playground, two girls grab a third and punch her in the stomach for flirting with the wrong boy. Throughout the corridors and classrooms, a palpable spirit of disorderliness and disrespect reigns.

The camera moves away from the suburb, past the old business district shown before, and into a truly devastated part of town where the nonworking poor live. Here many of the children and most of the adolescents no longer may be found within the walls of any school, even at the height of day. Some have formally withdrawn, others have never enrolled, and others simply never show up. Instead, they inhabit a subterranean world of crime, illicit deals, marketing in banned substances and flesh. Some run drugs, some run guns, others traffic in their own bodies. Few have any adults in their lives who are able to function as parents or guardians. For many of these youths, the grown-ups of their world have disappeared through choice or through misfortune, swept away by drugs, by criminals, by cops, or by the health hazards of poverty. Of the grown-ups who remain, few have little use for these neighborhood kids who roam the streets looking for trouble. The exception to the grown-ups who are indifferent are the hardened adults who prey on the youths by enlisting them as foot soldiers in dangerous and exploitative assignments.

The young people in this neighborhood band together in leagues of mutual protection. These are the street gangs that provide the youngsters with a sense of collective security as well as an opportunity for voicing some youthful bravado. The sense of security is as false as the bravado. Many of the children in this neighborhood will not see twenty with life and limb intact. Many of those who do will be hauled away for long stretches in prison, where they will learn even more effective ways of wreaking havoc on society.

Our science-fiction tale could show all this by documenting the tragic loss of child after child in this devastated neighborhood. Some would lose their futures quickly, through a flash of violence, a drug overdose, a criminal bust. Others would lose their futures gradually, through a steady deadening of expectations and loss of hope.

The real shock, though, comes when the camera steps back to place this neighborhood in a whole-earth perspective. We see the metropolitan area (including the leafy suburb) that flows into the neighborhood, the country that surrounds the city, and the world that surrounds the country. It turns out that this devastated neighborhood is not merely a pocket of despair in an otherwise thriving society. In all the world, wrecked neighborhoods flow together like seas that crash against a few well-guarded, frightened islands of affluence where children lethargically spend their youth on snacks and electronic entertainment. The metropolitan areas are surrounded by rural landscapes that are barren of young people because nothing is left there to hold them. As the camera scans the world, it reveals many versions of the same scene: a homogeneous global village with neither the elevated culture nor the friendly intimacy that was associated with this phrase in more hopeful times.

Back to the Present

I am not a science-fiction author, nor do I have aspirations to create fables or yarns of any sort. Happily for the average quality of fiction writing in the year that this book will be published, I shall not continue in this mode. But if this may be a small bit of good news for our culture, it is framed by some larger news that is far more serious and that is very bad indeed. Unfortunately for our society today, we do not need a science fiction account to render the circumstances that I have portrayed. *Every condition and event from the "futuristic" fictional nightmare that I have just sketched can be found in quantity throughout the world today*. Moreover, the prevalence of such circumstances is fast increasing. In fact, all such circumstances have grown in profusion for the past fifty years or more, in a trend that only can be described as steady acceleration.

Anyone who listens to the daily news has heard about conditions and events identical to the ones that I have just invented. We may perceive such events as aberrations, isolated misfortunes either confined to special populations or caused by unusual circumstances. There still may be a sliver of truth to this comforting sense of reassurance, but it diminishes with each passing year.

The truly bad news is that, in fact, all the news about the climate and prospects for youth development in our society is bad. As I shall show below, practically all the indicators of youth health and behavior have declined year by year for well over a generation. None has improved. The litany of decline is so well known that it is losing its ability to shock. We have become accustomed not only to the dreadful indicators themselves but also to their never-ending increase. As I recount the most recent facts and figures here, I am aware that they barely pack a punch anymore. Unfortunately, I also am sure that the data will be significantly worse by the time this statement reaches press.

Let us start with youth violence. Among teenagers living in the United States, homicide rates doubled in the decade from 1970 to 1980. After that, it doubled again in the next seven years; and by 1992 it had taken only five years to double again.[1] "Today," reports the National Commission on Children, "more teenage boys in the United States die of gunshot wounds than of all natural causes combined."[2] Girls, too, are joining in the mayhem, both as perpetrators and as victims of violence. Virtually every day now brings a newsstory such as the following:

A 13-year-old girl shot a cab driver to death to avoid paying a $6 fare, the police in West Palm Beach, Florida, said. The teenager was eerily calm during questioning, Sergeant John English said. "No tears, just cold," he said. "We're talking about a coldblooded, premeditated murder committed by a 13-year-old girl who shows no remorse. It's frightening."[3]

I did not conduct extensive research to uncover this anecdote: I simply reached for the newspaper on the table next to me, confident that something along these lines would turn up. It did. Today, as I revise this section, I do the same, and I find the following:

Two children pulled a gun on a high school teacher in her classroom and stole nearly $400 collected for a class picnic. A 12-year-old who allegedly fired at a pursuer after the robber Monday was caught. A second child got away with most of the cash. . . . The 12-year-old fired at the assistant principal before he was caught by police. A .357 Magnum was found in the bushes nearby.[4]

(Now some more weeks have passed, and my manuscript is entering final production—I have yet one more chance to recount the most recent news of youthful carnage. I do so sadly, with a sense that this will go on forever if we persist on our present path.) The date of this latest insert is Spetember 5, 1994. On page 6 of today's *New York Times*, the following story appears: "More sadness and disbelief in Chicago: Another eleven-year-old is accused of murder." The main subject of this story is a boy nicknamed "Frog" who has been arrested for beating an eighty-four-year-old woman with her cane, slashing her throat with a kitchen knife, binding her hands, and leaving her to die on her bathroom floor. The reason that the story's headline refers to "another" case is that earlier this week an eleven-year-old Chicago boy named Robert shot and killed a fourteen-year-old neighborhood girl. Robert's own life ended soon after that killing: according to police, he himself was executed by two teenage brothers in an act of vigilante justice.

But the catastrophes of this particular day are not confined to the urban streets of Chicago. Also on page 6 of the same edition we can read about a thirteen-year-old from High Bridge, New Jersey, who has just been accused of killing his longtime playmate, a "polite, shy, compliant" boy of ten. And it does not even stop there: according to police, two twelve-year-old boys from Wenatchee, Washington, have confessed to shooting a fifty-year-old migrant worker *eighteen times* in coldblooded sport. One final headline on the page announces what was perhaps the only accidental incident of the day; yet in context of the other killings, the news seems eerily prophetic: "Boy, 3, shot by brother, 5."

The current scourge of violence among the young is bad enough, but future trends look even worse. The most recent data show the *youngest* group of teenagers to be the most violent the world has ever witnessed. That is, within the *overall* increasing rates of youth violence, by far the most dramatic increase is taking place among children in their preteens and adolescents in their early teens. For example, in a five-year period from the late 1980s to the early 1990s, murder among children ages fourteen to seventeen rose 124 percent.[5] This does not bode well for the next few decades.

With growing frequency, children are killing—and being killed—at appallingly early ages. Among children between the ages of five and fourteen, murder now is the third leading cause of death in industrial countries. In the United States, a child dies of a gunshot wound every two hours. More children have been killed by guns in little over a decade than all the American troops that were killed during the Vietnam war—though with far less public protest.

Any urban medical intern can bear witness to the carnage wreaked on those who have been on the receiving end of the terror. On weekend nights, hospital wards in many of our cities and towns resemble battlefield clinics. Doctors and nurses care for once-healthy youth who, if they survive at all, will bear crippling impairments for life. Young people who witness this mayhem also are deeply affected. Speaking to Congress in the spring of 1994, a fifteen-year-old girl proclaimed through her tears:

> It is so bad that I am scared to leave my house in the daytime or evening. A friend of mine got shot and killed. He was standing right beside me when someone came up and shot him 17 times. . . . I have realized that something tragic doesn't only have to happen to bad people. It can happen to you.[6]

The vast majority of children who have been gunned down were shot by other youngsters. This grim fact in itself signifies still another grave problem. What happens to a young person's future once he has killed someone? (Or *she*: girls are rapidly catching up to boys in their readiness to commit violence.[7]) Or, for that matter, what happens to a young person who has *helped* to kill someone? Another disturbing present trend is the doubling of *jointly committed* murders among teenagers during the past five years.[8] Because such systematic violence among the very young is a new phenomenon, we do not know much about the ultimate fates of those who participate in such terrible activities. What kinds of social relationships will these children be able to have? What kinds of self-identities will they construct for themselves? To what purposes will they dedicate their future lives?

Whether they find themselves on the giving or the receiving end of the terror, many children are now preoccupied by it. Their daily energies are focused on avoiding, dispensing, or protecting themselves against violence—often through the same deadly means. The rapid rise in youth gangs is a response to this grim reality as well as a further feeder of it. A large portion of today's younger generation is growing up with the belief that they must either get a gun or fall victim to one. A fourteen-year-old from Washington, D.C., testifies:

> Guns have been part of my life since I was 12 years old. That was when my friend Scooter was killed with a gun. Since then, four of my friends have been shot and killed on the streets. One of them was my friend Hank. I heard gun shots. Then, right after that, I saw Hank lying on the ground. He wasn't dead yet, but he was lying there, twitching. It was a terrible thing, terrible, to see someone you know, someone who used to make you laugh, lying there, dying right in front of you.[9]

Homicidal violence is only one of the fatal dangers that children are turning to with ever greater frequency. Many young people who are not busy destroying others are doing it to themselves. Some are doing it indirectly through substance abuse. Others are doing it more directly and more purposefully than ever before.

Thirty years ago, our adolescent suicide rate was 3 per 100,000, already high by traditional global standards. Now it is 11 young people per 100,000, while adult rates have stayed pretty much the same.[10] A 1993 survey found that 20 percent of high school students had made a plan to commit suicide and that half of these students had made an actual attempt. The study also reported that these percentages had doubled *in just three years*.[11] After accidents, suicide is now the leading cause of youthful death in our society. It has maintained its grisly lead over homicide even as the latter races to catch up. There can be no plainer indication of youthful demoralization than suicide.

The less fatal indicators of youthful decline are just as discouraging. Each year over a million teenage girls throughout the United States become pregnant. A large and steadily rising number of the births resulting from these pregnancies take place outside of marriage. Largely because of teenage pregnancies, almost *one-third* of all babies born in the U.S. population at large have unmarried mothers.[12] Many unwed teenage mothers receive a temporary emotional uplift from the natural delights of parenthood, and some manage to draw upon their extended family resources in order to raise their children responsibly.[13] But generally the long-range consequences for both mother and baby are highly problematic. Indeed, in recent years some prominent social analysts have identified the rising numbers of unwed teenage births as one root cause of the societal disintegration that has threatened many of our communities.[14]

Drug use among the young stabilized a few years ago, though at a dangerously high level. Some recent unpublished indicators suggest that some forms of drug use may be increasing again. As for other types of juvenile crime, they all have continued to rise without respite. I have noted the data on youth violence earlier. Teenage robberies, muggings, and vandalism also have grown by leaps and bounds during the past three decades. The number of young people serving prison time for criminal activity rises yearly with relentless predictability.[16] Vast populations of teenagers today consider jail to be a dreary inevitability, something unavoidable that one adjusts to, almost like regular visits to the dentist. The average age of criminal offenders gets younger and younger with each passing year.

Then there are the quieter indicators of apathy and indolence among today's youth, seemingly less ominous in individual cases yet calamitous for society in the aggregate. Teachers everywhere complain of a host of behavioral problems among the students that they encounter today.[15] At the time of this writing, compulsive teenage gambling is reaching epidemic proportions among many sectors of the population. Accompanying the gambling is a cluster of deviant social and personal behavior, including petty theft, heavy borrowing, habitual deceitfulness, and irregular sleeping hours.

Even apart from those who are caught up in gambling and other obsessions, many of today's young people are having great difficulty separating day from night. School counselors complain that this generation of youth has "sleep problems" of a magnitude rarely before seen. So many students are arriving late these days that high schools have arranged clinical sessions to treat chronic oversleepers. Colleges are having trouble filling first-period classes, and students complain when required courses are scheduled early in the day. Many professors refuse to plan morning meetings with students, since so few show up. I have heard freshman-year deans say that some students spend the greater part of their first college year sleeping until noon.

In general, our students are less literate, and far less mathematically competent, than students were a generation ago.[17] Over a half million students a year drop out of our nation's high schools, usually with no good alternative in sight. A majority of our high school students cannot locate Greece on a world map, cannot compute the exact proportion of their spending money that goes for school lunches, and have never read a hardcover book that they were not forced to read.

And how do our young people spend their free time? During the week, the average U.S. child watches between four and five hours a day of television.[18] This is during the school week, when there are only about six or seven waking hours available (aside from meals, bathing, dressing, and so on) for discretionary activities. On weekends and vacations, with more time on their hands, American children on the average watch TV between *seven and nine hours per day*.[19] With this in mind, it may not seem surprising that childhood obesity rates have increased some 98 percent during the past fifteen years. "Children today are less physically fit than ever before in our history," according to one major national health organization.[20]

None of these indicators of decline—neither the illegal behavior, nor the educational failings, nor the wasted time and human potential—is confined to young people living in disadvantaged conditions. Today's disaffected and demoralized youth are widely distributed in our affluent suburbs as well as in our impoverished "underclass" neighborhoods. I shall make the case throughout this book that, although the problem may have different manifestations in different economic conditions, it is fundamentally the same problem with the same source.

Parents and teachers in communities of all types say that children's problems are becoming steadily more serious as well as more difficult to correct. One fifty-year comparison of teachers' concerns, widely cited in the media as well as the Congressional Record, claimed that in 1940 teachers worried mostly about gum-chewing and other "disorderly" conduct among their students, whereas in 1990 teachers were worried about violence, drugs, and dishonesty. Because this comparison was not made in a systematic manner, I do not wholly trust the data, and so I do not formally cite it here. But a well-designed study of parents' and teachers' observations over time was conducted between 1976 and 1989 and published in November 1993.[21] The results showed behavioral declines for children of all ages and both sexes during the study's thirteen-year period. In 1989, according to parents and teachers, children were far more likely to "destroy things belonging to others," to "hang around with others who get into trouble," to do poorly on their schoolwork, to be "underactive," "whining," "sullen," "stubborn," and "irritable." More children were lying and stealing; more were being held back a year at school; more were friendless; and more had chronic though minor physical problems such as frequent stomachaches. Fewer children were participating in sports or other healthy outdoor activities, and fewer had found any activity in life that truly engaged them, including their education.

The data that I have cited here pertain to the United States. To its credit, the U.S. federal government keeps good records of social indicators even though it has not been able to do much to stem the decline that these indicators reveal. But problems exist also in places where records are less well kept. The crisis that I discuss in this book is spread throughout the world today. We hear of the most vivid stories through the media: sport murders of children by other children in Britain, rampant drug use and prostitution among runaway youth in South America, drunken youth riots across Europe, skinhead gangs throughout Germany, an epidemic of teenage suicide in Japan, a rising tide of violence, theft, and gang membership everywhere. And, as in the United States, there are less dramatic stories as well—stories that may be even more foreboding in their commonality. Young people in Europe are "mired in the mud," in the words of one British social scientist.[22] They are dejected, they have given up; they are pursuing all the wrong goals; or they have no goals at all. There is a vacuum where there should be a tangible grasp of the present and a hopeful reach for the future.

Growing Up the Hard Way, Growing Up the Easy Way

Throughout the world today, young people grow up in a enormous range of conditions. Some young lives are spent "ducking the bullet," to borrow Milbrey McLaughlin's memorable phrase. These children risk their safety by walking down to the corner or home from school. They discover dread at an early age; violence is always on their minds. When asked to draw a picture for an art class at school or tell a story for an English class, a likely motif will be someone getting shot. Some of these children also have abusive parents, in which case their lives are as risky at home as when they are out on the streets. Some children have no functional parents at all. They have no one in their homes or their communities who takes the time, or has the ability, to guide them, to protect them, or to offer them advice, direction, solace, or nurturance. Some are seen solely as means of profit or pleasure rather than as children to be raised. Even their friendships turn out to be mean and exploitative.

At the other end of the economic spectrum, there are many children in the world today who have privileges that were once reserved for royalty. They are well fed, expensively clothed, and securely protected from harm. They possess their own bedrooms that overflow with playthings, and constant entertainment fills their lives. They have parents devoted to giving them the best of everything. Little is demanded of them beyond their own enjoyment of life. If they want something, it is theirs for the asking—especially if they ask strenuously enough.

The extremes seem to indicate separate worlds of childhood that are destined never to intersect. The young people who grow up in these disparate conditions look as if they are on diverging tracks, some headed for disaster, others for lives of luxury and ease. At first glance, this looks like an old story, a tale of two societies, one underprivileged, the other overprivileged.

If this indeed were the entire story, it would be appalling enough. It would mean that a significant portion of our youth population has been consigned to a present that is certainly bleak and a future that is likely so; whereas others in their cohort are drowning in ease and excess privilege. Although not a new story, it is a sorry one, and it grows more unacceptable with each passing year. Modern communications have made it impossible to shut out images of children with little to show but angry and hopeless eyes.

Yet this stubborn plight is only part of our present predicament. The conditions for growing up in one place these days have a great deal to do with the conditions for growing up elsewhere. Economically, culturally, and informationally, the world is growing closer together at every moment. In an era when modern media have created an almost universal human awareness, children's separate worlds have joined together.

The problems of youth cannot be isolated in today's world. The conditions may be more severe—in fact, literally more lethal—in places where children are murdered daily than in places where children drift aimlessly through schools and shopping malls. I do not mean to blur this distinction nor to understate in any way the tribulations of our most disadvantaged children. But *all* the complications of growing up in today's world have debilitating effects on the minds and morals of the young. Further, the problems tend to merge into one another, as the secure spots of yesterday become threatened, from within and from without, by the same types of destructive youth behavior that have decimated our inner cities. The problems arise from the same cultural vacuum and feed one another as soon as children gain awareness of how others in their society live. It may be possible, for a while, to barricade suburban streets against outsiders, but there are no walls that can block out the state of the world in a modern society.

The glaring spectacles of underprivilege and overprivilege feed a similar cynicism in the minds of young people from every sector of society. For a society concerned about the character of its children (and any society that is not concerned about this is surely on its way to oblivion), it is untenable to abandon certain members of its younger generation while heaping unearned entitlements on others. What message does this impart to growing children about what it means to be a person, or what it means to belong to a community? About personal and social responsibility? About the values and ideals of their respected elders?

Nor are there any barricades that prevent a culture's beliefs and practices from shaping the growing minds of children everywhere. *The mistaken beliefs that guide our childrearing practices are as prevalent in affluent communities as they are in poor neighborhoods. What is more, a diminution of standards and expectations for young people has occurred in every corner of the modern world.* As I shall show in later chapters of this book, young people everywhere today are lacking guidance. They listen fruitlessly for voices that do not speak.

A Tale of the Past

From time to time, reflections from the past can throw a glaring light on the present. Not long ago I first read a short story called "Youth," written around the turn of the century by Joseph Conrad. The story helped me bring into focus some disquieting perceptions that had been troubling me for some time but that I had not been able to articulate. A sea tale, it wakened me like a splash of cold water on a groggy morning.

Conrad's story tells about a young sailor on his first working voyage. The voyage was headed towards the Orient, a long journey fraught with peril, toil, and discomfort. Conrad has the sailor narrate the tale in first person, many years later, after he has become a middle-aged man.

If viewed with cold detachment, the young sailor's first voyage looked to be nothing less than a debacle. The ship was old and in disrepair, "all dust, rust, grime—soot aloft, dirt on deck." It leaked constantly and required frequent, strenuous pumping. Rats were everywhere. Two days out of harbor, the ship collided with a steamer and had to return for repairs. This and other setbacks led to interminable delays in leaving port. When the ship was finally at sea again, a gale forced another lengthy dock stay. Then the ship's cargo—coal—caught on fire through spontaneous combustion. The captain decided to plow on, which meant weeks of living with odiferous smoke and fumes. Even this miserable situation deteriorated further. The smoldering coal eventually exploded, the ship caught fire and sank, and the young sailor was left manning a lifeboat. After days and nights in an open boat, through drenching rains and burning sun, the boy finally rowed into an Asian port.

And what was the boy's attitude throughout this extended misadventure? He was thrilled about every experience along the way. Throughout the tale, the narrator barely can contain the exuberance that he felt as a young man long ago. At the darkest and most doleful part of the journey, the sailor recalls thinking "What next? . . . This is great! And as for me, there was also my youth to make me patient. There was all the East before me, and all life, and the thought that I had been tried in that ship and had come out pretty well."

The narrator goes on to conclude, ". . . tell me, wasn't that the best time, that time when we were young at sea; young and had nothing, on the sea that gives nothing, except hard knocks—and sometimes a chance to feel your strength. . . ." The miserable voyage had bestowed upon the boy nothing less than a sense of wonder and pride at the chance to test himself in every predicament that arose.

Now Conrad's piece is fiction, not science; and it is fiction that is laced with a thick air of nostalgia at that. Yet even romantic fantasies from another time can be revealing, especially when they are so different from our own. And of course this other time was not so long ago—a mere three or four generations past, on the cusp of the modern era.

Much indeed has changed. There are many stories that one can tell about today's youth, individual stories as varied as the conditions in which young people find themselves in our society. Some of these stories are happy ones. Many young people today are well-adjusted, well-meaning, and capable. But not many of today's stories will express the exuberance, the sense of confidence, the eagerness for adventure, the wholehearted hopefulness that Conrad's youthful sailor feels. Few stories of today's youth will show the same clarity of purpose. Few, in fact, will show a sustained commitment or an unreserved dedication to anything beyond their own immediate concerns.

Few pictures of today's youth could portray young people facing their world with a sense of *wholesome ambition*. Even this phrase seems antiquated nowadays, almost embarrassingly eager—or, worse, crassly assertive. Yet what, if not a sense of wholesome ambition, has enabled young people throughout the ages to plow ahead, through all the uncertainties of their first steps, to create a better future for themselves and their compatriots? Nowadays, even those on the right track seem timorous about their aims and guarded about their prospects.

Conrad's account struck me not because it represents a definitive picture of all that youth should be—it is, after all, a tale of only one boy's life—but rather because it contrasts so sharply with most of the pictures familiar to me in our contemporary social landscape. The story suggests a spirit that is very hard to find among today's young. Oddly, though, Conrad's account still rings true. It is as if it fills a natural category, an archetypical definition of youthful spirit that we shall always retain, even long after life in modern society would make it anachronistic.

But this, I hope and believe, will turn out to be too strong and too final a conclusion. The youthful exuberance expressed by Conrad's sailor is rare but not extinct. There are young people today who do have a coherent sense of purpose. Many other young people are desperately seeking one. Even those who seem truly lost have all the potential energy, intelligence, and courage with which young of our species have always been endowed.

Yet too many are demoralized, deeply so, in all the original senses of the word. When military strategists invented the notion of psychological warfare, one of the first tactics they turned to was "demoralizing" the enemy. To "demoralize" one's opponents, there were two choices. One could corrupt the enemy's morals or one could undermine the enemy's sense of hope. Either way, the will to prevail would be diminished.

Courage and energy would dissipate; a defeatist attitude would mush-room into a self-fulfilling sense of despair. As legions of armies have found to their regret, this is an effective strategy when successfully implemented. But the conditions must be right. Crude attempts often have the opposite effect. If troops (or civilians, for that matter) believe in the rightness of their cause, hardship, threats, brutality, and propaganda only bind them more strongly together in a spirit of determination.

Now I do not intend to go all the way with this military analogy. Although there are many casualties in the story that I shall tell, there are no real enemies. No one has waged a strategic campaign to demoralize our youth.

But demoralization is the right word for what I have seen in too many young people today. Although it has occurred through well-intentioned mistakes rather than through hostile calculation, the effects are pretty much the same. The legacy for many young people includes a cynical attitude toward moral values and goals; a defeatist attitude toward life; a lack of hope in the future; a thinning of courage; and a distrust of others as well as of the self. Above all, many show an absence of purpose, of commitment, of dedication—in a phrase, a failure of spirit.

The Present Once More:
Youth, Science, and Society

I have been a social scientist for all of my professional life, and I value the insights into human development that our great works in psychology, anthropology, and sociology have provided us. But for every valid insight there have been many myths. The myths, in turn, have led to harmful conclusions about the nature of youth and how to bring out the full potential of young people. Some of the myths have arisen from distorted coverage by mass media that pursue an easy popular market by overdramatizing and oversimplifying complex issues. Some myths have arisen from misconceived research directed towards preconceived social policy aims rather than towards objective scientific standards. Others have been fashioned by contemporary childrearing experts who do little more than unreflectively replicate the biases and illusions of the popular culture.

The most painful experience for someone who cares about scientific truth is to see a good idea twisted beyond recognition and then misused. As I shall discuss in Chapter 5, the notion of a "child-centered" approach to early development was a scientific breakthrough when it was introduced almost a century ago.[23] It allowed us to see that children are not simply "little adults" but that they have a unique perspective on the world as well as their own developmental needs. It enabled us to recognize the formidable skills and dispositions that children are born with. It opened the door to important discoveries about how children learn concepts, about how their values and character are formed, and about how we may best foster such positive developmental processes.

A child-centered stance not only helped us understand children more accurately, it also did much to improve our protective and nurturant behavior towards them. It gave us the push we needed to pass laws abolishing exploitive child labor. It has created interactive forms of instruction that make possible better communication between teacher and child in schools and other educational settings. It has made us sensitive to how abuse, poverty, and untreated disease affect children in especially pernicious ways.

But any truth can become a grotesque mockery of itself if stretched too far or taken out of context.[24] We are living in a time when the "child-centered" ethic has become a justification for every sort of overindulgent childrearing practice. As I shall show in Chapter 5, it is now the rallying cry of educators who have stripped the classroom of challenging intellectual material and rigorous standards. It has spawned a host of permissive doctrines that have dissuaded parents from enforcing consistent discipline in the home. It has focused our attention on elusive sensibilities such as the child's self-esteem rather than on substantive sources of pride such as achievement or responsibility. In the end, the once-valuable premise of child-centeredness has been used (or misused) to encourage self-centeredness in today's children and adolescents.

There are many such examples, and they are all part of a story of cultural decline that many observers have come to lament.[25] At the heart of any culture is its manner of raising its young. In fact, the very term "culture" derives from the root metaphor of *cultivation*, the essential function of raising the young. From time immemorial people have been aware that no culture will long survive unless it prepares its future generations properly. In modern times, we have strayed very far from our natural inclination to do so; and in every corner of our society there are signs that we may be in danger of losing the capacity altogether.

How could such a grave threat to our future generations come to pass with so little warning? I shall discuss the multiple causes of our present predicament in the initial chapters of this book. As I shall show, first and foremost among these causes is a misguided set of beliefs about children and what is best for them. We have been deluded by an inter-locking cluster of myths, misconceptions, pseudoscientific assertions, unexamined sentiments, and a host of other biases and distortions in our notions about raising the young. Since the early days of this century, these beliefs have spread throughout the modern world. They have been communicated by the mass media, legitimized by the misapplica-tion of scientific theory and findings, and supported by institutions that have grown up in their wake.

Misguided beliefs about youth pervade our childrearing practices in the home; they pervade our educational practices in the schools; and they pervade our public policies in the community. Misguided beliefs draw from and feed into a culture that has lost its compass for guiding children. Our culture prizes its children but nevertheless is failing them. It is failing them partly because it does so little to equip them with the skills and knowledge that they need. Even worse—much worse—it is failing them because it has produced a climate that discour-ages young people from building their natural virtues, from using their natural energies, in short from developing their own splendid natural aptitudes for character and competence to their fullest capacities.

Misconceptions of Modern Times

Many of our misconceptions began as valid new insights into the nature of childhood. Many have been fed by legitimate concerns for the wel-fare of children. But valid insights can be changed into fallacies when they are oversimplified or taken out of context. Legitimate concerns can become counterproductive when they are applied blindly or without careful constraints.

The childrearing literature of the past few decades has introduced parents to a host of notions that at best are easily misapplied and at worst are wholly misguided. Some of the misleading notions that I shall take up in this book include: parent/infant bonding during the first weeks of life; the fragility and amorality of children's natural dispositions; the incompetence of the young child; the hazards of "traumatic" early expe-riences such as failing at a challenging task; the irrelevance (some even say harmfulness) of parental discipline; the specter of the "hurried child"; the "pressures" of responsibility and the "stress" of early achievement; the need for adults to help children preserve their "magical" thinking; the value of self-esteem boosting; and the benefits of a lopsidedly "child-centered" approach to education and childrearing.

We have been led to believe that experiences which most children in the past have traditionally been exposed to—hard work, firm rules, consistent disciplinary practices, other people's religious celebrations, knowledge about the terrifying dramas of life and death or about the uncertain vicissitudes of reality—can harm young people and that they need to be protected from them. We have discovered (accurately enough) that young people have their own perspectives and values; but this valid insight has led us to defer to the views of the young, to treat children's sensibilities gingerly, to allow young people to drift rudderless in a sea of moral confusion.

At the heart of all our misconceptions is at least a grain of truth. Many of the errors have their source in sound writings on children's psychological development. In part at least, some of the notions have had some value in imparting insight about children or in preventing harmful practices such as child labor. But each of the notions at its periphery—that is, at its contact point with public consciousness—has seriously misled us. Of course this is not the fault of the notions themselves but of the ways in which they have been misapplied by our media, by many of our institutions, by some of our professional experts, and by most of our popular childrearing gurus.

Consider, for example, the notion of parent/infant bonding—the idea that an essential, psychologically lasting link between parent and child is forged permanently or not at all in the moments after birth. The bonding myth is an illegitimate offspring of the important "attachment" research tradition. With little scientific justification, the bonding notion rapidly gained currency among popular writers and other advice givers, spreading rapidly throughout the culture despite objections from the serious scholarly community. Before long, the idea of early parent/child bonding was being used to lure families into bizarre birthing rituals, to stigmatize adopted and handicapped children, and to induce guilt in parents who have obligations outside the household. In Chapter 5, I shall show that early bonding is a fraudulent notion, a perversion of attachment theory. Nevertheless, it is an idea that has been propagated in the popular press long after it has been scientifically discredited.

In books with titles such as *The Magic Years* and *The Hurried Child*, we have been told that childhood is a time of play and romance that must not be interrupted by the harsh realities of the grown-up world. To do so would be to stifle the child's nascent creativity, to overburden the child with responsibilities, to "stress out" the child. At the root of these warnings is the belief that children are fragile creatures with delicate sensibilities that are easily shattered and corrupted.

This is a belief that hails back to the romantic philosopher Jean Jacques Rousseau. It is not one, however, that has been substantiated in developmental research. In Chapter 6, I show that children are psychologically resilient and that they are born with a wide range of competencies, virtues, and positive social dispositions. Children are able spontaneously to interact constructively with others. They can create their own spirit of playfulness, and they eagerly seek out information about the real world. They need a framework of adult guidance in the face of life's complexities, not a protective bubble that shields out reality.

The idea that children will become overstressed, overburdened, and overwhelmed if we "hurry" them by urging them to achieve is diametrically opposed to the truth of the matter. Even at very early ages, children find the pursuit of talents, skills, and knowledge to be an uplifting experience, They are active and avid learners. The earlier we begin inducing children to learn and achieve, the more naturally they take to it. The longer we postpone such activities, the more they are likely to build up defenses, maladaptive habits, and unproductive interests. The stressed-out child is far more likely to be the one who has developed few proficiencies than the one who has thrived on the busy activities of exploration and achievement.

As for creativity, our childrearing experts have decried the destruction of natural creativity by traditional schooling that demands maturity from children. The notion is that creativity requires spontaneous, untutored impulses that may be stifled through too much discipline. The proposed solution has been to approach children's creative work gingerly, in a "child-centered" manner, holding back anything that could sound like criticism or instruction. The idea is that a laissez-faire approach is needed if the child's inborn talents are to be preserved. Fostering creativity, in this view, requires special attention, rewards, and license. Moreover, this romantic idea is accompanied by a determination that children should learn only what intrinsically interests them:

extrinsic rewards and other goads are seen as antithetical to the spirit of creative work.

At the present time in our post-modern culture, this is so much the dominant approach to early childhood education that there are few good alternatives to it. In Chapter 5, I discuss how this approach derives from outmoded Rousseauian sentiments and from misinterpretations of complex writings by great psychologists such Piaget and great educators such as Pestalozzi and Montessori. We have been left with watered-down pedagogies based on oversimplified notions. The result is a withholding of the encouragements, incentives, and constructive criticism that children need to develop true talents and skills.

Children need to be engaged not just in activities that seem easy and fun but also in challenging ones that can help them excel. In order to acquire creative skills, children need extrinsic feedback and reward just as much as they need work that is intrinsically interesting. They must learn to sustain their effort even when things get difficult and boring. Children do best in the long run when prepared to cope with the frustration and drudgery that is an inevitable part of creative work.

It seems that just about every parent, teacher, and guidance counselor today is convinced that building self-esteem is the answer to all childhood problems. If a child is unpopular in the playground, it is due to low self-esteem. If a child has a learning problem at school, it is because there is a failure of self-esteem. Even if a child is unruly, overbearing, and arrogant, it is chalked up to deficits in the child's self-esteem. The solution is available almost daily in the popular press: bolster your child's self-esteem. We are to assure children, at all times and regardless of the circumstances, that they are "terrific" in every possible way.

In Chapter 4, I show that self-esteem is a meaningless concept without a firm grounding in substantive achievement. Like happiness, it can be gained only indirectly, not through its own pursuit but through dedication to activities, talents, skills, and purposes beyond the self. This applies as much to children as to adults. It is an especially important principle for communicating to children, since they will quickly come to distrust both their caregivers and themselves if all they are given is empty incantations about how great they always are.

One of the special ironies in our misconceptions about children's development is that the myths often contradict one another. At the same time that we place self-esteem on a privileged pedestal, we communicate to children that they are not mature enough to be given real responsibilities; that it is too much trouble to get them to do something useful; and that they need to spend their free time "cooling out" from the rigors of their busy lives. In this and many other ways, we infantilize our children. This is especially destructive, because it robs them of a chance to acquire useful competence, thereby demolishing any valid claim to self-worth that they might acquire. Perhaps most seriously, the fiction of youth incompetence turns children inward, away from an orientation towards serving others.

In Chapter 8, I discuss how, throughout all the ages and around the world, children traditionally have been asked to help their families in many important ways. They have been given household chores, child-care responsibilities for younger siblings, and duties in attending to the elderly. They perform these services adeptly and benefit greatly from participating in them. Service also brings children into contact with other people, such as the elderly, who have much to teach children.

Our misguided views about what is good for children and about what they are good for have convinced us to let our children roam the shopping malls or lounge in front of the TV rather than ask them to help out. Modern affluence has permitted us the "luxury" of acting on our misconceptions by relieving children of their household obligations. The misconceptions and the affluence have created an unholy combination, to the detriment of our youth.

Affluence and permissiveness often go hand in hand: this is the downside of good fortune as far as children are concerned. It is a common tendency for parents to want "the best of everything" for their children. Unfortunately, too many parents interpret this to mean relieving their children of duties and indulging them with unwarranted privileges. The cultural *Zeitgeist* does not support the notion that what is really best for a child is the opportunity to develop a strong sense of personal responsibility.

The easy permissiveness extends to one of parenting's core functions, providing a child with discipline. As I discuss in Chapter 8, all young people need discipline in both a positive and a constraining sense. If children are to learn productive skills, they need to develop discipline in order to make the most out of their native talents. They also need to encounter firm and consistent discipline whenever they test the limits of social rules (as every child will do from time to time). The processes of accountability are similar in the two instances. Yet these also are under attack in the contemporary canons of childrearing. The belief is prevalent that children's vitality, their creative gifts, their very senses of self, may be crippled by too much "old-fashioned" discipline. Children, it is now strongly asserted, should be reasoned with, not forced; and all forms of compliance should be internally motivated. We shrink at making a child work to master a skill through laborious practice because we worry that drudgery will dampen the child's inspiration. Similarly, we worry that firm punishment will break the child's spirit. Chapter 5 documents our culture's descent into these permissive beliefs and will show how counterproductive they are to the growth of children's capabilities and character.

In a literal sense, the most dispiriting result of our myths about children is that we withhold spiritual messages from them. Our reticence springs from the myth of childhood incompetence. Many assume that it is an empty exercise to teach religious and moral principles to children, since they won't be able to understand them. In many educational settings today, spiritual instruction for children has become watered down to the point where it is hard to discern any meaningful core. We do not trust the child's intelligence or attention span enough to engage the child in serious consideration of transcendent values. We refrain from communicating other people's high ideals to them—or when we do, feel almost apologetic about it. This is justified by misinterpretations of developmental research, which is wrongly read as claiming that children cannot think about abstractions. In fact, children are fascinated by the timeless enigmas of life and death, are not at all threatened by talk of them, and are eager to be drawn into discussion about them. As I will show in Chapter 4, children are openly receptive to spiritual ideas and long for transcendent truths that can nourish their sense of purpose and provide them with a moral mission in life.

Today's children, like children throughout the ages, do best when they grow up within a cultural climate of purpose. There are still many pockets of the modern world that provide such a climate, and there are still young people everywhere who are thriving. But the trends are disturbing, because they have been in the wrong direction for much of the modern era. This is not to say that modernity itself is at fault; nor that cultural progress need be antithetical to the timeless spiritual needs of growing children. Spiritual needs may be fulfilled in a thoroughly modern way. In fact, the only realistic solution is to do precisely this.

The book's last four chapters present guidelines for raising children with an eye to their psychological and spiritual needs as well as to the modern world that they will inherit. I have drawn the guidelines both from traditional practice and from contemporary research in child development. The conceptual foundation for the guidelines extends backwards as well as forwards in time.

The guidelines in this book oppose much conventional wisdom of modern times, but they do not represent a return to a romanticized past. The guidelines do not, for example, advocate a "spare the rod, spoil the child" mentality. They do not suggest returning children to child labor in the town factory or the family farm. They do not suggest ignoring all the valuable things that we have learned during the past century about children's inner thoughts and feelings. Rather, the guidelines present age-old standards in the context of present-day insight and knowledge. They are informed, as they must be, by our most recent knowledge about the children and adolescents who are now struggling to grow up in our society. For it is these particular children who are imperiled today. It is to these children that we must speak. It is for their futures that we must help them prepare. In doing so, we must fashion a new approach that is both ancient in its wisdom and youthful in its readiness for changing times.

2
Growing Up the Easy Way

Modern life has brought comfort, convenience, and affluence to middle-class homes the world over. Compared with any other time in history, the typical household earnings in today's industrial nations buy an astonishing array of services, consumer goods, and electronic gadgets. Chores that once took the better part of a day are now accomplished by the push of a button. Televisions and VCRs have made cheap, round-the-clock entertainment available to people everywhere. For large numbers of well-off people today, the home has become less a place of work and drudgery than a place where one is fed, sheltered, and entertained as a matter of course.

It was not, of course, always so. Until the last century, the family itself was the main source of social, emotional, and material support for most of the world's population. Even the upwardly mobile American society was grounded on families that operated largely as self-sufficient economic and social units. Many were farm families that needed the cooperation of every member, including the children. Girls and the very young worked around the house. They cleaned, folded laundry, chopped vegetables, and put up the farm's produce. Older boys helped plant and harvest the crops.

In those days, families employed their children's services because the services were deemed essential. The mutual well-being and, in many cases, the survival of all the family's members depended upon the children's contribution. There was nothing discretionary about asking children to perform family services, and all social policy regarding children was guided by this economic necessity. For example, when mandatory public schooling was begun in the nineteenth century, a long summer break was mandated so that children would be available to help with the crops during the high farming season. (The legacy of lengthy summer vacations remains with our schools today as just one of many indicators of our schools' resistance to revising archaic practices.) One of the grimmer manifestations of the pressing need for children's economic services in earlier times was the endurance of child factory labor in many urban settings until well into the twentieth century.

Nowadays, in most of the modern world, three sources of social progress have relieved children of work and service obligations: technology, affluence, and a public awareness of child labor's exploitive evils. Many families have benefited from all three sources of social progress; virtually all have benefited from at least one. As a result, children have gained the opportunity to enjoy their childhoods and to spend time acquiring a wide assortment of skills and knowledge.

Accompanying this change has been a sea change in how our society values children. No longer viewed as an essential means to their family's well-being, children now are seen as an end in themselves, the target of their family's care and concern. Parents strive first and foremost to enhance their children's well-being. Childrearing has become the family's primary stated goal.[1] The modern family exists to provide for the children and not the other way around. Rather than expecting economic contributions from their children, families are ready and willing to dedicate an enormous share of their own resources towards childrearing expenses.

Some of these resources are financial: for the decade of the 1990s, the projected average cost of raising a middle-class American child prior to college totals $186,000. College will add another sum at least that large for children born today. The other valuable resource that many of today's children enjoy, despite popular beliefs to the contrary, is a large amount of leisure adult time. Today's middle-class children have greater access to adults during times of leisure than children at almost any time in history, simply because their elders have been relieved of so much excess work and drudgery. (The only exception to this was one brief period after World War II, when many mothers had both the luxury of modern conveniences and the advantages of a low cost of living that enabled them to stay home from work.) Most modern families spend much of their leisure time with their children. More than this, they feel a responsibility to care for and amuse their children. In most cases, middle-class families can provide sufficient adult time to see that this responsibility is reasonably well discharged from their children's birth through the end of their childhood. So many years of sustained adult attention is a privilege that not many children throughout history have had.

The transformation of children's social value during the twentieth century represents a radical reordering of society's priorities with regard to youth. There is much wisdom in the new priorities. The future of any society lies in its younger generation. It is both natural and enlightened for a society to dedicate itself to the proper raising of its young. When affluence and social progress free up resources to aid with this most essential task, so much the better. In areas such as health and nutrition, many children's lives have been tangibly improved by the fruits of social progress.

The shift away from viewing children as economic resources also has refocused our efforts towards the goals of raising and educating them in the finest manner possible. Because we now consider children to be invaluable ends in themselves, we center many of our social policies on their welfare. We orient our laws and practices toward "the best interests of the child," with many favorable results. This orientation has led to vast improvements in child protection laws, in child health care, and in the many facilities that we dedicate to children's intellectual and physical growth: schools, museums, parks, playgrounds, and so on. All of these good things have been made possible through the enlarged resources of modern times and through our willingness to use them to advance children's interests.

The benefits that affluence and social progress have brought to middle-class children today are unquestionable. It would be foolish to allow the course of such good fortune for so many to be reversed. But, like much good fortune, these benefits have come with risks that must be guarded against. Many of the risks still are largely unrecognized. Because we have not yet learned to identify the risks, we have not yet learned how to avoid or control them. The result has been too many casualties among children who ought to have auspicious prospects and too much half-fulfilled potential among children who ought to have endless promise.

Neither affluence nor social progress can offer us a solution for how to foster positive youth development. They may provide welcome tools in this endeavor, such as valuable time and resources, but they do not provide directions for how to use these tools. And they come with dangers that must be recognized if they are not to end up as destructive rather than constructive forces. It is as if a new machine had been invented, with great power to serve humankind, but also bearing lethal side effects that are masked by the glitter of the thing. I am reminded of the days when children (myself included) found hours of fun wriggling their toes under fluoroscopes at the shoestore. Luckily the dangers were spotted before too much harm was done. The misuses of the technology were controlled, and the medical benefits of X rays became worth the risks.

The improved nutrition and health care available to modern middle-class families clearly redounds to their children's welfare, but the benefits of other elements of the modern lifestyle are not quite so clear. Take entertainment for an example. In the industrial world today, children have access to a world of entertainment that would have been unimaginable as little as fifty years ago. Children who live in the most minimally advantaged circumstances have bounteous opportunities to amuse themselves. Television has penetrated virtually every household, with VCRs and CDs not far behind. No longer is a child's affection confined to a precious figurine or two, laboriously handcrafted and caringly looked after for years: most children's closets now are stuffed with an amazing array of gadgets, dolls, and toys. New theme parks for the young are built almost monthly, with attendance high enough to make this one of our strongest growth industries. We spend freely for children's consumer goods, including designer clothes and sneakers, fine furniture, special fun foods, and fancy bikes. It is estimated that U.S. families spend over fifty *billion* dollars yearly on their children's food, clothing, entertainment, and vacations.[2]

There is nothing wrong, and much right, with children having fun. Yet we must examine the nature of the fun available to children in today's world. We must view children's entertainment activities and their consumption patterns from the perspective of the objectives that we hold for them. We must examine how our children's competence and character are affected by the TV watching, the dazzling toys, the brand-name clothes, and the copious time that they lavish on such pursuits. Even more important, we must determine what our children are *not* doing while they are watching television or roaming the shopping malls. Has something gone out of their lives that might have contributed to the development of their competence and character? What are today's children learning, at play, with their friends, and in school?

Today's Good Life, Child Style

We may begin with a quick look at a day in the life of a middle-class American child during this last decade of the twentieth century.[3] The activities and events that I shall cite are so commonplace that they may seem wholly unnoteworthy. This is part of my point. Practically without notice, our expectations for youth have changed to an astonishing degree. In our shared vision of childhood and adolescence, mediocrity has become the norm. This is ironic as well as tragic, for youth has always been, and should always be, the time of highest hopes.

From ages five through eighteen, the lives of most middle-class children are organized around a school day lasting approximately six hours.[4] On most weekdays, this leaves somewhere around eight to ten hours free for other matters. In the United States, public school typically runs 180 days per year. This leaves another 185 days, during weekends, holidays, and summers, that are wholly open to the child's and/or parent's discretion. By my calculations, this means that just about one-third of an American child's life is spent in school and two-thirds of it outside of school, adding together after-school time with nonschool days. I refer of course to the child's waking life (though there are some critics of contemporary education who would question whether that adjective accurately captures the in-school part).

Let us begin a brief tour of the middle-class child's life with a glance at the school day. In a recent wave of consternation about the current state of schooling, there have been many evocative accounts of schooling in the United States and other Western nations. Some of these accounts are harshly critical, others are sympathetic but concerned.[5] The more critical accounts have described our schools in such terms as wastelands, prisons, shopping malls, and havens of mediocrity.[6] The kinder accounts have noted the inspired commitment of some dedicated, yet thoroughly frustrated, teachers but have decried the overcentralized, bureaucratic, and inflexible conditions in which such teachers must work.[7] All the accounts have one thing in common: they portray contemporary schooling as a failed compromise between society's need to educate the young and the mindless, inefficient, and thoroughly anti-quated institution that we have entrusted to accomplish this purpose. *None* of the accounts describes today's school life as rigorous, demanding, or engaging.

As with all things human, there is wide variation in schools and students. I have noted earlier—but it bears repeating—that my comments in this book pertain to *trends* and *harbingers*; they are not intended to generalize across every childhood condition in the world today. In communities everywhere there are still many hard-working students who are learning up to their full potential, who devote themselves to their homework, to school newspapers, to projects for science fairs, to sports teams, to community service, to the performing arts. Through participation in these and other activities, these young people are acquiring personal responsibility, a capacity for sustained commitment, and a taste for the joys of accomplishment. There are still many fine teachers and fine schools that do everything possible to encourage their students to discover and develop their talents. It would be wrong to suggest that any of these have become wholly extinct within our society. But I do wish to assert that they are becoming too rare; that, unfortunately, the trends are all in the wrong direction; but that, fortunately, it is in our power to set the trends right again.

Despite some ideological differences among the recent critics of our schools, there is broad overlap in their comments. Three themes emerge from the perceptions of those who have observed school life today. First, students are passive and disengaged. Second, they are not learning anything close to what they will need to know if they are to thrive in the world of the twenty-first century. (Here an ideological split arises among critics who would like to see students learn to think better versus those who would like to see students acquire more knowledge about the world; and then there are those, present author included, who would insist on both). Third, the critics note that many teachers have become cynical after years of disappointment with their apathetic students, with their disjointed instructional requirements, and with the insensitive and invalid tests that they must use to evaluate their students and, by direct implication, their own teaching performances.

One of the original, and still most trenchant, critiques of this muddle was Theodore Sizer's portrayal of a prototypical teacher named Horace who labored cynically through the motions of his high-school job. Horace's own particular "compromise" was with his students. The tacit deal that he made with them was as follows: If you let me get through my day without causing me too much trouble, I will let you pass through this place with a minimal amount of effort on your part. What's more, if you put your time in quiescently, you will receive your required credential, the high school degree. Sizer's analysis has had enormous influence because it immediately triggered that shock of recognition that comes whenever a solid truth is uncovered.

Today's students take readily to the compromise that many teachers like Horace offer them. I think of a high school student whose family I know well—I will call her Susan here. She is as bright and gifted a youngster as one could hope for. Susan comes from a home where intellectual achievement is valued, and she does well in one of our top schools. There is nothing particular to worry about with this pleasant young person, yet her parents have found something in her attitude puzzling and perhaps a bit troubling.

It came out most recently on a vacation that the family took to a French-speaking sunspot. Susan had studied French for years. Her grades were exemplary, and her teachers had no complaints. The parents naturally thought that Susan would jump at the chance to try out her French in the real world, to hone her skills, to display her hard-won expertise. They remembered the thrill that they received from trying out a foreign tongue when they were students. On the trip, Susan's parents went out of their way to make contact with local people who could communicate only in their native language.

To their surprise, every time that someone tried to speak French with them, Susan clammed up. Susan avoided speaking French even when it would have been helpful for the rest of her the family, who were untrained in the language. She acted as if listening to the sounds or mouthing the strange vowels were painful acts. Susan's parents never thought of their personable daughter as shy. What was up, they asked her? Susan told them without hesitation that she was on vacation and had no intention of doing anything that vaguely reminded her of school. Besides, she said, she had always hated French. Her parents expressed disappointment. Susan responded with some agitation: Wasn't it enough that she would grind away to get her grades? Wasn't it enough that she would suffer through four or five years of the stuff on her road to college? What did they expect, anyway?

What the parents had hoped was that Susan would get some pleasure and pride from all her work. That she would show some inclination to use the fruits of her labor for a genuine purpose. That she would take some initiative. That she would see this as an opportunity to refine and improve her skills. Her parents found the episode disturbing because it was not singular. They could not remember when their daughter took the effort on her own to pursue something worthwhile. She met her obligations reliably and intelligently, but she rarely showed a zest for further accomplishment or exploration.

Susan is among the top sliver of our high-achieving students. In today's schools, she is outnumbered by many counterparts who look practically illiterate in comparison—the ones, that is, who cannot write a coherent paragraph or compute an algebraic formula without their teacher's help. Despite her apathy, Susan is a solid student, part of a fortunate minority with good prospects for eventual success in our society. Still, no adult in her life—parent, teacher, or counselor—believes that she is living up to her full potential.

For too many of our children, school activities seem devoid of meaning and isolated from the rest of their lives. As students, they see no compelling reason to invest their energies in anything that their teachers tell them to do. Their schools have made no academic subject interesting enough to capture their full attention for the present. Nor have their schools made literacy and numeracy skills seem important enough to appeal to students' awareness that they may need such capacities in the future. For many students today, the academic agenda of schooling—the subject matter, the problem solving, the famed "three Rs"—is all taken as beside the point, useless, something that one does out of drab necessity. Their performance is perfunctory, a cheerless going-through-the-motions.

It is a principle of human development that, over time, one becomes what one does.[8] A person's actions, performances, and participation in various social relationships all create a personal history that shapes the person's outlook and habits. This is especially true during the formative years of childhood and adolescence.

A child who spends her precious years of school life in ritualistic, barren exercises learns a pattern of vacuous response that can diminish the child's future efforts and future aspirations. Going through the motions of learning out of dreary obligation is not a benign experience for a child. It is a deadening one. It can lead to an intransigent sense of disinterest in learning and achievement.

Recent school critiques have told us in dreary detail about what is not happening to students in our schools.[9] Students are not learning the basics of math and science, they are not able to find Canada on a map, they are not learning how to write a coherent paragraph, they are not throwing themselves into their schoolwork, they are not behaving properly in gym, and so on. The critiques, however, have left unanswered the question of what *is* happening to all the children who are sitting for hours in mental states that approach suspended animation. I will venture an answer here: developmentally, these children are acquiring habits. These are not habits that will serve them or society well. They are habits of idleness, of getting by with the least possible effort, of cynicism about the very possibility of achievement. They are habits of shirking, of ineptitude, of willed incompetence.

In general, our schools are not providing students with environments that stimulate intellectual and moral growth. But perhaps there is a tendency to blame the schools too extensively for everything that is wrong with today's society. Schools are but an integral part of society, not in any way isolated from the cultural forces of our day. Schools can do little more than reflect the priorities and values that define the culture at large. Moreover, as I have noted, a child's school life subsumes only about a third of the child's waking time. What is happening, and what is *not* happening, to children during the rest of their time?

For children from today's middle-class families, there is one fact of life that stands out. Almost all the activities that occupy most children's nonschool time are directed towards their own pleasure-oriented diversions. There is a vast amount of time watching TV shows filled with silly humor or gratuitous violence. This is time that is ill-spent, because it wastes precious hours that could be invested in exploring the world and in building skills and character. The same can be said for many of the other sources of popular entertainment available to young people today, including the more widely distributed movies, videos, and CDs.

Some of the enrichment and friendship activities that children pursue do have some value, especially when they are entered into with vigor and intelligence. I do not wish to imply that there is anything wrong with all of today's pastime activities per se. For example, the music and dances lessons, the sports teams, and the assorted youth clubs are unquestionably worthwhile for those children who invest their energies in them. Time spent playing with friends offers developmental benefits as well as important emotional satisfaction. Yet when we consider the sum total of a modern child's out-of-school life, it is striking how much time is frittered away in idle amusements. It is also striking how little time or effort is spent in activities that are devoted to the needs of others.

Throughout history and in much of the nonindustrial world, children traditionally have been expected to help out in the family and in the community. They lend a pair of hands in the kitchen, they care for sick and the elderly, they watch over infants and younger siblings. They run errands and do chores. This is normal, and it imparts many benefits both to the family and to the child. For the family, it relieves some of the pressures of having too many things to do. For the child, the benefits may seem less obvious, but they are even more profound. Performing serious service confers a sense of personal competence and a sense of social responsibility. These virtues are central to the child's character development. The earlier that children begin acquiring them, the more surely they will flourish.

In our society, middle-class parents commonly offer three reasons why they refrain from requesting service of their children.[10] First, they say that it is more trouble to get children do something right than simply to do it oneself. Second, they worry that their children are already overwhelmed with activities and "stressed out" from all the demands of modern life. Adding more to the child's burdens would raise the emotional ante. What their children need is more time to cool down from the pressure-cooker life that they have been subjected to. Third, they believe that children have a "right" to their own time—that children have their own things to do, and that it is somehow unfair to ask them to give up their time for other purposes.

Such beliefs are pervasive throughout modern society. They are at least as prevalent among experts and intellectuals as among laypersons. At a recent high-level academic conference on human development, I heard a presentation by a distinguished economist on what he called the "mundane" topic of child help around the house. The economist's conclusion was that it is irrational for parents to request any chores from their children, since (in economic terms) the costs of the request (nagging, scolding, redoing the child's imperfect job) far outweigh the benefits that parents get from it. This economic conclusion was accepted without remark by social scientists from the disciplines of psychology, linguistics, and cognitive science. In fact, the analysis led to a lively discussion about the new ways in which children's time ought to be valued. During this discussion, one developmental psychologist began with the assumption that, in a household, the child's time and the parents' time must be equally valued. Therefore, any duties that take children away from their own activities must be fairly compensated—that is, paid for with material rewards. *Again, there was no dissent from the group*. Instead, some of the conferees commented on how busy children's lives had become. Another psychologist reported the lengthy negotiations that one must go through with children today in order to get them to help out. Inevitably, this participant noted, parents either cajole a child into thinking that the chore may be fun or, more likely, find some other way to get it done.

In Chapter 4, I shall examine the sources and the validity of parental concerns about expecting their children to offer some regular household help. For now, let it simply be noted that today's concerns go far beyond the fears for the child's well-being that justifiably sprang from exploitive child labor practices of earlier times. Today's concerns revolve around the parent's convenience, the child's emotional comfort, and the shared sense among parents and children that fairness demands fully respecting children's time prerogatives. The concerns do not include worries about the child's future growth prospects.

Affluence and our modern sensibilities have removed hardships from most children's lives, and this is certainly fortunate. At the same time, they also have removed many external demands on children's time and effort—so much so that the value of effort itself is called into question. The notion of effort as a virtue in itself—the so-called "work ethic"—is rapidly going out of fashion, even in the United States, where it once was considered almost definitional of the national character. Recent student surveys have found that barely more than a quarter of American youngsters place top priority on working hard, as opposed to almost three-quarters of Japanese youth.[11] High school teachers from well-off school districts routinely quote today's brightest students as saying: "It's cool to wing it; to do the least work possible and get away with it;" or, "It's the American way—to get the best results with the least amount of energy expended."[12]

Predictably, the "best results" flowing from this stance have not been very good. No matter how we measure it—test scores, creative projects, or just plain eagerness—the learning performance of today's students generally is limp. Outside of school, most children have little to show for their time beyond TV watching, shopping at the local mall, and an occasional music lesson accompanied by perfunctory practice. For many young people, the lack of effort has shown up in their physical fitness as well. "American kids are fatter than their counterparts of 20 years ago," reads one recent news story.[13] Since the early 1960s, the number of obese children has risen by over half and the number of highly obese children has doubled. The story reports that "fitness organizations and media cry out that our youth comprise a new generation of flab, unable to lift themselves from a stupor of TV watching and potato chip chomping."[14]

In many well-off sectors of modern society, the attitudes of young people also have deteriorated markedly. Scientific research has been slow to investigate this attitudinal change, but it has not gone wholly unnoticed. A small crop of impassioned grass-roots books, often self-published, have sprung up in recent years. These books warn of the clear and predictable decline in children's attitudes resulting from current tendencies to coddle and lavish them with comforts. One author writes of today's "cornucopia kids" who expect little of themselves but demand the best of everything from everyone else.[15] Another author, in a book somewhat peevishly called *Spoiled Rotten*, writes:

> This book grew out of my increasing frustration with the behavior of young people. . . . Ethics of work and behavior are declining at an alarming rate. I am *amazed* at the underachievement of many of our young, as the easy way becomes their chosen way. And I am tired of seeing parents cater to their children's every whim, giving so much of themselves, yet frequently receiving so little in return.[16]

Yet the heart of the matter still remains the loss of all obligation to serve anyone beyond oneself. Even if our children were being raised to become the best informed, most artistic, and healthiest children that the world has ever seen, it would all come to nothing unless they found some things beyond themselves, and indeed some people other than themselves, to devote at least a part of their efforts to. Even if children took their math homework and piano lessons far more seriously than they do now, they would still need to develop a sense of social responsibility. They would still need to care for other people, to work for the good of others, to live according to shared social rules, to control their own behavior, and to develop a capacity for fruitful social relationships. Otherwise they could not live together in a decent society, nor pass along what is left of the culture to their own children.

Without each new generation of children learning a collective sense of social responsibility, society can have no future. Without learning an obligation to serve and respect others, children cannot develop a sense of social responsibility. Exactly this is the gravest danger in societies that have lost touch with the need to foster in their children an obligation to serve others. Societies that have lost this knack may be not much more than a generation away from ceasing to be civilized societies at all.

The Good Life, Fraying Around the Edges

Beyond the apathy, the lack of effort, the mediocre performances, and the wasted hours and months of precious time, there is a still grimmer story of middle-class childhood today. It is a story that follows directly from the undeveloped sense of social responsibility that we have allowed to persist in so many of the younger generation. Because of the self-centeredness and poor conduct of rising numbers of our young, suburban life has begun to look less safe and less comfortable and less convenient. The easy life is becoming harder, largely because too many young people are not learning to accept their part in society's bargain.

Young people always have been inclined toward mischief: this is an inevitable part of the exuberance of growing up. But there is a hard edge to it these days, even among many of today's middle-class youth. Many young people seem to have a moral blind spot when it comes to pursuing their kicks. A friend told me of an incident that occurred when she and her husband left her suburban home for a three-day trip. Their eighteen-year-old son saw this as an opportunity to host an extended drinking party for a large number of friends and acquaintances. My friend came back to a home reeking with liquor, crammed with empty bottles, and in a state of wild disrepair. Her greatest shock, though, was when she confronted her son and observed his attitude. The boy was reluctant to admit that he had done anything seriously wrong. He had been to dozens of these parties at others' houses, the boy said, and the other kids' parents had learned to live with it.

Later, on another occasion, I spoke with the officer in charge of youth affairs at the local police station in my own home town. The officer told me that "trashing" homes in this manner is now a favorite teenage activity when parents are away. Each year in this small, solid middle-class community, the officer is called out to report on several homes that, in his (perhaps somewhat exaggerated) words, "get totally wrecked." The officer stated that he does not think that any parents these days can trust a teenager with the responsibility of staying home without supervision. He noted that he would not have imagined this to be the case when he was a youngster growing up in these parts.

In every society, there are young people who turn toward antisocial pursuits early in their lives. They come from every station in life, rich as well as poor; although strong family support systems do provide incentives and deterences that usually keep youngsters from such families from drifting into crime. Today the old incentives and deterences are failing, even in sectors of society that seem most equipped to support them. As a result, behavior that was once considered marginal has worked its way into the center of our most solid communities. What is more, a new sort of behavior that is truly appalling—frightening beyond anything in our society's historical experience with its younger generations—has begun to appear on the fringes of even our "best" neighborhoods.

In July 1993, a page one news story in the *New York Times* announced a disturbing trend with the headline: "Gang Membership Grows in Middle-class Suburbs."[17] This was hardly news to policemen and school principals across the country, nor to maintenance staff who have been removing gang-related graffiti from suburban buildings with increasing frequency. Still, the substance of the story was revealing. Youth gang activity has penetrated deep into the preserves of the affluent. "There is vandalism, from graffiti to property destruction. There is violence too, although the victims are more likely to end up in the emergency room than the morgue."[18] We cannot take too much reassurance from this last comment, the story goes on to say. Gang fights among middle-class youth "are steadily becoming more dangerous." One seventeen-year-old is quoted as saying, "It went from punches to razors, bats, and bottles, and now to guns."[19]

The truth is that the news media just now are discovering a phenomenon that has been worrying police officers and social scientists for years.[20] Youth crime and violence, organized through gangs, is steadily on the rise; and the trend shows absolutely no sign of abating. Long ubiquitous in the cities, youth gangs now are growing fast throughout the once-safe suburbs. The involvement of suburban youth is not new: it is just that the locus of their operations is spreading. In the past, middle-class youth have traveled to the inner cities whenever they felt the urge to engage in antisocial activities.[21] They would traffic in drugs and stolen goods with the city gangs, and they would drink and act rowdy in someone else's neighborhood. Now they are forming their own gangs and bringing the action home.

Some of the action is not very different than the kinds of misadventures that young people have always pursued, just more organized and more persistent. At Taylor Allderdice High School in the prime Pittsburgh suburb of Squirrel Hill, students collaborated in a systematic cheating ring.[22] They bought and sold homework from one another, stole and exchanged tests, and smuggled reference books into exams. The atmosphere at Taylor Allderdice High School became so consumed with this corruption that one student summed up the ethic as "Cheating pays."[23] Naturally, the staff of Taylor Allderdice was publicly embarrassed when the news broke. But this one school should not be singled out as an anomaly. Three-quarters of college students today admit to have cheated during high school, a contrast with only one in five as recently as fifty years ago.[24]

Cheating in school is not a propitious sign of early character development, but neither is it a foreboding type of behavior with a socially warped quality to it.[25] Children have always cheated in school and no doubt always will—though hopefully not with such regularity and such dedication as did those at Taylor Allderdice High. Childhood cheating is in large part situational. It is not especially difficult to prevent in schools that give a high value to honesty and at the same time provide students with meaningful work.

The same cannot be said of the other antisocial behaviors now appearing on the youth scene across every sector of our societal landscape. The Marmotte League, a confederation of eight high schools that play sports together, has banned an old tradition: the post-game handshake. Since the league's inception, it had been considered good sportsmanship for losing teams to congratulate winning teams with handshakes and "high-fives" after the game. In recent years, however, this moment of intended graciousness had become an occasion for scuffling and insults. When school officials sensed that such hostilities might escalate into real violence, they banned the ritual for all of the sports that the league plays. The course of greatest wisdom, they decided, was to prevent any contact between opposing teams.

Peer relations between boys and girls also have run into trouble recently. Many who work with young people have noted a surge of sexual harassment among today's teenagers. In 1993, a survey by the

American Association of University Women found that two-thirds of all schoolchildren—82 percent of girls and 51 percent of boys—say that they have been sexually harassed *by a peer* sometime in their school careers.[26] Almost one-third of the girls claim that unwanted advances from other young people occur frequently. Because the AAUW study defined sexual harassment broadly (including items such as glances and wisecracks), it may have overstated the extent of the problem. Still, the study provides one indicator of how much the quality of relationships among girls and boys is deteriorating. Heterosexual relationships are becoming more a forum for cheap amusement and macho self-testing than a source of intimacy or romance. It may be that this quality has always characterized some portion of boy-girl relations among immature young people; but today's young seem to be intent on growing into rather than out of their immaturity.

A recent summertime fad among preteens is a practice called "whirlpooling." A ring of boys traps a girl in the middle, closes in on her, and then "anything can happen," in the words of one gleeful participant.[27] A 1994 National Council for Research on Women report describes the activity this way:

> At a local swimming pool, a throng of boys surrounds a girl to fondle her and pull at her bathing suit. No one protests; the lifeguard looks away, figuring "boys will be boys." The demeaning game—called "whirlpool"—becomes routine; most girls choose to sunbathe rather than swim and eventually another girl is physically assaulted in the pool."[28]

This is simply one step further along a pathway of sex-for-sport that young people have been walking down for years. Although such conduct has been associated in some accounts with inner-city or disadvantaged youth, this is not the case at all. Children in middle-class communities have shown exactly the same tendencies. The best known example of this was the 1993 "Spur Posse" incident in the town of Lakewood, California.

The Lakewood incident has been well documented, and it is instructive.[29] On 19 March 1993, eight students from Lakewood High School were taken into custody by Los Angeles County Sheriff's deputies. The students were accused of raping and molesting girls as young as ten. What caught the public's imagination about this incident was not simply that youngsters were committing sex crimes against other youngsters. In fact, it has been well known for some time that minors themselves are responsible for a major portion of today's child abuse plague.[30] The spectacle of youth preying on one another no longer has much surprise value. But the Lakewood incident did have a newsworthy twist. The boys were competing with others in their gang (the "Spur Posse") to win points through sexual conquest. Each "score" won a point; it counted the same whether the girl consented or not. A rape was as good as a love affair. This group of boys had gone about as far as one could go in reducing their girlfriends to objects in a sexual game.

It turned out, though, that the gang's antisocial exploits were not limited to their sexual gamesmanship. Upon further investigation, the gang was found to be at the center of criminal activities that had been quietly terrorizing the community. Members of the gang were accused of burglary, assault, arson, and finally the detonation of an eight-inch pipe bomb that, according to a member of the arson squad, was intended to kill a target of retaliation. People throughout the town, and particularly the children, repeatedly had been intimidated by the gang's use of such tactics as driving menacingly past homes as if they were trying to run people down.

Of all the striking features of this incident, the most revealing (and the most chilling) was the sense of normalcy with which the community absorbed the gang's activities. "It was well known around the school, this point system," the police lieutenant said matter-of-factly. "It didn't matter whether the girls consented or not. If they consented, it was a point. If they didn't consent, it was a point." The same lieutenant reported that some residents of the community were taking the attitude that "boys will be boys."

The high school's principal apparently was so unconcerned about the gang's activities that he failed to act on early warnings before things blew up. When later challenged, he said, "It was not a school problem." Taking his lead from the principal, the school's physical education teacher was quoted by the New York Times as saying, "You should know that this incident was blown out of proportion." In fact, in writer Joan Didion's follow-up interviews with residents throughout the community, she found the phrase "blown out of proportion" to be something of a mantra. She noted that residents were treating the news coverage and not the boys' behavior as the town's real problem.

With this kind of muted community reaction, the boys could hardly be expected to take their misdeeds to heart. When interviewed on the inevitable talk shows after they had achieved national fame, they responded with a kind of feral pride and swagger. They were full of what they had been told was "self-esteem"—I shall have more to say about this in Chapter 4. For now, I quote from Joan Didion's incisive observations:

> The boys seem to have heard about self-esteem, most recently at the "ethics" assemblies (date rape, when no means no) the school had hastily organized after the arrests, but, hey, no problem. "I'm definitely comfortable with myself and my self-esteem," one said on "Dateline." "Yeah, why wouldn't I? I mean, what's not to like about me," another said when asked on "Maury Povich" if he liked himself.[31]

Was the Spur Posse an anomaly or a fulfillment of the direction in which young people from all sectors of society are now drifting? There is no answer to this question just yet. As a society, we may change course in the way that we raise our young. If we do not, I would guess that we shall see many more Spur Posses in our future.

Nor should the Spur Posse be seen as the far-out fringe of antisocial youth. Police blotters all across the country have records of youth crimes that likely would curl the hair of the most hardened Spur Posse member. Every county D.A. will tell you that he could fill a book with the horror stories that he has investigated in the last few years, and the pace is quickening all the time.

Some of these stories, but not nearly all of them, make their way into the media. A teenage president of his class in Missouri joins with two classmates to bludgeon a classmate to death with baseball bats. A fourteen-year-old in New Jersey cuts his mother to pieces and then takes his own life. A sixteen-year-old in Oklahoma City shoots his parents point-blank through their heads while they are sleeping. Three young teens in Atlanta spend a long night torturing to death a man who had been crippled from multiple sclerosis.[32] In the spring of 1994, a gang of eight boys and girls in Houston blithely videotaped their own crime spree for sport. When a woman reported the boys and girls to the police, they torched her house and destroyed her car. In the bucolic country setting of Rochester, Massachusetts, a fifteen-year-old admits to coldbloodedly murdering his parents and younger sister on a lovely fall evening in 1993. The case is eerily reminscent of Didion's Spur Posse account: the boy's father had always excused his son's long history of antisocial behavior with the comforting defense that "boys will be boys." All of these recent crimes have taken place in middle-class suburbs, committed by children raised with the many reputed advantages of a middle-class upbringing.

According to Joan Didion's report, the young people in Spur Posse also were from a solidly affluent background—and they took pride in their advantages. They considered themselves upper-middle-class, well educated, and well bred. They certainly did not suffer from lack of parental attention. Didion writes of one member's family: "This is a family that has been, by its own and other accounts, intensively focussed on its three sons. . . ." Didion quotes the mother as saying, plaintively, "We'd walk into Little League and we were hot stuff . . . people would come up to me and say, 'Your kids are great.' I was so proud . . . I've been Mother of the Year. I've sacrificed everything for my kids."[33]

This chapter began by noting the comfort, ease, and safety that modern affluence has brought to middle-class families. The chapter ends, though, with descriptions of family life that no longer seems as comfortable, easy, or safe as it used to be; and with forebodings of a future filled with fear and disgrace. What has happened to the middle-class dream?

In fact, the middle class *is* in danger of falling apart—not because, as many have written, its affluence and material benefits are threatened, but because its future generations are slipping away. In this regard, the advantaged of our society are in the same boat as the disadvantaged. The two social worlds are merging, swirling together in a whirlpool of present-day youthful disenchantment. This common predicament is a hard but inevitable fate: it is, after all, one society that we must inhabit. It is a society that will recover only when we find ways to inspire the best in every young person, rich and poor alike.

3
Growing Up the Hard Way

The squalid and dangerous conditions surrounding many children living in disadvantaged neighborhoods are well known to anyone who glances at the morning newspapers. Barely a day goes by without a story of a child who has been shot, abandoned, abused, or neglected to the point of lasting damage. I do not refer here only to stories in the national or world news. In virtually every locality—certainly in our cities, but even in our smaller towns and rural villages—the mayhem in our less fortunate children's lives is a daily event, carried out with grim regularity.

Also widely reported is the havoc that many young people themselves are wreaking on their own homes, their own schools, and their own communities. It is not just that children are getting shot, abused, and exploited. The most shocking part is that they are doing much of the damage themselves. And they are often doing it to one another. In many bleak corners of our society, children are not only the victims but also the perpetrators of the most savage types of crime, from mayhem to murder.

As I write this chapter, today's newspapers report that a local teenage girl has been killed in a drive-by shooting. Earlier this week the same papers told of a twelve-year-old boy shot to death by a friend. Last week there were other stories, and next week there will be more: they blend into one another with their numbing regularity. There is nothing special about any one week, nor about the particular area in which I live. The violent death of a child by the hand of another child is now a commonplace event. One barely winces anymore when hearing of it. The problem for those of us who would bring such calamities to the public's attention lies not in finding outlets for exposing the damage but in keeping the dreary onslaught of childhood disasters from deadening everyone's sensibilities. What was once horrific has now achieved normalcy. When this happens, people inevitably tune out.

A 1993 National Academy of Sciences report on the deteriorating conditions in many young peoples' lives stated baldly: "We believe that the problems of America's young people are getting significantly worse, not better. This is a human tragedy, and it is a national tragedy that will have a serious impact on all of us."[1] The National Academy of Sciences is not an organization that is known for using hyperbole to make its points. The report's executive summary concludes: "For more and more children and adolescents—especially those who are poor and those who must deal with discrimination—the settings of their everyday lives fail to provide the resources, the supports, and the opportunities essential to healthy development and reasonable preparation for productive adulthood."[2]

I shall not repeat here all that is known about the dangers and difficulties in the lives of today's less fortunate children. Journalists and social scientists in the past few years have provided us with enough documentation of these deplorable conditions to shame the most hardhearted citizen. (The title of Alex Kotlowitz's most compelling account itself tells much of the story: "*There are no children here.*") Rather, my purpose here will be to underline a few facts that have especially ominous portent for these children's development—and, by implication, for the future of our society. I also intend to counter some misimpressions that have been spread about the nature of these children and their families. At the close of this chapter, I shall offer some less-than-orthodox views about what has gone wrong and why. Then, in the latter parts of this book, I shall discuss what we can do about it.

I begin with a quote from a seventeen-year-old boy, code-named "Arturo Morales," living in Brooklyn, New York. The quote comes from Mercer Sullivan's rich ethnographic study of youth delinquency in the inner city.[3] Arturo was a subject in the study. On his own initiative, Arturo wrote the following document to explain his motivations for engaging in crime:

Let's say it was right before the burglary with a serious armed robbery charge on me and pending. How was I thinking then? If I was to write my thinking about myself in a scale of 1 to 10, it was a "2," if I was lucky.

1. Didn't care if I got caught by police, prepared to do any crime. Down to shoot, stab, not fatal thoughts, though. Mug, rob anybody, burglarize any property.
2. No job at all.
3. No girlfriend or person to count on.
4. School, I gave up on that.
5. Family, let down.
6. Real tight dirty relationships.
7. Try to get over on cheap shit (crime in general).
8. Thinking to do a job for some money.
9. Wasting time on absolutely nothing but to think of nasty and dirty things to do.
10. Damaging myself physically on a day-to-day basis without doing any positive thinking for myself.
11. Almost every penny to get high or find dumb pleasures.
12. Didn't handle boredom the right way.
13. Being in the neighborhood 90% of the time.
14. Hanging out with the wrong people 85% of the time I hang out.
15. Thinking that I had authority to rob and steal.
16. Not think about the future at all, or serious things not to do, especially at such a young age.
17. Just falling into hell.
18. Not using nothing at all as lessons.
19. Not knowing all I was doing was wrong and later going to be punished for it.
20. Letting money problems get to me thinking I was slick, having a "let's do it" attitude.
21. Nothing to be happy about.

This is a remarkable document, not because the boy's feelings and motives are unique—in fact, they are replicated millions of time over throughout the world today—but because the boy has expressed so much of the standard bundle in one coherent, though discouraging, statement. In his list, the boy opens a window onto some ways of growing up in today's harder places. He also presents us with twenty-one facets of youthful demoralization.

The most striking items in Arturo's list decry the absence of supportive relationships in this life. Who does this boy have to keep him on the
right track, to comfort him when he's been hurt, to set him straight
when he is wrong? Not his family, not a girlfriend, no contact with any
people who genuinely care for one another. Just "real tight dirty relationships"—associations in which, very likely, people are treated like
objects for one another's gratification and exploitation. It is difficult for
a child to develop respect either for others or for the self in a social
world where people are treated as means to ends rather than ends in
themselves.[4]

What the boy does develop respect for (as well as affection) is
money—and particularly for the instant pleasures that money can
bring. As Cornell West has written in his trenchant discussion of communities that rouse material rather than spiritual goals in young people,
"the result is lives of what we might call 'random nows,' of fortuitous
and fleeting moments preoccupied with 'getting over'—with acquiring
pleasure, property, and power by any means necessary."[5] Arturo is well
aware of how empty such material pleasures turn out to be. Yet these are
the only things that he has found in his young life to motivate his energies. School certainly hasn't; nor has work of any kind. This leaves lots
of room for thrill seeking and other empty pursuits, boredom, crime,
self-destruction, and ultimately despair. He acknowledges all of this.
The greater pathos, though, is that none of his life experience leaves
him with much hope for the future. Arturo's demoralization is complete with his recognition of this void.

At least Arturo is able to recognize what is missing in his life. He has
an awareness of certain higher standards against which he may compare
his own spiritually impoverished circumstances. He knows that something is wrong, that there is a better way. Otherwise, he could not
inveigh against his lack of good relationships, his sense of lawlessness,
his failure to learn from his mistakes. He could not complain about
"falling into hell" unless he had some intimation of a different sort of
place. Arturo will not allow himself to be fooled into thinking that his
materialism will ever lead to happiness. There is an astuteness, a wisdom in Arturo's comments that belies the common stereotype of the
savage youth—the all-around loser who is as short on wits as he is on
conscience.

In an insightful attack on this misleading stereotype, the study's
author Mercer Sullivan points out how bright and adaptable these

wayward young people really are: "Some of these youths' criminal activities were indeed reckless and thrill-seeking, but others displayed considerable and often successful ingenuity. *The assumptions of low intelligence and blind pathological motivation as the chief driving forces of criminality do not square well with such evidence*" (my emphasis).[6] The problem clearly is not in the nature of the young people but in the direction in which they are heading.

Why aren't they able to find a more promising direction? The first thing that comes to mind when we think of young people who live in disadvantaged conditions is the adverse impact of material disadvantage on their health, their education, their communities, and their prospects. The many deleterious effects of poverty on youth are a serious matter. They cannot be lightly dismissed, as some romantic social Darwinians are prone to do.[7] It is dispiriting for people of any age to be surrounded by crumbling buildings and downtrodden people, and children are no exception. Whatever their homes are like—and there is wide variation there—children in today's poorer communities trek daily into schools that are without a trace of physical or emotional cheer.[8] Their neighborhoods are in decay. Moreover, some of our children are malnourished, some are ill clothed, some have untreated maladies, and some need eyeglasses or hearing aids without knowing it. These are serious and unconscionable obstacles to children's learning and development.

Yet material poverty is only one part of the story. Children throughout the ages have grown up well in desperately poor conditions. Immigrant families in our own history, as well as in the history of many other places, have had access to far fewer material resources than families on public assistance do today. Despite their economic disadvantages, these earlier immigrant families normally raised their children to avoid trouble and to succeed in their own lives. It has not been unusual, in fact, for children to rise from dire disadvantages to achieve great heights in life. One developmental psychologist sums up an important bit of evidence this way: ". . . reporting on the childhoods of over three hundred famous [and successful] individuals in the study entitled *Cradles of Eminence*, the authors conclude that in the great majority of cases, poverty, illness, alcoholism, parental death, and violence were prominent features of their early family contexts."[9]

Poverty can be a severe handicap, and it is certainly an unfair disadvantage for a child born into it, but it by no means determines the child's destiny. It is a handicap that can be overcome if the society presents other, more fundamental advantages—in particular, social-relational, moral, and spiritual ones. Unfortunately for children throughout our society today, these advantages have become largely unavailable, because they are no longer valued highly enough within the culture at large.

Our cultural drift has adversely affected children of the rich as well as children of the poor. But the damage that it has done to the poor has had more immediate and more deadly consequences. It is important to recognize that the lethal damage to youth in even our most disadvantaged communities is not the result of poverty alone, but rather that it stems from the particular way that poverty combines with current childrearing standards and practices. In affluent communities, the loss has been centered mostly around misdirections in the standards and practices—still with potentially devastating consequences. In less affluent communities, *both* the economic and the cultural climate of childrearing have disintegrated in an interwoven tangle of missteps and wrong turns.

In a landmark ethnographic study entitled *Streetwise*, sociologist Elijah Anderson documents the economic and cultural decline that has decimated a contemporary African-American community.[10] Although not representative of all African-American communities in this country, the tragic stories that Anderson tells are heartbreaking. They reveal the ways in which deteriorating social conditions, combined with a kind of cultural amnesia, can rob children of the guidance they need from concerned adults. They also show how the same unwholesome combination can devastate the community's capacity to maintain a spiritual core. The African-American community that Anderson describes no longer supports the older men and women who for generations have acted as mentors to the young. To aggravate matters further, the community has lost its capacity to support churches and other institutions that once provided sources of shared purpose for young and old alike.

Until as little as a generation ago, boys and girls in African-American communities had access to the wise elders—Anderson calls them "old heads"—who would provide invaluable mentoring for the young. "An old head," Anderson writes, "personified the work ethic and equated it with value and high standards of morality. . . . The old head was a kind of guidance counselor and moral cheerleader who preached anti-crime and anti-trouble messages to his charges."[11] There was nothing subtle or indirect about the guidance. Both the child and the old head accepted the socializing agenda of the relationship. The old head would tell the youngster to shape up, to make something out of his life, and to copy the examples of elders, like the old head, who had succeeded.

Children would meet old heads in small jobs that they might take, in their churches, in their schools, or simply on the street corner. An old head might be a friendly local policemen, a shoeshineman, a favorite teacher, or a hairdresser in the beauty parlor. Many of the female old heads were known for their special links to the life of the local church. The old heads took an active interest in the community's young people, and the youths in turn would respond with ready deference. For many children who had no father or mother, an old head offered much-needed surrogate parenting. They were sources of consolation, sources of advice, sources of occasional help (including financial), and, above all, sources of moral values, well laced with doses of street wisdom.

> In the old days young boys would gather around an old head on a street corner or after Sunday school to listen to his witty conversation and moral tales on hard work and decency. They truly felt that they were learning something worthwhile from someone they could look up to and respect. One of the primary messages of the old head was about good manners and the value of hard work: how to dress for a job interview and deal with a prospective employer, how to work, and how to keep the job. Through stories, jokes, and conversations, the old head would convey his conception of the "tricks of the trade."[12]

These pillars of social support for urban youth are largely gone now. Their ranks have been decimated by the economic and social decline of city neighborhoods. Many of the old heads now are unable to find work in their communities. Many have become victims of crime. Others have moved away in fear of being caught in the incessant war between the drug lords and the cops. Some have even fallen prey to violence at the hands of young people who at one time would have come to them for advice.

Most of the old heads have gone, and the few remaining in place have lost their drawing power. Their ability to galvanize the young was always contingent on the shared perception that their road, with its moral overtones, was the road to both survival and well-being. As the social position of all the neighborhood's adults has disintegrated, this perception has lost its validity. Because jobs with living wages are not widely available in disadvantaged communities, no longer can an old head credibly send out the message that young people will have fine prospects if they model themselves after their elders.

As a result, the quality of social life for young people in inner cities has changed drastically. In the place of constructive mentoring relationships with concerned adults such as the old heads, young people have drifted into exploitive associations with drug traffickers, pimps, and gangs. A generation or two ago, relationships were based upon mutual trust and care. The newer ones too often are founded upon instrumental ends rather than interpersonal ones; and they are conducted with deceit and self-protectiveness rather than honesty and respect. The child is now a means for someone else's profit and pleasure. Children are best advised to look out for themselves, because no one else can be counted on. As I shall maintain throughout this book, children learn values most readily from their own direct experience in relationships. If a child's social experience precludes honesty, respect, and caring, and if it instead reflects deceit and mistrust, the child will come away with a cynical view of the social world and a tendency towards the manipulative use of other people.

The economic blows to the old head tradition have gone hand in hand with the cultural ones. In fact, it is impossible to separate the two. The decline in meaningful work has been accompanied by a lost faith in the work ethic that the old heads professed. Skepticism and rebelliousness have replaced respect for authority, and guile has replaced social responsibility. I shall argue throughout this book that this skepticism about moral values is culture-wide. Along with the economic factors, it has led to the rapid decay of the communities from which the old heads are disappearing. For the few old heads who remain, the culture's repudiation of their most cherished values is especially painful when embodied in the behavior of young people who were once considered to be the old head's charges. Anderson quotes one old head as lamenting: "These young boys today just don't want to work."[13]

They don't want to work, that is, *in the settings that our society now presents to them*. Their schools do not engage their talents and energies. Nor can they find decent jobs that spur their ambitions. This is not to say that these young people are short of talent, energy, or will. In the right setting, they will readily display all of these virtues. The "right settings" are ones that offer young people genuine challenges, that require young people to accept genuine responsibility, and that give young people an opportunity to develop skills that they recognize as useful for their future prospects. In the absence of such, skepticism about the core vales of work and responsibility quickly takes root. The problem for too many young people today is that the "right settings" for their healthy growth are becoming increasingly unavailable. This is true all over, and especially so in our more troubled communities.

In a careful examination of three inner-city neighborhoods, Milbrey McLaughlin has chronicled the loss of what she calls "nurturing settings" for youth development.[14] McLaughlin describes how violence has made these neighborhoods into threatening environments for children rather than places for them to find friends and mentors. "The notion of neighborhood as a nurturing setting where older members watch out for and over neighborhood youth and where networks of 'local knowledge' and intergenerational intimacy weave sturdy systems of support for young people and their developing identities, is far from the reality that contemporary inner-city youth experience. Such notions of nurturing neighborhoods embody, at best, times gone by."

McLaughlin also shows how schools, churches, and workplaces no longer hold much attraction for young people in the inner-city. The schools have crumbled, many of the churches are gone, and the workplaces no longer offer good jobs. These once-valuable contexts for growth, writes McLaughlin, "do not add up to much for inner-city youth." As a result, children develop little sense of what it is like to work; nor do they acquire the habits, values, and beliefs that could support their abilities to work. These youngsters cannot imagine themselves as people who could handle serious responsibilities, enjoy working hard, and contribute something of value to society. "In this context," writes McLaughlin, "the deep pessimism, low self-esteem, and destructive behavior that correspond to this (disconnected) sense of personhood are not surprising, nor is the hope of the youth advocate that they 'just live, just duck the bullet.'"[15]

But the same young people will come alive when given a modicum of opportunity. At a community center in Los Angeles, inner-city children help organize neighborhood clean-up campaigns.[16] In Camden, New Jersey, disadvantaged adolescents care for the elderly in nursing homes, plant community gardens, and take leadership positions on city boards.[17] At a residential treatment center in New Hampshire, teenagers who were once considered dysfunctional have built sturdy cabins and lean-tos that withstand the harsh winter weather. In after-school programs and clubs across the nation, children put on plays, write newspapers, and conduct science experiments.[18] In every instance, observers have remarked how *smart* the children's performances are, how filled with zest and vigor.

Often these are young people whom everyone else has given up on. Yet they look wholly different when they find engagements that galvanize their natural strengths. In new settings that present them with tasks that they can understand and take seriously, their broad array of natural intelligences shines through. At the same time, the history of disappointments and failures that they bring with them recedes into the background. Eventually, these young people build upon their old strengths; they acquire new strengths; and they begin to believe in their own potential. They share their newly invigorated views about themselves with others in their social world, and in turn this mutual communication reinforces the positive directions that their lives have taken.

Scattered throughout our cities and towns are a few remaining settings that still do provide nurturing environments for young people. Milbrey McLaughlin and her colleague Shirley Brice Heath have examined some of these. In particular, Heath and McLaughlin have identified some invaluable grass-roots organizations that shelter young people and offer them worthwhile activities, safe peer relations, and informal counseling from concerned adults.[19] Boys and Girls Clubs, theater groups, sports teams, charities, and local community centers are among the organizations that are providing nurturant settings for youth development. Heath and McLaughlin's analysis of these successful youth organizations is instructive, partly because it pinpoints what is missing in other, less successful settings and partly because it provides clues about what kinds of settings we need to create if we are to reclaim the future prospects of young people everywhere.

First and foremost, successful youth organizations ensure the physical survival of the children who attend them. They provide safe havens from the perils of the streets and, for some children, from the unpredictable hazards of their own homes. The organization gives the child a place to go to get away from trouble; and, just as importantly, it gives the child an identity as a member of an organized group that will look out for him. Youth workers are aware of the protective value of such an identity and use it freely. One worker is quoted as saying: "As long as you are involved in something—school, sports—the gangs will leave you alone. It's the unaffiliated youth that they are after."[20]

Other characteristics of organizations that succeed in providing nurturing settings for inner-city youth include local community credibility and stability in their staffing. Workers who know the local scene well, and who are committed to remaining on the job year after year, are able to reach even the most difficult youth because they can be trusted. Trust is a feeling that is sorely missing in many of these young people's lives.

Trustworthy organizations also take pains to include all the youths who seek them out, as long as they follow the rules and are not disruptive of the group. Moreover, they engage young people in activities that reflect a sense of purpose. The purpose may be competitive—such as winning the community basketball league—or charitable—such as providing food for the needy. Either way, the purpose creates a sense of solidarity within the organization. Just as importantly, the purpose serves to bring youngsters out of their own self-centered concerns.

Most striking of the characteristics that mark a successful youth organization is the nature of its expectations for youth. Successful organizations hold a high positive regard for their young members. They hold high expectations for young people's behavior, requiring strict adherence to community regulations. The organizations also hold high expectations for their young members' abilities, giving them demanding tasks to perform. They give their young members real responsibilities without doubting that they can shoulder them. All of this stands in sharp contrast to the approach that most public agencies and other service organizations take when they come in contact with today's youth.

Many of our government agencies and other service institutions radiate condescension for the young people whom they are in business to serve. They see disadvantaged youth as helpless victims with problems to be fixed. McLaughlin quotes one child in a public project as saying, "People just don't expect much of you."[21] To exacerbate matters, many public agencies project the idea that the youth problems are too deep and complex to be directly remedied; and, in any case, they (the agencies) have not been given enough resources to do so. What follows is a plea for more resources that may serve the agency's self-interest but fails to address the vacuum of expectation in these young people's lives. It is little wonder that so many young people come away feeling helpless and hopeless after contacts with such organizations.

Young people everywhere search for challenges. This is part of their natural drive to develop skills, to test themselves, to demonstrate competence. If a society is to provide a healthy climate for youth development, it must offer young people vigorous challenges with honorable purposes. Otherwise, and inevitably, the young will look elsewhere. They may explore the underground with all of its illicit and dangerous associations. They may confuse reasonable risk-taking with self-destructive danger-seeking. The young will continue to seek out channels for their natural talents and energies, but they will do so without moral guidance from people who care about them. In short, they will expend their youth in a frenzy of empty encounters, many of them angry or frightened. They will come away with nothing more than a hostile sense of self-protectiveness and a feeling that they have been cheated by society.

On this matter, their feelings are right. They are cheated, certainly, by the bad economic hand that they were dealt at birth. But, more than this, it is the combination of the economic deal with the drift of contemporary culture that has proven particularly malevolent for these youths. The crises of violence, crime, self-destruction, and despair among disadvantaged youth is an interactional phenomenon. It cannot be explained by economics alone. *Nor can it be remedied through purely economic solutions.*

At the heart of the crisis is a failure in our society's capacity to guide the development of young people in productive directions. This is a failure that stems from misconceived notions about what children are like and what they require for healthy growth. The failure is culture-wide, although it affects young people differently in different sectors of society. That is, the failure interacts in one way with affluent conditions and in another way with impoverished ones. In affluent conditions, as I have noted in Chapter 2, it can lead to narcissism, depression, under-achievement, and to a host of antisocial and self-destructive behaviors— often, though not always, of a mild-to-moderate sort. In impoverished conditions, where many other social supports for the young have been ripped away entirely, the failure of societal guidance can bear more bitter fruit. It is then that we see youth gangs terrorizing neighborhoods and schools. We see prison rates for young men and pregnancy rates for young women soar. Less dramatically but most hauntingly, we see a generation of young people grow up devoid of hope or dreams for their own future.

A recent National Research Council report on adolescents in high-risk settings shows us how the life settings for disadvantaged youth have crumbled in recent years:

Over the past two decades, the major settings of adolescent life have become increasingly beleaguered, especially where the numbers of families living in poverty have expanded and where their concentration in the inner cities of large urban areas has increased. Schools in such areas do not have the resources needed to sustain their mission, school buildings are in disrepair, and there is often the threat of violence in classrooms and corridors; neighborhoods are more disintegrated, buildings more dilapidated, and streets often physically dangerous; communities are also fraying as ever-rising mobility destroys personal ties and traditional institutions, such as churches, and local businesses suffer from disinvestment; families are more frequently headed by a single parent, often a working mother unable to obtain competent child care or by two working parents with less time for childrearing because they are striving to maintain their standard of living in the midst of a general decline in wages. Such settings have become the crucible in which the lives of increasing numbers of America's youth are being shaped.[22]

The litany of decline that the National Research Council presents is appalling beyond question. In its analysis of the problem, the NRC identifies the usual candidates: loss of family income, truncated federal spending programs, and a general decay in the economic climate of urban neighborhoods. Yet the crisis that the NRC describes has a fundamental cultural side as well. This side is not illuminated in either the NRC document nor in most other government and social science reports. The cultural side has to do with the beliefs and practices of people throughout our entire society—with beliefs and practices that have been allowed to wither during the present era. It has to do with the loss of guiding relationships between adults and children; with the loss of institutions that once provided guidance for the young; with the loss, or corruption, of shared standards for youth conduct; and with the deterioration of our expectations for our young.

A dilapidated building is a demoralizing sight to look on, and there is no doubt that buildings fall into disrepair for lack of resources to fix them up. But buildings do not put graffiti on themselves. Only people do that—usually young people. And there is nothing more demoralizing than a building, dilapidated or not, that is splattered with graffiti. I do not know of any statistics on graffiti trends over the past hundred years, but I would guess that the practice has been rapidly accelerating in places where youth congregate. In this and in other ways, the material decay of places where young people grow cannot be understood in isolation from their behavior. Economics plays its part, but the culture's declining standards for youth behavior also have been a highly active agent in the mix.

In the end, the gravest threat to our society may come from the least likely source: the optimistic venture of reproduction. Birth, the renewal of human life, calls for celebration whenever it occurs. Yet the calamitous mix of poverty and cultural decay has triggered an explosion of teenage births that could yield further societal disintegration beyond anything that our society has witnessed. In some communities, nine out of ten children are born out of wedlock, and the numbers spiral upwards with each passing year.[23] As the numbers of children born out of wedlock soar, these children face ever dwindling chances that their communities will be able to provide them with proper support and guidance.

Poverty sets the stage for teenage motherhood because, as Joelle Sander has written, "living in poverty strongly adds to many children's feelings of deprivation, disadvantage, degradation; to their need to get out of their homes; to their overall sense of instability."[24] Throughout the ages, in many parts of the world, the less affluent generally have started families earlier and have had larger families than the wealthy. In part, this was seen as necessary for the family's economic survival. Yet there is a different quality in today's teenage births. It is an out-of-control quality that promises neither economic advantage nor a responsibly raised family. This out-of-control quality cannot be explained by poverty alone, because it rests in large part on our culture's failure to impart a sense of social responsibility to its young.

As anthropologists have pointed out, societies the world over limit the reproduction rights of their members.[25] Some traditional societies do so by demanding that prospective parents own goods, land, dowries, and the like. Others bestow parenting preference on those with social status, secure incomes, or good education. In modern democratic societies, such biases have vanished; but until now there has remained an expectation of commitment, as demonstrated by a marriage vow. The rationale behind all these means of social control is the same: this is society's means of ensuring that those who are born will be properly raised. Social control of reproduction is an elementary mechanism of societal self-preservation.

Such social control has disappeared in many sectors of our society, to its great peril. Teenagers with little education, no demonstration of commitment, and no financial means are allowed the opportunity to produce children. In fact, in some ways they are encouraged by their social norms to do so. Far from fearing social sanctions for producing children out of wedlock, many teenagers perceive a rise in their social status by becoming parents, whether married or not.[26] The fathers achieve a boost in their self-image, and the girls achieve public assistance, a home of their own, and enhanced status. There is of course an important economic background here—the rewards would not be so attractive if the girls had better alternatives—but the main story is cultural. And the culture truly has lost its bearings on this matter. As Mihalyi Csikszentmihalyi has written:

> Nowadays spokespersons for the disadvantaged bridle at any hint of restricting the procreation of the poor and accuse the more affluent classes of attempted genocide. Such critics blame the racist, capitalist nature of our society for even thinking in these terms. If this be genocide, however, it is a form that has been practiced by every society, on every continent, as far back as human memory goes. It is hard to imagine how any society could have survived without making sure that children were raised by parents who took responsibility for them.[27]

What happens to a society that not only fails to raise its young properly but that then sets up *these same young people*—many of whom have shown little interest, capacity, or commitment for raising children—to be parents of a yet another unguided generation? We do not know. It has never been tried in recorded history. Or perhaps it has been tried, but the societies that did so passed away too enfeebled or too preoccupied by chaos to record their misadventures for us.

One thing, though, is known. Young people who throw themselves into parenthood with few resources, little education, and shaky networks of social supports cannot be expected to recreate the culture on their own. They will not reverse the decline in expectations. Nor will they correct the misconceptions and myths that permeate our contemporary childrearing practices. They will gaze upon the fallen standard, and leave it where it lies, for they will know of no higher possibilities.

These are young people with all the natural potential in the world. They have the ability to understand social responsibility and to shoulder it fully. Yet although we can expect much from them, we cannot expect them to develop their potential wholly on their own. They cannot learn responsibility until we assume *our* responsibility to know what these youngsters need and to provide it to *all* of them. Our first step in this direction must be to see past the myths and misconceptions that have been blinding us in recent years. I examine these in the next part of this book.

Part II
The Misdirections

4
Misconceptions of Modern Times, I
The Elevation of Self and Derogation of the Spirit

The vast economic and technological progress of the past two centuries has brought with it a cultural sensibility that has been loosely called "modernity." For some, the modernist sensibility has seemed liberating, whereas for others it has seemed corrupting. Those who raise children in modern times have had a vantage point on both experiences. No one can doubt that modernity has affected childrearing in many profound ways. Some changes have been unquestionably to the good: for examples, our advanced medical sciences and our improved capacity to produce food for the world's children. In most parts of the world, happily, young people now routinely survive their childhoods without fear of disease or hunger. Others changes have been clearly for the ill: for example, the dissolution of familial and community bonds that has cut millions of children loose from the guidance and protection that they need during their formative years. In its most extreme incarnation, this dissolution can be seen in the large numbers of children who make their homes on the streets, scrounging out a living and threatened dail-

by violence and exploitation.[1] Less extreme manifestations include many kinds of youth demoralization and conduct problems that I am discussing in this book. Many changes brought about by modernity have positive as well as negative elements. These include new beliefs that combine valid insight with dangerous myth and new practices that are at the same time well intentioned and wrongheaded.

At its core, modernity represents the shared conviction that we can make progress over the constraints of nature and tradition.[2] Modern science and technology indeed have dominated nature, to our great material advantage; and social change has made tradition seem anachronistic in many ways. Yet among the victims of modernity's victories has been our traditional sense of community. For many of the early moderns, this was a fully intended victim. They longed to consider themselves free-spirited and chafed under the petty confines of traditional communities with their "small-town" mentalities. They believed that, in a society unbounded by arbitrary conventions and close personal affiliations, people would have more opportunities for self-realization and less arbitrary injustice in their lives. As sociologist Amitai Etzioni has written:

> It's hard to believe now, but for a long time the loss of community was considered to be liberating. Societies were believed to progress from closely knit, "primitive," or rural villages to unrestrictive, "modern," or urban societies.[3]

Etzioni points out that the loss of community has had a bleak side that was unforeseen by those who thought that it would be simply liberating. When community vanishes, writes Etzioni, the fundamental sense of "we-ness" that establishes the very basis of morality cannot long endure. In its place emerges a disconnected, self-centered, and aimless quest for personal advancement. In a social world made up only of "free" individuals, people may argue about their rights but forget their responsibilities. They may promote their own needs but ignore those of others. In the process, they may drift into crime and other antisocial activities; and they may lose sight of the cherished social traditions and moral values that once were passed on from generation to generation. When people pursue private goals, the risk is that they may never acquire an ennobling sense of a purpose beyond the self. "The ancient Greeks," writes Etzioni, "understood this well: a person who is completely private is lost to public life."[4]

Ever since its aversion to unimproved nature and the traditional order of things became apparent, modernity has drawn its share of critics. One of the more flamboyant initial statements to this effect was Friedrich Nietzsche's *Will to Power*. The nineteenth-century philosopher threw down the gauntlet at what, to him, was modernity's worst demon: the nihilism at its core. In our modern attempt to control nature through reason and science, Nietzsche wrote, humanity was negating its most vital sources of energy and power.[5] Nietzsche's writings were passionate, intemperate, and ultimately inflammatory, and they presented no credible alternative vision. Yet over the years more and more social critics have echoed Nietzsche's concerns and have added others that they see as related.

In particular, two themes emerge in recent critiques of modernity: the ascendence of self during the modern era, and the derogation of spirituality and faith.[6] At present, as the cultural sensibilities of the day escalate into post-modernism and some of its frenzied excesses, the familiar themes of nihilism, egoism, and faithlessness are becoming increasingly dominant in many brands of social criticism.[7]

In discussing modernity's shortcomings, my purpose is to reveal some unfortunate byproducts of our modern cultural sensibilities. I intend to expose some mistaken beliefs that shape popular conceptions of children and influence our contemporary approaches to raising them. My focus here is restricted to the mistaken notions and not to the entire cultural setting surrounding them. The beliefs indeed have arisen from, or have been shielded by, the features of modernity that our social critics have attacked. But I do not believe that such links are inevitable. Many families who live thoroughly modern lives have resisted the misconceptions. In the future, as we strip away the mistaken notions from the invaluable advantages that modern life has brought our children, I hope that we may be persuaded to resist the false ideas. One of this book's aims is to show how it is possible—indeed, essential—to improve our understanding of children's needs, and to reform our present childrearing practices, without rejecting the many insights and opportunities that progress has granted us.

Of the three themes that I noted above—nihilism, egoism, and the derogation of faith—it is only the latter two that can be readily detected among many modern families. True nihilism does prevail in a few circles, and it may set a tone—even a direction—for the society as a whole; but in its most blatant forms it is still a fringe phenomenon that has little direct impact on most families' childrearing beliefs and practices.[8] In contrast, the aggrandizement of self and the loss of faith are powerful currents in the mainstream of modern living. They each exert a strong influence on our collective approach to children. It is true that each may draw from, and contribute to, an overall tone of nihilism in the culture, and they no doubt reinforce one another; but they also operate on their own accord, as formidable voices of moral influence. About the aggrandizement of self, the sociologist Daniel Bell has written:

> . . . in the nineteenth century, the sense of the self came into the fore. The individual was considered unique, with singular aspirations, and life assumed a greater sanctity and preciousness. The enhancement of the single life became a value for its own sake.[9]

About the loss of faith, Bell writes:

> The real problem of *modernity* is the problem of belief. To use an unfashionable term, it is a spiritual crisis, since the new anchorages have proven illusory and the old ones have become submerged. It is a situation which brings us back to nihilism; lacking a past or future, there is only a void.[10]

The elevation of self and the loss of spirituality are not in themselves responsible for all the misconceptions about childhood that prevail in contemporary society, but they have created a cultural context where the misconceptions have flourished. They have established a receptivity to ideas that once would have been ridiculed or dismissed out of hand. They have desensitized us to the inane nature of some currently fashionable childrearing practices. Moreover, these misconceptions about children have contributed to their own perpetuation; for the consequences of the misconceptions have been precisely to promote self-centeredness and a spiritual void in the generations of youth who have been raised in their wake.

The Primacy of Self

A common refrain in today's popular discourse about human development is the primary importance of self-esteem. The idea, baldly stated, is that it is impossible to respect, cherish, or love others without first learning to respect and love oneself. The refrain runs throughout pop music, Hollywood movies, pulp literature, and newspaper advice columns. It can be heard on talk shows, in lay psychoanalysis, and during confessional conversations of every sort. Self-love is considered "the greatest love of all," in the words and title of one pop song at the top of the charts in recent years. In this and other formulations, self-love is the first source of one's personal fulfillment, happiness, and positive feelings towards others.

The popular phrase most bandied about in recent years has been, of course, "self-esteem." The phrase has attained a certain notoriety in the wake of some especially foolish extravagances, such as an infamous California state commission dedicated to raising self-esteem among its citizenry. The vacuousness of such uses of the idea have been well-revealed in social commentary such as, for example, Wendy Kaminer's brilliant exposé of the self-help industry.[11] Still, the notion of self-esteem has retained its appeal in many circles, professional as well as public. In fact, self-esteem boosting not only persists as a stated goal but prevails in most educational and service institutions. Teachers, clinicians, and guidance counselors everywhere speak first and foremost about the primary importance of self-esteem. They see a lack of self-esteem at the root of every problem and an increase in self-esteem as the hope for every recovery. Many professionals believe self-esteem to be the key engine of both intellectual and personality growth.

The "how to" childrearing books are liberally dosed with tips for bolstering children's self-esteem. Many explicitly claim that self-esteem is a *prior* condition—and a necessary one—for a child's optimal psychological development. They also emphasize the importance of early experience in either establishing or permanently impairing a child's self-esteem. This, of course, places a major onus on the parents. Any parent who wishes to raise healthy children (and what parent doesn't?) is advised that praise, expressions of love, and other direct efforts to build children's self-confidence will make all the difference. Here are some versions of the idea, drawn from well-established parental guides:

> Every parent wants his child to grow up to be secure and self-reliant, and much of this is based on his feeling of self-esteem. It is the parents themselves who are most responsible for the desired results. . . . The self-esteem established during the preschool and school years is the basis for self-assurance and self-esteem during the teen-age years and adult life.[12]

> Self-esteem—how we feel about ourselves—affects us in all areas of life. It is a reflection of all our early experiences, especially how our parents feel about us and how they convey that feeling. Good self-esteem is the enzyme

in whose presence emotional, intellectual, and creative enterprise flourishes. Self-esteem determines degree of sense of ownership of ourselves—the continued feeling that we really do own our inner assets. This provides for appropriate independence and serves us well in all areas of life.[13]

Helping your children grow up with strong self-esteem is the most important task of parenthood. The child with good self-esteem has the best chance of being a happy and successful adult. Self-esteem is the armor that protects kids from the dragons of life: drugs, alcohol, unhealthy relationships, and delinquency.[14]

Self-esteem—or the lack of it—is critical in people's lives. Positive self-esteem has been found to be related to high motivation or drive for achievement—in sports, in work, in school. Studies also show that youngsters with high self-esteem have more friends, are more apt to resist harmful peer pressure, are less sensitive to criticism or to what people think, have higher IQs, are better informed, more physically coordinated, less shy and subject to stage fright, and are more apt to be assertive and get their needs met. High self-esteem is considered by some to be the essential core, the basic foundation, of positive mental health.[15]

None of these statements is unusual or especially notable. They are all typical of the way that childrearing experts—and, as a consequence, the public—view the role of self-esteem in human development. In fact, these statements come from books that I selected largely at random from the shelves of my local public library: I am confident that if I had grabbed other books, I would have found similar statements. They are fair reflections of today's conventional wisdom.

The conventional wisdom is flawed on several grounds. As the last statement expresses most clearly, self-esteem is assumed to cause many positive and important developmental outcomes, ranging from intelligence to mental health. (Intriguingly, the last statement also notes physical coordination, which may be a stretch of the imagination even for diehard self-esteem enthusiasts). The notion that self-esteem is a *prior cause* of these positive outcomes derives, illegitimately, from correlational studies that show no more than simple association between measures of self-esteem and measures of achievement, health, and so on. Every statistics lesson taught anywhere begins by explaining that *correlations do not establish causality*. No matter how many correlations are found between self-esteem and anything else, self-esteem is just as likely to be a *result* of the positive developmental outcomes as it is to be a *cause* of them.

This is not just an academic dispute. It is a matter of serious consequence for young people whether we believe that self-esteem precedes healthy development or whether it derives from it. At the present time, there is a shared assumption among many that the direction of the relationship leads from self-esteem to healthy growth. According to this assumption, we should build self-esteem in children before we do anything else, using direct means such as extensive praise.[16] Then and only then it can become possible to move on and encourage them to achieve, develop skills, and so on. If this assumption is wrong—if, that is, it has the developmental relationship backwards—many of our childrearing practices are futile as well as counterproductive. By following such practices, we are overlooking the true source of self-esteem and in the process allowing the child's potential to lie fallow.

Early in my daughter's kindergarten year, she returned home with a three-by-five index card containing two words: "I'm terrific." Each child in her class had been given a similar card with the same two words. My daughter told me that her teacher had asked all the children to recite the words in class, to remember them, and to keep the cards for a further reminder. I asked my daughter what it all meant. She said that she was terrific and that her friends were terrific. She had no particular ideas about what they were all terrific at.

Such exercises are not unusual in today's elementary and preschools. I have seen many similar versions of "self-esteem boosting" in my visits to classrooms nationwide. These kinds of efforts are based upon the widespread assumption that self-esteem is the first business of child development and early education. Most teachers, day care workers, and clinicians I know refer immediately to "low self-esteem" when children in their charge are having problems. Their solutions, naturally, are to find ways to encourage children to think well of themselves.

Now this practice is certainly admirable in its intent and message. All children *are* good—and, yes, terrific—in the sense that they are all valuable and special. There is nothing wrong, and everything right, with communicating this sentiment to young people. But we must realize that self-esteem is not a virtue that can be directly transmitted through abstract injunctions. Exercises such as "I'm terrific" do not implant the point in any sustainable way. Even more troubling is the ancillary message that such efforts often carry. As I discuss below, a young mind often interprets an abstract incantation for self-esteem as an invitation into self-centeredness.

In and of itself, self-esteem offers nothing more than a mirage for those who work with children. Like all mirages, it is both appealing and perilously deceptive, luring us away from more rewarding developmental objectives. While capturing the imagination of parents and educators in recent years, the mission of bolstering children's self-esteem has obscured the more promising and productive possibilities of childrearing. We would do better to help children acquire the skills, values, and virtues on which a positive sense of self is properly built.

A primary focus on a child's self-esteem provides no useful point of entry into the child's psychological world. For one thing, the notion of self-esteem per se lacks grounding in anything that the child considers real. From a young child's perspective, there is no objective referent to generalized statements such as "I'm terrific." Young children have little appreciation for idealized or abstract statements about persons. Their concerns are far more tangible. When thinking about themselves, young children focus on what they look like, what they do, where they come from, and how they feel from moment to moment. If they are to have any impact, communications about what a child is like must be embedded in concrete statements about *actual* personal qualities, capacities, and activities. Holistic messages that "you're great" are empty of meaning to a young child, because they are devoid of information that children care about. Disembodied compliments that are intended to bolster a child's self-esteem are unlikely to be processed, or even heard.

In this light, the common practice of empty praise may seem like nothing more than an ineffectual though harmless exercise. But it is more damaging than this, and for several reasons. The most serious problem with this practice is that it is based upon a kind of white lie, a benign falsehood similar to the appealing "Lake Wobegon" conceit—that there can be a place where "all children are above average." It would indeed be mean-spirited to complain about such a gentle fib, especially when meant in humor. But when intended seriously, the message is, in fact, less than honest. Even when spawned by the best of intentions, less-than-honest communications to children inevitably create unfortunate complications. One such complication is that, sooner or later, children see through all inaccurate statements about themselves.

Children are remarkably bright and active when it comes to figuring out who they are. They have a searching understanding of self that few adults fully appreciate. They are aware of what they can and can't do; and they constantly probe their surroundings for feedback about their capabilities.

From birth onwards, children receive feedback about themselves from many sources—including parents, peers, teachers, relatives, and their own experiences in the physical world. People tell them that they are short or tall, that they are learning to read well, that they can dance or play baseball, that they are generous or thrifty, bold or shy, and so on. Children listen hard for such feedback and keenly digest it. They construct from this multiple-sourced feedback an objective framework through which they appraise any new messages about themselves that they may hear.[17] It is not possible to deceive them for long with statements that do not fit into this framework.

What happens when a child receives a pleasantly meaningless message to the effect that the child is the greatest in every possible way? There are several possibilities. Some children will simply tune out such messages. The abstractions mean little to them anyway. They may repeat the phrases on occasion but do not take them to heart in any enduring sense. The messages change nothing about their notions of who they are.

But other children do become affected by such messages, though not at all in the way intended. Some develop an exaggerated, though empty and ultimately fragile, sense of their own powers. Some dissociate their feelings of self-worth from any conduct that they are personally responsible for. (Witness the case of the boys from the Spur Posse, with their "I'm all right" attitude, as discussed in Chapter 2.) Other children develop a skepticism about such statements and become increasingly inured to positive feedback of any kind. In time, this can generalize into a distrust of adult communications and a gnawing sense of self-doubt.

Repeated shadings of the truth inevitably tend to undermine the listener's confidence in the message bearer. There are many ways that parents and teachers may shade the truth to children while trying to build up a child's self-esteem. Strategies include empty rhetoric, transparent flattery, bland distortions of reality, inappropriate comparisons between the child and others, and so on. Even though these are white lies intended to help rather than to deceive, children can and do see through them. If repeated often enough, these deceptions will undermine the child's trust in the adult's veracity.

This would be problematic enough if the ill effects of such messages were confined to children's distrust of certain statements made by the benevolent adults in their lives. But the distrust generalizes much further, eventually turning backwards on itself. The unfortunate irony of this is that empty self-esteem messages work directly against the exact condition—low self-regard—that the adults are trying to ameliorate. If children have fragile feelings about their own competence, mistrusted messages can only unsettle these feelings further. Children are perfectly capable of asking the same questions that we would ask when faced with empty flattery: Why do people feel they need to make up things about me? What is wrong with me that people need to cover up? What are these stories about me trying to prove?

There is no question that adult encouragement can play a supportive role in helping children acquire skills. Children thrive on genuine accomplishment. They should be urged to try new things, and they should be told that success is within their reach. When linked to the child's real effort and real achievements, adult praise can serve a useful purpose. But bland admonishments that "you're great" with no particular referent weaken the adult's credibility with the child. New achievement is a slow, gradual, step-by-step process. If an adult has the patience to guide a child through this process, the child will not only develop new skills but will build a solid self-confidence grounded on something objective. There are no easy shortcuts to this. The child cannot be quickly inoculated with self-confidence through facile phrases such as "I'm great" or "I'm terrific."

Researchers in child development have conducted multitudes of studies reporting reams of data on children's self-esteem and its correlates. An examination of these studies reveals that this is one of the many areas where popular mythology is wholly out of touch with the scientific findings. Overall, research on the abstract type of "self-esteem" that I have been discussing has been one of the great disappointments in empirical studies of child development. Scientists rarely have been able to connect, in a direct or unambiguous way, a child's global sense of self to any important behavior or skill in the child's social, emotional, or intellectual life. The most authoritative review of self-concept research in the past twenty years was conducted by psychologist Ruth Wylie.[18] Wylie's conclusion about the studies relating children's global self-esteem to important developmental outcomes is the following: "the most impressive thing which emerges from an overview of this book is the occupance of null or weak findings." This despite the fact, as Wylie revealingly notes, that "conventional wisdom very confidently predicts strong trends."[19]

Self-esteem research is usually conducted by asking children to rate themselves on a number of generally phrased items like "I'm a good person," or "On the whole I am satisfied with myself." Children are asked to agree or disagree with such statements and the extent of the child's agreement determines the measure of the child's positive self-esteem. Since many child-care professionals believe self-esteem to be the root of most children's problems, there has been a widespread expectation that such measures of self-esteem will correlate with all sorts of indices of the child's performance. That is, by the common line of reasoning, the extent to which a child expresses agreement with these positive self-statements should predict how well the child is adapting to life. But evidence supporting such common-sense predictions has proven elusive. Studies that purport to link children's self-esteem with their intelligence, their achievements, and their social and emotional maturity have not even provided convincing correlational data, let alone evidence of causal connections, as is commonly believed.

In the past few years, the news media have frequently publicized a purported finding to the effect that girls in our society "lose" their self-esteem when they reach adolescence.[20] The finding has been circulated in many news stories, popular books, and newspaper opinion columns. As a consequence, the finding has captured the public eye. Schools and teachers have been urged to make special adjustments for female students in order to combat this "loss." At the time of this writing, there are even rumors of an expensive government program now in the works to remedy this "problem."

Yet the scientific support underpinning all this clamor is as shaky as jello. There have been few reports of such gender-specific losses in reputable professional or scientific journals, and gender differences of this sort rarely appear in longitudinal studies of childhood and adolescent self-understanding.[21] In cases where such differences have been claimed, they can usually be accounted for by wide variations in the meaning of "self-esteem" among different groups of youth. For example, boys with conduct disorders—those who routinely cause trouble—often score extremely high on many self-esteem measures. The inclusion of such boys in studies of adolescent self-esteem could well explain the supposed "drop" in female scores, because the exaggerated scores of the troublesome boys raise the overall male average. In other words, the reason that adolescent girls look as if they are "losing" their self-esteem is that they are being compared with a group that includes boys with high self-esteem scores that are based on braggadocio. The concept of high self-esteem is so nebulous that it can just as readily indicate swaggering miscreancy as self-assured learning and productivity.

For many reasons, there is no credible self-esteem methodology that could establish a "drop" in adolescent girls' self-esteem. The entire construct of self-esteem is simply too flawed for such a determination. How can a young girl's statement about her "self-esteem" (whatever that might mean to her) be compared with statements that she makes about this diffuse notion when she is a teenager?[22] By what standard could the two be compared? The notion of self-esteem is so elusive and ephemeral to begin with that it cannot possibly provide the basis for a valid comparison among either age groups or gender groups. Yet the cultural climate is so receptive to concerns about children's self-esteem that large-scale social policy decisions are considered in the light of spurious claims about alleged "losses" of such among girls.

A child's generalized sense of adequacy can not be readily accessed through glib, abstract statements like "I'm a good person." Such statements mean little to the child in real terms. Rather, the child's self-confidence is spread across a host of small, specific skills. It is noteworthy that the one self scale which has reported some success at reliably predicting children's adaptation is Susan Harter's "Perceived Competence Scale." This scale measures children's impressions of their own abilities across several well-differentiated areas of performance. The rating items are grounded in concrete activities that children are directly familiar with, such as sports, artistic performances, reading, and math. The measure does not assume that children abstract an overarching, global message from the sum total of these activities. As a consequence, the measure seems to have some core validity and some real meaning to children.

Parental and teacher communications to young children also must have validity. They must be meaningful and they must be forthright. They also must be oriented towards purposes that adults can fully and consciously endorse: that is, they must encourage children to develop specific skills and values. With this as a goal, children know what they must do, and they can see tangible signs of progress when they learn the skills that help them meet the goal. In this way, the skills and values will bring intrinsic rewards of performance and accomplishment to a child. Only these kinds of truthful and specific messages can impart to the child a self-confidence that is grounded in real capabilities.

In contrast, trying to orient a child toward the overall "worth" of the self means communicating with the child in terms that children are unfamiliar and uncomfortable with. It means speaking loosely and non-literally; and therefore it means teaching children not to take adult words seriously. In some cases, it also may mean raising questions about why this peculiar message is being transmitted at all. Ironically, questions such as these can trigger the child's self-doubt, aggravating the exact wound that the original message was intended to heal. I have seen this happen on several occasions. An adult offers a child who is having trouble a generalized self-esteem boost: "you're the greatest," "you're just fabulous," or some such phrase. From the child's point of view, the message comes out of the blue. A quizzical look crosses the child's eyes. The child protests, verbalizing her own self-doubt and dismissing the adult's message. The child's self-doubt is strengthened and a potentially helpful channel of communication is discredited.

Our contemporary obsession with children's self-esteem no doubt stems from the historical shifts in our attitudes towards the young. The obsession derives from an entire movement away from imposing external demands on children and towards nurturing their internal sensibilities. This movement has not been all bad. It has increased our sensitivity to the special nature of young people's thinking, and in the process has opened new communication channels between adults and children. But our heightened concern with children's internal mental states has combined with the increased child-centeredness of modern times to create crippling imbalances in children's views of themselves and the world. When we tell children that their first goal should be self-love, we are suggesting to them that they are at the center of the universe. By contributing further to the already child-centered orientation of modern culture, this emphasis can push a child towards a narcissistic insensitivity to the needs of others. We should not dispute the value of self-love, but we should question its utility as a primary goal in raising and educating children.

The development of character and competence means much more than getting in touch with one's personal feelings. It means more than acquiring a favorable opinion of oneself—especially if that opinion is based on little more than a generalized desire for high self-regard. It means more than loving, respecting, or even improving oneself. Growing up means learning to participate constructively in the social world. It means developing real skills, getting along with others, acquiring respect for social rules and legitimate authority, caring about those in need, and assuming personal and social responsibility in a host of ways. All of these goals necessarily bring children out of themselves. They require children to orient towards other people's needs and standards.

The psychological danger of putting the child at the center of all things, of making children too conscious of themselves and their own feelings, is that it draws the child's attention away from fundamental social realities to which the child must adapt for proper character development. When children learn to place themselves first, they learn to care more about their own personal experience than about the feelings and reactions of others. They come to ignore the guidance and feedback of others, because they have never learned to value it. They fail to establish a firm basis for respecting others, including even the important adults in their lives. In the long run, they learn to act as their own sole moral self-referents, which is not a good way to develop a balanced moral sense.

I recall a police interview with a fourteen-year-old who had just been caught mugging an eighty-year-old blind woman. Not only did the boy steal her purse, but he beat her so badly that she was hospitalized with intense pain and possibly permanent impairment. When asked why he had chosen such an unlikely victim, the boy cavalierly said that it was best to rob blind folks since they would have a hard time identifying you. But the real shocker was the boy's response to the question of whether he had no feelings of sympathy for the old lady in the pain that he had caused her. "Why should I?" the boy asked bewilderedly. "After all, she isn't me."[23]

Without objective moral referents beyond themselves, children cannot acquire a stable sense of right and wrong. The child-counseling literature is full of cases where children have become accustomed to denying misdeeds even when they have been caught red-handed. An older brother intentionally pushes a younger sister off her bike, perhaps because he wants the bike or perhaps just for the fun of it. The act is done in plain sight of the parents. Although the sister howls from pain, the boy strenuously asserts that he has done nothing wrong. He clearly means it. Indeed, in this child's mind there was no misdeed. Because the boy has learned to respect only himself, he is the only one whom he needs to convince. Over time he gets used to convincing himself of his rightness, whatever the objective evidence to the contrary. Since he has not found reason to care what others think, the objective evidence makes no difference to him. So the boy tells himself only what he needs to hear in order to feed his self-image. The truth counts only insofar as it serves the self-image: this, after all, is a long-standing pattern for the boy. The pattern of denial, which began as a series of benign white lies intended to bolster self-esteem, has hardened into an enduring propensity towards deception. The deceptiveness is directed as much toward the self as toward the outside world. Out of such seeds grows a stubborn disregard for objective truth and external standards. In more extreme cases, such disregard can develop into pathological lying and other clinical disorders.[24]

Just as children need to acquire real skills in order to provide an objective referent for their feelings about themselves, they also need to be held to consistent standards, firmly enforced, in order to develop respect for persons other than themselves. Children must learn to cope with stubborn realities that will not change as the children's moods and feelings change, and that will not vanish when the children's complaints grow loud enough. Failing to give children firm rules and guidelines is a sure way to breed arrogance and disrespect. It leads to another facet of the inflated sense of self-importance that is fed by our culture's overemphasis on self-esteem.

It is essential that children learn a deep and abiding respect for others in their lives. This is at least as important as respect for oneself; and it is in fact ultimately required for it. Stable self-respect cannot be built in a vacuum. It requires the support of constructive relations with persons whose judgment and feedback one respects. For this reason, perhaps ironically, humble persons are often the most secure. Conversely, the most aggrandized expressions of self-regard are often the most shaky. Children in particular rely on their positive feelings for others when they shape their own identities and senses of worth. It is a matter of grave concern when young people, in their attitudes and conduct, show little spontaneous respect towards the elderly or towards adults in general. For those raised in other times and places, or for anyone who has had the opportunity to observe adult/child relations in a more traditional culture, the dearth of respect between children and adults in our society always seems unsettling, and properly so.

Children must learn to hear negative as well as positive feedback, to care about it and to act on it. This can only occur in relationships where they have full respect for the person who offers the child feedback. It is best for children to learn this while young, well before the adolescent years. It is best, too, for them to learn it through actions rather than words. Exhortations to "Listen when I talk!" or "Respect your elders!" are just as futile as "You're terrific!"—and for much the same reasons. In both cases, the only effective route is through a continuing succession of specific actions and achievements, such as taking on genuine family responsibilities around the house. The process must be sustained, in small and large ways, over the years. There is no quick fix. Only through long-term exposure to these kind of socializing experiences will children come to realize that their own opinions and reactions cannot remain their sole, or even their primary, reference point. Only through such experiences can children develop a healthy sensitivity to the judgments and guidance of others.

The pursuit of self-esteem is everyone's right. It is an important part of psychological adjustment to cultivate the sense of well-being that lies at the center of personal happiness. But the pursuit of self-esteem *in and of itself* is a misdirected quest. It is a logical *and* a psychological contradiction in terms. One cannot "find" self-esteem in isolation from one's relations to others because it does not exist apart from those relations.

I noted earlier that feelings about oneself must have some grounding in reality if they are reliably to serve any positive psychological function. Similarly, they must be compatible with one's feelings towards others. Even the most basic sense of self-worth (a sense, that is, that "I am worthwhile simply because I am a person") is inextricably linked to one's respect for other people. One cannot say that "I respect myself simply because I am a person, yet I have no respect for other persons." Even for a young child, this conclusion is untenable logically and unmanageable psychologically.

Like happiness, self-esteem is a goal that cannot be pursued directly or for its own sake.[25] A successful quest for good feelings about oneself will take many circuitous paths and must subsume many types of accomplishment. The acquisition of skills and knowledge is a part of this quest; and so is the building of positive social relations with others. Acute self-consciousness rarely will aid the quest, and it can be a serious distraction. Parents and teachers serve their children best when they guide their children towards the skills, knowledge, and relationships that eventually lead to genuine self-esteem. Parents serve their children poorly when they engender in them an artificial belief in their own importance. There are no shortcuts to the real thing.

Nothing to Believe In

When we teach children to concern themselves first and foremost with their own senses of self, we not only encourage self-centeredness but also fail to present a more inspiring and developmentally constructive alternative: that they should concern themselves about things *beyond* the self and *above* the self. We fail, that is, to convey to them a sense that there are other important things in life beyond their own individual circumstances and feelings.

Even at early ages, children need something beyond themselves to believe in. One mantra of our modern age is that we should all "believe in ourselves" and that we should urge every child to "believe in yourself." The sentiment is understandable, but the phrase has a very different meaning than it once had. Not long ago, to "believe in yourself" meant taking a principled, and often lonely, stand when it appeared difficult or dangerous to do so. Now it means accepting one's own desires and inclinations, whatever they may be, and taking whatever steps that may be necessary to advance them.

Self-centered goals cannot provide a constructive foundation for a child's development. Children will not thrive psychologically until they learn to dedicate themselves to purposes that go beyond their own egoistic desires. They will not thrive unless they acquire a living sense of what some religious traditions have called *transcendence*: a faith in, and devotion to, concerns that are considered larger than the self. In a child's world, the clearest example of this is a sense of service to others. But it also may include beliefs about profound matters such as the meaning and purpose of life.

A sense of transcendence, an orientation of service to others, an intimation of life's deeper meaning are all elements of the capacities that I refer to when I write of children's need for spirituality. The notion of spiritual needs has not been a fashionable one in scientific or professional circles, in part because of its connections with religiosity. For decades it has been difficult to locate a mention of spirituality in any child development text or childrearing manual. This, of course, is no more than a reflection of a long-standing trend in secular societies.

As for religiosity, the very mention of it raises either anxiety or scorn in many educational circles. As Nel Noddings, a moral philosopher and Stanford University's dean of education, writes: ". . . educational theorists have been ignoring religion as if the enlightenment project had succeeded."[26] What began as efforts to remove prayer from public school classrooms has escalated into a movement to remove from nondenominational settings everywhere all forms of religious display, including Christmas carols, menorahs, and the ceremonial use of the name God. As Noddings complains, even the formal *study* of religion, with no advocacy concerning belief or nonbelief, has become off limits in many schools.

Yet religiosity has been humanity's primary means of imparting a sense of spirituality to its younger generations. Despite the suspicions of social scientists and educators, religiosity has been shown to have clear benefits for children. In developmental psychology's landmark study of children's adaptation to difficult circumstances, religiosity proved to be the only "non-negative" quality that protected children from risk.[27] In other words, each of the other effective protective "factors" amounted to the *absence* of something—the absence of drug use, the absense of hormonal imbalances, the absense of parental conflict, and so on. Religiosity was the only *positive* force enabling some children to adapt to stressful and burdensome life events. This finding, I believe, would be replicated many times over if social scientists were not so leery of including the benighted notion of religiosity as a variable in their research with children.

In just the last few years, some of our most noted authorities on child-rearing have woken up to the glaring omission of spiritual messages from our children's lives. Some of these authorities have tried to awaken a society that is forgetting how to give its children something to believe in. In a recent statement, Benjamin Spock wrote of the importance of spiritual beliefs and values for children.[28] Dr. Spock defines spirituality as, among other things, "feelings such as love for others, dedication to one's family and community, courage, the response to music and scenery." He goes on to write:

> I have hopes that enough people will come to recognize the social ills and tragedies stemming from our spiritual poverty, or be shocked by some economic or environmental disaster, or be inspired by a spiritual leader, so that they will dedicate themselves to the ideal of service to their fellow humans, whatever their gainful occupations, and inspire in their children a similar

ideal. I literally believe that without such a conversion, our singleminded dedication to materialism will do us in. I'm not basing this on religious or moral grounds but simply on the evidence that our society is disintegrating.[29]

In calling for a spiritual enrichment of our children's lives, Dr. Spock notes first and foremost how important it is to encourage in children a dedication to service. But despite the injunctions of such an influential childrearing guru as Dr. Spock, there still is a strong bias in our society against expecting service from children. As anthropologists have concluded, this is one of the most striking contrasts between modern and traditional cultures.[30] In traditional homes, children routinely are asked to help look after younger siblings, help care for the elderly, and pitch in on many household tasks. Children are given real responsibilities, and their assistance is taken seriously. This is not the case in most parts of the modern world, where children are shielded, even discouraged, from assuming duties that provide essential services to others.

There are many reasons why parents now shy away from expecting service from children. I noted several of these in Chapter 2. Some of the reasons are legitimate: the sad saga of child labor in factories and sweatshops during the industrial revolution makes decent people leery of anything that smacks of child exploitation. Moreover, affluent families are justifiably grateful for their ability to provide their children with sufficient time and resources to pursue activities of self-improvement, from reading to sports to piano lessons. These are all valuable experiences, and children's lives would be poorer without such opportunities.

But these activities subsume only a relatively small portion of children's time today. Amidst all the TV watching and hanging out at the mall, there should be some spare time left over for helping others. Yet here some other, less legitimate, reasons intervene. The first common reason is that parents believe it to be too inconvenient—"more trouble than it is worth"—to get their children to do something useful. The second reason is that parents worry that their children may be too busy, too "stressed out" from all their other activities and obligations, to add one more set of burdens. This second reason derives from the common apprehension that today's children are growing up "too fast, too soon," an idea that has been widely advanced by experts in popular childrearing books.[31]

The first reason is a self-fulfilling prophecy. The surest way to breed incompetence (and low self-esteem of the *real* kind) in a child is to treat the child as incompetent. If a parent assumes that a child cannot be counted on to accomplish a task, the child takes that message to heart. The child thinks that "I am not the kind of person who can . . ."; and a negative belief in one's own capacities forms. In the process the child loses the opportunity to develop the skills required for the task, and so the negative belief creates its own validity.

In actuality, children are far more competent at early ages than adults in our society give them credit for.[32] They thrive on challenges and on chances to prove themselves. Competence motivation is a natural part of every child's repertoire.[33] If encouraged, it enables children to develop their capacities with zest and vigor. Still, we have found many ways to discourage children's native competence drive. Not the least of these are our unfounded doubts about children's abilities to be helpful.

The second reason—that children are already "stressed out" without adding further to their burdens—is as ill-founded as the first. Children are hardy creatures. They do not become overburdened by participating in a reasonable share of industrious activities. They do not need to come home after their six-hour school day and "cool out" in front of the TV. They *do* need to have their energies fully and joyfully engaged in worthwhile pursuits. Stress for a child is not a function of keeping busy; rather, it is a function of receiving conflicting messages about the self and experiencing troublesome life events beyond one's control.[34] Activities that children gain satisfaction from, and accomplishments that children are proud of, relieve rather than induce stress. Activities that provide genuine services to others are ideal in this regard.

Even in our recent history, there have been times when families have needed to ask their children for help, despite any misgivings they may have had. Some of these occasions have been temporary: a natural disaster such as a flood, a severe family illness, a calamitous accident in the home. Because such occasions quickly come and go, it is hard to know how children respond to the extra demands placed on them during the crisis. But within recent history there has been a prolonged economic crisis—the "Great Depression"—that historians and social scientists have documented extensively. Some of the records include data on children's development in families that were hard hit by the economic stresses of the day.[35] These data show no overall ill effects of asking children to provide daily household help and other family services. On the contrary, all indications from the data are that children adapted to such demands as a matter of course. They pitched in with energy and pride, with all the natural vigor of childhood. Such experiences gave these children invaluable opportunities to learn personal and social responsibility. In an old-fashioned phrase, they were character-building experiences. In contrast to the worries of many parents and professionals today, the demands were neither stressful nor debilitating for the children.

I am continually astonished by the extent to which children's nature is misunderstood throughout contemporary society, even among circles of experts in child development. Some years ago, I organized a team of educators to create a demanding after-school program for children from a disadvantaged neighborhood.[36] The idea was to provide dynamic, engaging, and educational activities for children who were having difficulties learning during the regular school day. Often these children had nothing much to do in the afternoons other than hang out on the streets and look for trouble. The program that we designed combined exciting instructional projects, community service, and tutoring in literacy and numeracy. We wrote a proposal for the after-school program and shipped it off to a respected funding agency. The agency had a distinguished panel of child development experts who were charged with reviewing the proposal. The critique came back from the experts: Children would not have the energy to accomplish anything in the afternoons because they would be "burnt out" by then. They needed that time after school for themselves, to "recharge their batteries."[37]

Sparing children from demanding challenges, and in particular from all expectations of service to others, does *them* a disservice; because it robs them of opportunities to establish their sense of competence and the sense of social responsibility. It imparts to children exactly the wrong pair of messages: (1) that they are incapable of accomplishing anything and (2) that they are living only for themselves. The first message belies the child's natural endowment of intelligence, hardiness, and energy. The second goes against the grain of what it means to be a fully developed human.

Removing service from children's lives is misdirected enough. But many families in modern society go even further. Not only do they relieve children of the expectation to serve others, they alleviate them of responsibilities for their own personal care. Busy parents get children dressed long after the children are able to dress themselves, because the parents believe that it is quicker and easier that way. Parents make their children's beds, clean up after them, make them sandwiches and snacks, drive them distances that could be easily and safely walked or biked—all out of a sense that asking such things of children would be either too much trouble for the parent or straining the capacities of the child. Once again, the sense of personal incompetence becomes a self-fulfilling prophecy. The child quickly acquires the belief that the bed is too hard too make, the distance too far to be walked. I cannot imagine a set of beliefs that could be more crippling for a child's developmental prospects.

In systematically underestimating the child's capabilities, we are limiting the child's potential for growth. In withholding from children the expectation to serve others as well as the expectation to care for themselves, we are preventing them from acquiring a sense of social and personal responsibility. We are leaving the child to dwell on nothing more noble than gratifying the self's moment-by-moment inclinations. In the end, this orientation is a particularly unsatisfying form of self-centeredness, because it creates a focus on a personal self that has no special skills or valued services to offer anyone else. Paradoxically, by giving the child purposes that go beyond the self, an orientation to service results in a more secure belief in oneself.

In the same vein, fostering children's spiritual beliefs nourishes children's psychological development as well, enabling them to realize their full intellectual and social potentials. This principle, benign though it may sound, is not widely accepted in today's culture. The present climate of childrearing beliefs is skeptical and guarded about the notion of spirituality—so much so that Dr. Spock himself takes on an apologetic tone when he invokes the notion.[38]

The final set of misconceptions that I shall take up in this chapter has to do with children's spiritual beliefs. Three misconceptions in particular have been especially constraining. One is the fallacy that young children are unable to understand or appreciate spiritual messages. The second is the misplaced fear that children will be damaged by exposure to other people's spiritual and religious beliefs. The third is that spirituality itself is somehow maladaptive—or at least quaintly irrelevant—in our modern, technological society. All of these misconceptions have arisen from misreadings of various psychological theories, and they have become pervasive in today's public consciousness.

Now spirituality and religiosity are by no means synonymous. Spirituality, as I have been discussing it, is the broader concept. Still, religious convictions have been a common expression of spirituality, in childhood and beyond. Much of what we know about children's spiritual potential comes from observations of their statements and feelings towards God. Many of the misconceptions about the risks of exposing children to spiritual messages derive from controversies concerning religious tradition. In the remaining section of this chapter, I shall draw much of my argument and my illustrations from analyses of children's religious beliefs.

The psychological sciences have provided too few coherent accounts of children's religious beliefs. Most child psychology textbooks ignore the subject. Researchers are wary of the harm that dabbling in such a "soft" and ethereal area might do to their scientific reputations. Even clinicians treat the matter gingerly, not sure whether to take a child's religious expression as a maladaptive symptom or as an adaptive insight.[39] Within psychology, the roots of this wariness go back to Sigmund Freud's antipathy towards religion. Freud wrote that "religion is comparable to a childhood neurosis," a "poison from childhood onward."[40] Certainly this perspective leaves little room for accounts that could show the positive contributions that spirituality might make to children's development.

The non-Freudian perspectives also have shed their share of skepticism on the subject of children's spiritual development. Jean Piaget was notably unfriendly toward religion and dismissed children's statements about God as "magical" or "animistic" beliefs that normally are outgrown in the course of development.[41] To confound matters more, many of Piaget's followers have misread Piaget's writings as having claimed that children are incapable of abstract thinking. Piaget did write that children have trouble disentangling the concrete from the abstract, and that they often cannot manipulate abstract symbols for the sake of quantitative operations; but Piaget did not claim that children are incapable of abstract thinking. This misreading of Piaget has led many within educational settings to refrain from engaging children in discussions about the meaning of life, death, and other metaphysical issues. It is remarkable, therefore, that the same theory has been used to dismiss children's spirituality on two contradictory grounds: first, that religious beliefs are nothing more than immature childishness, and second, that children are incapable of the kinds of abstract thinking that it takes to engage in metaphysical discourse.

We should know better on both counts, especially in the light of writings by some researchers who have stepped beyond the previous boundaries of the old Freudian and Piagetian traditions. Studies have clearly demonstrated children's capacity for profound religious thought. These studies also have confirmed the value of faith in children's lives. Psychoanalyst Anna Maria Rizzuto, who has opened up the area of religious development for psychiatric study, writes of young children's early capacities for religious understanding:

> In dealing with the polarities of life from the earliest moment, the child has already formed complex representations of both parents, of the divinity, of the order of things, and, most important, of himself or herself as a unique individual. The private interpretations that the child has formed about these matters constitute something like a proto-religion, with a child-centered private godhead, private psychic rituals to deal with it, and complex beliefs, all of which carry the force of convictions of emotionally lived experiences.[42]

In a program of research designed to extend the Piagetian "cognitive-developmental" tradition into hitherto uncharted territories, psychologist James Fowler has documented the rich religious faith and beliefs of children in the earliest years of life.[43] Fowler discusses at least three belief systems present in young children: "primal faith," which characterizes the infancy and toddler years; "intuitive-projective faith," found among preschool children; and "mythic-literal faith" that appears during the elementary school years and beyond. Fowler shows how the progression of these belief systems follows the general direction of the child's intellectual growth during this period. He also shows how each system, in its way, helps the child sort out the meaning of the child's relationship to the universe.

It can be as frightening for children to gaze into the void beyond their existence as it is for adults. Like adults, children naturally rely on systems of belief and faith to fill that void with meaning. This is a primary function of religious belief for many children. Fowler cites many examples of how religious conceptions serve this function for the very young. The conversation quoted below took place between a four-year-old who had just lost her mother in a car crash and a family minister:

JULIE: Why did God take away my mommy to heaven?

MINISTER: That's a hard one to answer, Julie. When your mother was hurt so badly in her car accident she was in a lot of pain. Maybe God did not want her hurt so much, so he took her to be with him in heaven.

JULIE: But why did God make that man run into my mommy's car?

MINISTER: I guess I don't think that God made that happen, Julie. Sometimes things happen that God doesn't do. I think he probably felt very sad when your mommy was hurt.

JULIE: When Tabby [the family cat] died, Mommy said that God took her to heaven. Didn't he take mommy away too? I want her back. Why doesn't God bring her back?[44]

There can be no answer to Julie's heartrending final question, of course. It is the language of the discourse, not the possibility of a solution, that is important here. Julie's response to her unimaginable loss is to search for meaning through religious ideas. As Fowler writes, "That she is willing to use religious language, even at age four, is a strong indication that she will struggle to make sense of her mother's death in terms of how she understands God."[45] Julie's questions show signs of a spiritual quest in a four-year-old's world: a faith that there must be a larger meaning, even in the face of an incomprehensible tragedy; an active search for meaning through personal examination and social communication; and a resolute persistence even when intellectual tools such as logic have been exhausted.

In another recent ground-breaking work, child psychiatrist Robert Coles uncovered a rich world of spiritual beliefs and ideas in children's drawings, spontaneous musings, and conversations.[46] Coles also notes the functionality of children's religious beliefs: "Children try to understand not only what is happening to them but why; and in doing that they call upon the religious life they have experienced [and] the spiritual values they have received. . . ."[47] Typical among the many children that Coles observed was a nine-year-old girl who thought of God as "a companion who won't leave;" she said that "God is in heaven, but He is in my mind, too."[48] Coles makes the point that the girl's statement demonstrates the close connection between spiritual and psychological development for many young children. This connection can lead children into profound and fruitful directions as they forge their sense of values and their understanding of life. It can be a central support of a child's character development. In an insightful statement, Coles writes:

The task for these boys and girls is to weave together a particular version of a morality both personal and yet tied to a religious tradition, and then (the essence of a spiritual life) ponder their moral successes and failures and, consequently, their prospects as human beings who will someday die.[49]

Among adults today, so much confusion surrounds children's religious interests that children often are actively discouraged from expressing their spiritual concerns at all. In the worst cases, children's intentions are misunderstood and even maligned. Children's needs to reach for faith and to fashion transcendent beliefs in the face of profound mysteries become devalued, to their great chagrin. I am reminded of an incident that I observed on a speaking tour and recounted in *The Moral Child*.[50] I repeat it briefly here because the story illustrates how adult misconceptions about children may interfere with the children's natural need to acquire and use spiritual concepts in their search for meaning.

The background to the incident was the stormy national debate over religion in the classroom. A young teacher had begun her first year teaching in a typical school district composed of worshippers from many diverse religions. The local school board had decided that the best way to ensure the protection of all beliefs was to prevent teachers from offering religious opinions to their pupils. The board expressly issued an edict to that effect. The young teacher in question, just new to the profession, had been advised of this rule in her preservice training and had accepted it without any question.

The incident began with a classroom science project in which the teacher's first grade pupils were asked to raise some fish in a controlled environment. Each child had a fish to care for. After some time, one girl's fish died. The girl wanted to know what would happen to the fish now that it was dead. Would it come back to life somewhere, would it still be happy, would it remember the little girl who had cared for it? The teacher immediately recognized the metaphysical implications of these questions. She simply reassured the girl that the fish was in no pain and that they could bury it outside in the school yard. She told the girl that they would never see the fish again, and suggested that she raise a new one.

The next day an irate principal called the teacher into his office. How, he demanded, could the teacher tell her pupils that fish go to heaven when they die? Apparently, the little girl had relayed to her parents the story of her fish's death, but had embellished the teacher's statements with some comments about heaven and afterlife. The parents, who belonged to a religion that professed the spiritual discontinuity between persons and animals, objected to their daughter's learning in school that fish have could have an afterlife.

When I met the teacher, she told me that she was left with lingering doubts about the little girl. She could not help but wonder if the girl had acted mischievously, in order to stir up some trouble. Was the girl perhaps dishonest by nature? Or did she hold some undisclosed grudge against the teacher? These uncomfortable questions mingled in the teacher's mind with her basic belief that the little girl was just a child, acting childishly. But why, then, the provocative miscommunication to her parents?

Every adult in this story had failed to understand the child, her intentions, or her developmental needs. The parents somehow thought that if the child got their church's precise dogma wrong, the child's religious future would be impaired. The teacher thought that the child must have been up to some mischief with her fabrication. And the principal appeared to be unconcerned with anything more spiritual than covering his own rear flank. In actuality, the child was doing what comes quite naturally to six-year-olds: using a tried-and-true religious idea to cope with the profound and troubling problem of death—a problem for which clearly no one had given her a more satisfactory answer.

In attempting to understand the death of a valued loved one, the little girl turned to the helpful notion of an actual heaven where good creatures find their just reward. This, of course, is a concept widely available in our culture. It is also a concept easily understood by children accustomed to thinking of spiritual ideas in terms of things and places that one can easily imagine. In contrast, the young girl was less likely to be impressed by her teacher's cryptic answers about the fish's disappearance. For the young girl, her parents' abstract distinctions between the spirituality of humans and the nonspirituality of animals inevitably left something of a conceptual vacuum, however well-grounded such distinctions may be in classic theology. The girl filled this vacuum in a creative manner characteristic of six-year-olds. This resulted in an embellished version of what the teacher had told her. Whether the girl realized that her version of the teacher's explanation did not match the teacher's is something that we shall never know. But we may be sure that the girl's story was a function of a six-year-old's need to understand a confusing and disturbing event and not some incipient character flaw. Nor was it a wrong turn in her spiritual development. It was, in fact, a step forward that should have been encouraged by all those interested in the girl's personal development. Instead, everyone in the situation got mad.

Our society discourages children's spiritual growth in countless ways. I mentioned earlier in this chapter two ways that likely are linked to one another: the fostering of self-centeredness and the withholding of expectations for service. Here I add to these a third, more direct kind of discouragement that arises from our wariness and fear of children's spiritual beliefs themselves. This wariness extends both to children's own expressions of spirituality and to their observations of other people's expressions.

For well over a generation now, a fierce battle has raged over public displays of religious symbols such as crèches. Schools have become the front lines in this battle. The hot subject of school prayer is only the tip of the iceberg. In my own community, I have seen effective campaigns launched against children singing Christmas carols, bringing Jewish menorahs to school, and singing spiritual requiems in afterschool singing groups. (I have also seen the cynicism in children's eyes when they heard that groups of people had been complaining about their wholesome and aesthetically beautiful performances.) Other examples are everywhere. In a small New England town, a minister reports on requests to stop his carillon from playing hymns because they are offensive to nonbelievers and their families. In Texas, a parent prevents the free distribution of Bibles to children on their way out of class. In Rhode Island, a parent sues the school system because a class valedictorian refers to God during her graduation speech.

I do not wish to dismiss the legal or civil liberties implications of this intricate issue. I certainly respect the principle of tolerance for people with diverse beliefs, and I understand that a monopoly on religious expression by a powerful majority can be oppressive. Still, from the perspective of children's development, the protests that I have observed can only have a stultifying effect. The protests are heard by young people not as protecting religious freedom but as discouraging the very idea of faith. And they are based on a wholly fallacious notion: that young people need to be shielded from expressions of other people's beliefs. This is yet another case of our underestimating the natural strength and intelligence of the young.

Children are not so easily wounded or led astray. They are resilient, purposeful, and intellectually capable—no doubt far more so than most adults give them credit for being. Children are not so brittle as to be shattered by exposure to beliefs that are different from their own. Nor are they so plastic as to be immediately remolded by such exposure. To the contrary, a sincere display of another's beliefs can hearten and inspire a young person. Such a display can result in an affirmation of the child's own spiritual inclinations, instead of—as in the danger of religious censorship—an implicit denial of the validity of faith. As in so many other ways, misguided attempts to shelter children do nothing more than interfere with their own natural needs and inclinations. These attempts mistake the nature of the child and end up using children to play out our own spiritual conflicts. We do better, and children do better, when we recognize children for who they are. Then we may help them build character upon the firm foundations that their natural strengths provide.

5
Misconceptions of Modern Times, II
The False Oppositions

Of all the distortions in today's public conversation about youth, the most disturbing is the unnecessary polarization of opinions about education and childrearing. Oppositional thinking rules the day. In education, we argue about whether we should teach children subject matter *or* thinking skills; whether we should make school playful *or* rigorous; whether we should teach reading through phonics *or* whole language; whether we should emphasize character *or* academics; and whether we should encourage children to acquire good habits *or* to develop their capacities for reflection. In the home, we argue about whether parents should emphasis freedom *or* duty, self-expression *or* discipline. In the community, some argue for increasing children's rights, others for increasing children's responsibilities, and firestorms develop over issues such as whether children should be directly told to abstain from drugs and sex *or* whether they should be given more detailed instruction about the nature of the risks.

In each case, debates proceed as if the alternatives all were mutually exclusive, standing in opposition rather than potentially linked. Political and civic leaders define overly simplistic positions and create yawning gaps between these positions. Many do so intentionally in order to place themselves on one side of a contentious issue and their opponents on the other. This is the contemporary political strategy of creating emotional "wedges" as means of attracting votes. Where complex societal problems are concerned, the tactic is both irresponsible and dishonest. The truth always falls in between the false oppositions, lost in the gap.

Beyond the havoc that it wreaks with the truth, polarization around matters of childrearing leads to paralysis among the groups of elders who should be mobilizing to provide young people with guidance. The paralysis created by oppositional thinking has been a main contributor to the lack of direction that plagues so many young people these days. In order to combat widespread youthful demoralization, responsible adults need to show solidarity rather than discord with one another.

A striking example of the crippling effect of oppositional thinking has been our failure to mount a nationwide initiative in character education. It is not that citizens disagree about whether schools should teach values, or even about which values schools should teach. There is, in fact, widespread public accord about the need for programs that communicate core community values to young people. A 1993 Gallup poll revealed that over 90 percent of U.S. parents agree that public schools should teach the following core values: the golden rule, moral courage, caring, tolerance of people from different racial and ethnic backgrounds, democracy, and honesty.[1] (Honesty, in fact, was endorsed by 97 percent of those polled; which may lead one to wonder what the other three percent were thinking.)

Such a consensus indicates the kind of shared public concern that ought to make possible forceful public policy. Yet in the spring of 1994, a modest congressional resolution to support a conference and some demonstration programs promoting character education was soundly defeated in committee by a lopsided 23–6 margin. It was the seventh time that Congress had turned down a character education initiative in recent years, despite the fact, as one lonely congressional supporter lamented, "The whole country is crying out for this."

The reason? Politicians chose to ignore the vast areas of consensus over young people's values and to focus instead on the hot areas of disagreement that divide the citizenry: abortion, homosexuality, abstinence, religious expression, and so on. As one reporter put it, "Liberals fear the character-education movement may be a backdoor effort to mix religion with public education. . . . Conservatives, meanwhile, fear character education as an attempt to spread political correctness and undermine parental authority."² One would think that, given the public's shared concern over youth conduct, the two sides might agree to support character education programs that concentrate on honesty, caring, democracy, and so on, and to leave the other issues in the private domain. But the constant polarization over the more contentious matters has worn away the possibility of any such cooperation.

The paralysis has spread across the entire field of education and beyond. As a reporter who covered the character education quagmire wrote, "The controversy in Washington has much to do with the fact that federal involvement in almost every aspect of education virtually guarantees years of discord."³ Governmental efforts to combat other grave youth problems, such as drug use and premature pregnancy, have been disabled by similar debilitating quarrels. It seems that we would rather fight with one another than form a united front to provide young people with the guidance that they need.

Why it is that the oppositional atmosphere persists in the face of our many serious social problems, we may only speculate. Some have pointed to a destructive "culture of critique" fostered by the rapacious sensationalism of modern media. One observer has written: "If public discourse is a fight, every issue must have two sides—no more, no less. . . . The culture of critique is based on the belief that opposition leads to truth."⁴

This state of affairs is especially problematic with respect to matters of youth development. While there are many areas of public life in a democratic society that may indeed be well served by vigorous debate, too much oppositional conflict on matters of youth development is counterproductive. It erodes the consensus of values that we adults need to project in order to ensure the socialization of all our children. Many of our communities are failing to provide positive direction for their young people precisely because they are no longer able to arrive at such a consensus.

It has not always been this way. Although philosophers and social scientists have always argued over the course of youth development and how best to nurture it, such debates were not turned into oppositional political spats within the public arena. For one thing, the intricacies of human development were recognized as complex and irreducible to simple slogans. Problems of education and child medicine were seen as technical matters that required some degree of expert analysis. For another thing, moral issues such as children's character development were seen as private rather than public affairs. Normally such matters were left to the church and the family. Within most communities, there was a general consensus about what was best for children.[5] Where there were differences in opinion about such things, they were kept private.

All this has changed. In recent years, public figures have sought political advantage by taking strident positions on education, "family values," and childrearing. Alternative approaches to youth development have become sharply differentiated and polarized. Explicit efforts in this direction have become a central part of the new political strategy of creating cultural "wedge" issues that separate political candidates from their opponents.

In both the 1988 and 1992 presidential elections, for example, both major parties made conscious decisions to throw education into the arena of political debate. Leading public figures made stump speeches about educational issues such as school choice and student test scores. They also argued about family issues, such as the difficulties of single parenthood and whether women should become working mothers. Political opponents were castigated for their views on childrearing matters that once were considered deeply personal.

What has made this strategy rewarding for politicians is the growing public awareness of the youth problems that I outlined in the first part of this book. Unfortunately, the political rewards of the strategy are not matched by any value that it might have for defining a sensible manner of raising our young. In fact, as I shall show, the polarization itself is aggravating the very social problems that it addresses—including the frustration of today's parents and the demoralization of today's youth.

To ensure the futures of our young, we need to rebuild what one social scientist has called a "youth charter"—that is, *an unwritten community consensus about the behavior and the goals that young people should be guided towards*. In a study of over three hundred American cities and towns, Frances Ianni found that such a "youth charter" is a far stronger predictor of wholesome youth behavior than are such widely heralded factors as affluence, ethnicity, geography, family structure, or social status.[6]

This will come as no surprise to anyone who appreciates the importance of multiple sources of influence on children's social development during their formative years.[7] Young people receive messages about what is right and what is wrong from *all* the people in their lives (including even the public figures whom they hear on the airwaves). As I discuss in Chapter 7, it is important that the multiple messages work in synchrony to guide a child in a beneficial direction. When they clash, the messages lose their coherence. This can be one primary source of confusion and demoralization in a young person's life.

The polarization has yet other unintended deleterious effects. It oversimplifies the alternative solutions for today's youth problems and isolates these solutions from one another. As a consequence, none of the solutions remains adequate for addressing the challenges that we face. The problems of crime and violence, the troubling spirit of apathy among the young, the underachievement, the self-centeredness, the wave of demoralization that threatens to engulf an entire generation, are all complex and multidetermined problems that elude any simplistic cures. A serious attack on them needs to draw on many ideas from many sources. It requires the combined—and cooperative—efforts of every sector in our society. No single answer by itself will suffice, particularly when the answer has been crafted for the roundabout purpose of staking out a highly visible and easily digestible political position.

In this chapter, I consider a number of false oppositions that arise from, and in turn fuel, the overly politicized public discourse about today's youth. My theme throughout this chapter is that our oppositional mentality has been blinding us to the more subtle and complex truths that we must grasp if we are to provide children with proper guidance. Until we see past the false oppositions to the real nature of children and their developmental needs, we shall leave young people to flounder in their apathy and their cynicism.

Many of the false oppositions spring from competing visions about the proper relationship between children and adults. The fundamental polarity here is between "child-centered" and "adult-centered" inclinations. The polarity has led to fierce divisions on issues such as children's educational needs, their rights and responsibilities, and about parental disciplinary practices. I shall argue that the polarity has created twin sets of imbalanced positions—one a child-centered set and the other an adult-centered one—as well as extreme and irrational swings between the two sets. The polarity also has given birth to a set of false oppositions concerning the nature of the child. Here the controversies revolve around how capable, versus how incapable, children are; how tough and resilient, versus how tender and fragile, they are; how they learn literacy and other skills; and how they can best develop character and competence. Each of the false oppositions masks the truth and draws our attention away from the urgent effort to find constructive approaches for raising all of today's young people.

Child-centered Imbalances

If ever there was a case where rhetoric has become reality, the history of the phrase "child-centered" has been one. In many ways, it is an auspicious history, one of progressive enlightenment concerning the unique perspectives and needs of children. In other ways, though, it is a history of simplification and obfuscation. Scientific insight has been systematically misinterpreted, and complex scientific truths have been reduced to slogans that run counter to the truths themselves. Usually the worst excesses have come from the use of the child-centered approach as a doctrine that stands in opposition to more traditional, adult-centered positions.

The past two centuries have witnessed a revolution in the way that adults view children. Although attended by less tumult, it has been an intellectual shift every bit as profound as the Copernican revolution that removed earth from the center of the universe. This time it has been the perspectival world of adults that has been dislocated. The searing new insight that came from child study was that children could not be understood simply as little adults. Children have their own special feelings, wishes, and fantasies, and they see all things very differently than do adults.

There have been many milestones in our dawning awareness of this. Centuries ago, paintings and literature reveal a vision of children as half-grown, roughly shaped miniatures—not dissimilar to adult midgets—showing no physical or behavioral qualities associated with their young age.[8] Children, it was assumed, simply knew less, not *differently*, than adults. An early objector to this adult-centered view was the philosopher Jean Jacques Rousseau, who wrote that "childhood has its own way of seeing, thinking, and feeling, and there is nothing more foolish than the attempt to put ours in its place."[9] In the nineteenth century, art, literature, and science began recognizing children's unique inner worlds. Young people's dreams and fears were explored through poems, stories, and *Bildungsromanen*; and eminent scientists such as Charles Darwin and William Preyer took an interest in children's thoughts and emotions. But the greatest leap forward took place during the twentieth century, with the landmark writings of Swiss epistemologist Jean Piaget.

Again and again, over a career spanning six decades and dozens of seminal scientific studies, Piaget made the point that, from day one, human development is a process of radical reorganization.[10] Psychologically, this means that a person's ideas and beliefs can change utterly from one developmental phase to the next. To take one of Piaget's favorite examples, at an early age a child may believe that there is more to drink in a tall, skinny quart of water than in a short, fat quart. Two years later, the same child may say that they are the same, and may even reject his earlier statement as an illogical absurdity that he never could have uttered. Researchers in the Piagetian tradition have provided literally thousands of examples of such developmental reorganizations during infancy, childhood, adolescence, and adulthood. Some pertain to logical conceptions, others to ideas about the self, others to moral beliefs, and other to the nature of the physical and social world.[11]

Piaget's first books in the 1920s hit the intellectual world like a storm, forever changing the way that writers, educators, and eventually parents understood children's mental lives. Four decades later, Piaget's theory, by then bolstered by a vastly greater empirical base and more intricate mathematical formulations, enjoyed a renewed surge of interest worldwide. During this resurgence, Piaget's work for the first time gained true acceptance in the discipline of scientific psychology and its academic relatives. The notion of developmental reorganization spread through child psychology, sociology, personality theory, psychobiology, and the new discipline of cognitive science. The somewhat less theoretical notion that children have their own worldviews spread into the applied fields of education, clinical psychology, psychiatry, medicine, and law.

That children have their own way of understanding things is a benign and accurate enough notion, especially as it was intended in Piaget's own sympathetic analyses of the peculiarities in children's logic. In more recent years, serious scientific work on children's intelligence has benefited enormously, in method as well as in its factual base, from Piaget's insights on this matter. The important contemporary field of cognitive science is founded on the Piagetian idea of the active processor of information who learns while doing.

But what the insights have come to mean in applied fields has been less accurate and less helpful. In education, the notion that children have their own ways of thinking has devolved into what is widely known as the "child-centered" approach to learning. This is an approach that has become synonymous with a lack of academic rigor and a lack of clarity about pedagogical goals. As I shall show in Chapter 9, a developmental approach that springs from true Piagetian and cognitive science theory has little in common with the loose "child-centered" approaches that prevail in our schools today. It is unfortunate that the two have become confused in the public mind. As is so often the case, distorted versions of a good idea can do more damage to the credibility of the idea than direct attacks on it.

Among parents, child-centered beliefs have encouraged exaggerated concerns about children's momentary feelings. They also discourage efforts to inspire accomplishment among young children; and they have eroded the foundations of parental discipline. In the clinical professions, child-centered notions have spawned confusion about how to interpret and work with children's fantasies. In the legal profession, they have created erratic and groundless imbalances between the rights and responsibilities of young people.

In each of these cases, the valid insights of science have been degraded by polarizing debates that have set child-centered approaches in opposition to adult-centered ones. As the two perspectives have been wedged apart, they both have lost their balance as well as their core wisdom. In recent years, the newer child-centered approaches have been gaining on the more traditional adult-centered ones. But even as they have gathered some momentum within the practicing professions and elsewhere, the child-centered approaches have proven increasingly inadequate to the challenges that they have been called upon to deal with. This will always remain the case as long as the use of false opposition creates imbalanced, one-sided positions.

In all parts of the modern world, child-centered doctrines are fast dominating schooling, especially in the early childhood and elementary grades. In educators' terminology, "child-centered" generally means a laissez-faire approach that allows children to proceed at their own pace, pursue their own interests, and learn from their own actions. It follows from what is known as a "constructivist" perspective on learning—a position also widely attributed to Piaget.

Constructivism assumes that children construct knowledge of the world through their own mental and physical actions rather than through information provided to them by others. Educators do best, therefore, to create settings where children act spontaneously and receive enlightening feedback from such activity. Constructivism, a now entrenched movement with its own grass-roots organizations and newsletters, argues that schools should de-emphasize formal instruction, general requirements, mastery of facts, learning by rote memory, external inducements (such as grades), and standardized tests. It strongly endorses the idea that learning should be fun, engaging, and intrinsically motivating.

Much like any truth, these are all worthwhile ideas when taken in context; but they quickly lose their value when oversimplified and overextended. There is no question that constructivism has made crucial contributions to our understanding of children's learning. The insight that children learn about the world through their actions has transformed scholarship and practice in child development permanently for the better. No longer are we chained to the unfruitful and unlikely assumption that children soak up knowledge passively, like sponges or tape recorders. No longer do we assume that all people, including children, receive and interpret information the same way, as B. F. Skinner and fellow behaviorists once held.[12] It is valid as well as beneficial to treat the child's inner world as having special properties unlike those of any adult.

But current educational applications of these ideas look more like the passionate, one-sided sentiments of Jean Jacques Rousseau than the careful and complex science of Jean Piaget and his developmental followers. In truth, Piaget was not only a constructivist but also an *interactionist*. When Piaget wrote that children learn through their own actions, he did not mean that they learn in a vacuum. Essential to the learning process, as Piaget formulated it, was *feedback* from the child's actions on the real world. Learning is not just an action but an interaction. The child pokes at something, it moves, and the child learns a bit about moving objects from this *interaction* with a real one. Moreover, another person—a parent, teacher, or peer—may have something to say to the child about this experience. As a result, the child also learns something from the *social interaction*. The child's own original actions were critical to the learning experience, but this does not mean that these actions alone taught the child everything she needed to know.

In most of his research, Piaget emphasized the child's interactions with the physical world, but he also wrote extensively about the contributions of social interaction to children's learning.[13] Neo-Piagetian theories, and recent writings from other traditions sympathetic to Piaget's active-child model, have gone even further in emphasizing the social-interactional bases of all learning.[14] Virtually all serious theoretical work in child development now assumes that learning is neither a solipsistic expression nor a passive experience for the child but rather that it results from complex, extended, and multifaceted engagements between learners, teachers, and the rest of the real world.

Few of our educational programs for young children reflect this wisdom. Only one side of Piaget's interactionist mix, the child-centered side, has been preserved in our present-day educational applications of constructivism. At the same time, the constructivist perspective has come to dominate the educational scene, particularly among teachers in the early grades. As a consequence, early childhood education in most places has become a grab bag of loosely structured storytelling, singing, untutored arts and crafts, play activities, and frequent partying. The normative expectations increasingly are that young children need to express themselves, to "connect" with their own inner interests, and to build their self-esteem: their skills and knowledge can wait. There is also a spreading sense that hard schoolwork introduced too early could stifle a child's creativity and permanently impair a child's academic motivation.[15] The exceptions, such as the more tightly organized Montesssori programs—which started out as child-centered in the original, more rigorous sense of the term—are either dwindling in popularity or capitulating to the norm. Moreover, not only is this perspective rapidly spreading through the ranks of early childhood programs, it is spreading to the higher elementary grades as well. The ages at which students are expected to learn literacy and numeracy skills and begin to master the basic disciplines of knowledge are being pushed ever higher.

For children as well as for all humans, low expectations breed low results. Postponing the introduction of rigorous academic work leaves students incapable of doing much more than playing, creating the impression that this indeed is all they can or want to do. Tragically, the students who suffer most from this approach are those who have had little academic preparation in their homes: these are the very students who most need a productive school experience. Their school failure becomes ensured by a philosophy that refuses to give them serious opportunities to learn. But the self-fulfilling prophecy of low expectations affects the fast as well as the slow, the prepared as well as the unprepared, because it robs all students of the chance to build the foundations of understanding at ages when they are eager and fully ready to do so.[16]

The child-centered perspective not only underestimates children's capacities, but it also mistakes the nature of learning. It does so on two counts: intellectual and motivational. Earlier I discussed the constructivist fallacy that overlooks the interactional roots of all intellectual achievement. Simply put, children cannot learn wholly on their own: for intellectual growth, they need to be instructed, prodded, challenged, corrected, and assisted by people who are trying to teach them something. Whatever fancies may have been spun in ancient philosophy, learning is more than a matter of realizing one's incipient inner intimations.[17] It requires an external structure of reality, of information, of communication, and of social supports. Above all, it requires an organized presentation of a systematic body of knowledge.

David Cohen, a distinguished critic of present-day educational practices, observed a California teacher (whom he names "Mrs. O") trying to teach math to second-graders through an activity-based approach geared towards children's spontaneous interests.[18] The teacher was committed, eager, and well-intentioned. The problem was, she seemed to have little interest in the subject matter: "Mathematically," writes Cohen, "she was on thin ice." Her focus was on her students' *experience* rather than on the mathematical concepts that she was teaching. Mrs. O's efforts were guided by a popular (and typical) constructivist treatise called *Math Their Way*. Cohen describes the treatise's philosophy this way:

> . . . experience is vivid, vital, and immediate, while books are all abstract ideas and dead formulations. *Math Their Way* also claims that concrete materials are developmentally desirable for young children. Numbers are referred to many times as an "adult" way of approaching math. That idea leads to another, still more important: If math is taught properly, it will be easy. . . . The book's claim also helps to explain why it gives so little attention to the explanation of mathematical ideas. . . . Appropriate materials and activities alone will do the trick.[19]

Guided by such principles, Mrs. O can only present a confusing and uninstructive lesson for her students. She entertains the students with games involving beans and charts but manages to get across little mathematical understanding. In all of Cohen's observations, there is no indication that Mrs. O has challenged her students' abilities at all, or that she has prodded them to learn anything new. Inevitably, the entertaining games lose even their motivational appeal: "Everyone was flagging long before it was done. . . ." writes Cohen. In her efforts to make math easy and fun for her students, Mrs. O has lost sight of the ideas and skills that lie at the heart of the subject matter. The unhappy irony in this case is that it is precisely the prospect of learning these ideas and skills that, in the long run, provides the most powerful motivator for students.

The motivation to learn cannot come solely from within. It is built on an amalgamated foundation of inner and outer inducements—including a teacher's expectations, support, encouragement, and grades. In recent years, the phrase "intrinsic motivation" has attained almost biblical status. Of all the notions affiliated with constructivist and child-centered doctrines, this has become the least questioned of all. Educators everywhere believe that school materials must intrinsically motivate children if children are to benefit from them. Once again, however, the facts are not that simple. Extrinsic motivation—goading children through rewards, pressure, and other incentives—also has its place in real-world learning. School programs that rely on students' intrinsic motivation alone cannot teach students to work through the inevitable frustrations and drudgery that eventually accompanies any pursuit. In short, such as approach cannot teach children the work habits that they need for sustained accomplishment and true mastery.

Recent research supports this conclusion. In a comparison between students from school programs emphasizing intrinsic motivations and students from programs with more traditional learning incentives such as required assignments and grades, psychologist Mordecai Nissan found that the extrinsically motivated students did far better in the long run.[20] They had developed not only the skills but the motivational tenacity required to stick with a subject even when it becomes difficult or boring. Students who were used to relying on their inner lights alone often quit as soon as they lost interest. They were not able to gain the ensuing satisfactions that come from hard, disciplined work.

From a teacher's point of view, trying to guide instruction primarily by children's interests and feelings is like trying to guide a ship on a foggy night without a compass. Without a stable grounding in academic goals and standards, both teacher and student get lost. It is of course necessary to present information and tasks in ways that engage children. No one wants to return to the days of empty drill, when students' only refuge of meaningful escape was to stare out the window or into their own daydreams. But engaging children does not require setting aside a rigorous instructional agenda. In the long run, children will be most captivated by challenges that lead them into the rich world of understanding that our disciplines of knowledge offer them.

On many occasions in recent years, I have observed teachers flounder in the foggy quest to guide their classrooms by student's whims and feelings. They shift nervously among classroom projects, hoping to find one that will capture their students' attention. Without realizing it, teachers following such poorly grounded practices are further fostering the wandering attention spans that they are trying so hard to cope with.[21]

The unstable grounding leads to a confusions of goals and as well as to contradictions between intention and practice. Some of the contradictions are so blatant, and yet so unnoticed, that they would be amusing if they were not so detrimental. I recall a typical example from a classroom encounter that I once observed. In conversation prior to the taped session, the teacher expressed the belief that her primary job was to raise her students' self-esteem. But, as I discussed at length in Chapter 4, self-esteem is not a substantial enough quality in itself to provide a target for educators. In this case, the teacher associated self-esteem with the vaguely generalized feelings of her students about themselves, their schoolwork, and their relations with her. Above all, she wanted her students to feel good about those things.

The teacher's classroom practice revealed quite a discrepant story. A few moments into the session, the teacher began losing her students' attention. She tried with little success to get them interested in the tasks that she had presented them. She pulled aside individual students, showed them how to go about working on the tasks, and expressed her own fascination with the materials, all to no avail. Spurred by the restlessness of the most distracted students, the class slipped further and further from the teacher's control. Her final response was a study in the kind of desperation that one can sink to without a steady standard to provide a more reliable frame of reference. The teacher gradually raised her voice until it reached a loud and angry pitch. She cajoled, she pleaded, and she threatened. Before long she was hurling invectives at any student who was disobeying her. "You are just the worst listener!" she said to one; "What's wrong with you?" she asked another; "Don't be such a moron," she said to another; and in a final fit of frustration to one little boy she exclaimed "You are just a complete and total waste!"

In discussions afterwards, the teacher complained about how difficult this group of students had been. She did not budge from her conviction that her primary purpose as a teacher was self-esteem building.

The disjunction of purpose and practice that ensnared this teacher stems from a confusion that is culture-wide at the present time. I cannot say how common such incidents are, although I strongly suspect that they are not at all rare. My point is that teachers and students have been led astray by a lack of clear, external standards to guide them in their learning quest (I shall discuss the essential standards for education in Chapter 9). The standards that children need have become obscured and destabilized by a one-sided concentration on children's fluctuating inner worlds.

To the extent that any developmental theory has been used to spawn or justify this approach, it is an oversimplified and distorted version of the theory. Any such approach overlooks an essential component of development: children's need for guidance as they assemble their skills and their habits. An exclusive focus on children's feelings creates an imbalance. So, too, does an exclusive focus on the adult's perspective, a mistake that many traditional practices have made. Imbalances always lead to uncontrolled swings from one unsatisfying extreme to the other. The teacher's switch from solicitously boosting self-esteem to hurling harsh invectives stands as a prime example of such swings—and of the futility of trying to gain control from an imbalanced position. Neither child-centered nor adult-centered approaches can lead to a balanced relationship providing sure guidance for the child. Only a focus on the quality of the *interactions* between child and adult can create a balance. As I shall show in Chapter 7, this means paying attention to the characteristics of effective communication between adults and children and replicating those characteristics in all the contexts—instructional, familial, community—where adults and children mingle. I shall have more to say about these characteristics and how to replicate them in Part III of this book.

I began this chapter by noting the oppositional thinking that has been created by the present politicization of matters pertaining to families and youth. The field of education is rife with such oppositional thinking. There are incessant fights between progressives and traditionalists, between privatization and public school advocates, between those favoring "excellence" and those favoring "equity," between those who would track children and those who would integrate them, and on and on. Such polarities provide fertile ground for jingoistic, oversimplified thinking about complex problems.

The child-centered versus adult-centered polarity is the most widespread and debilitating example of this in education today. It has appeared in a thousand guises, all of which obscure the central problems of our disaffected and underperforming youth. From this polarity has arisen constructivism's distortions and simplifications, as I have discussed above. At the opposing end, the polarity has spawned an equally simplistic reaction from those who have criticized child-centered education under the banner of "cultural literacy."[22] In these reactive critiques, the subtleties and positive contributions of educators ranging from John Dewey to Mortimer Adler have been left behind in the dust of controversy. The oppositions are pointless on both ends. As I shall show in Chapter 9, we have available to us today sound educational strategies that could respond to the concerns of both camps. At the close of the present chapter, I shall touch on yet another casualty of this same pointless opposition: the attempt to foster character growth in young people through moral education.

On the family front, the debates between child- and adult-centered views are less theoretically driven than in the field of education, but they can be just as extreme and unproductive. Moreover, the debates reflect ideological polarities similar to the oppositions that have obfuscated educational discourse. The ideological component is not always articulated when it comes to family matters; but whether articulated or not, it feeds a sense of divisiveness about cultural values that is precisely contrary to the consensus that young people need to thrive. As in education, recent years have seen child-centered views gathering momentum in family affairs. As in education, these views have created wild imbalances that in turn have triggered equally one-sided oppositional responses.

Studies of the beliefs that parents hold about how to raise their children have shown a steadily increasing concern for children's momentary feelings over the past century.[23] Early in the century, many considered children's enjoyment to be irrelevant, or even deleterious, to their development. Childhood playfulness was ignored or discouraged; making things "fun" for children was of little concern. A study at mid-century already showed a rapidly changing picture.[24] Parents by then were attempting to insert fun into every demand that they made of their children. A spirit of playfulness now had become an unwritten criterion of good parenting. Parents had come to believe that they should make eating, going to the doctor, going to the potty, learning to get dressed, learning to read and count, all into enjoyable activities for their children. The researcher who first observed the trend towards the fusion of play and seriousness in mid-century childrearing called it "the fun morality."[25]

By now, at the end of the twentieth century, play and seriousness again have become disentangled; but this time it is play that has become elevated and seriousness downgraded. Children's enjoyment is the priority of many families today. Parents avidly pursue whatever they believe will please their children and avoid anything that they believe will upset them or cause them stress. People who market children's products have learned this full well. A recent study of advertisements geared towards parents found that "less than one third of the advertisements made explicit statements about the growth-promoting potential of their product."[26] Moreover, the authors report:

> Virtually none promoted a product on the basis of its educational value alone. Instead, products that were claimed to increase academic skills—teach reading, numbers, prepare the child for school, and so forth—did so in the context of teaching the child that "learning is fun." Apparently, learning in and of itself is not sufficient to promote a product. . . . [The same was true] in the area of safety, health, and hygiene. Food needs to be more than nutritious, dental care needs to accomplish more than the prevention of tooth decay. These things should also be fun and enjoyable for children.[27]

Adult-Centered Imbalances

In 1992, a young developmental psychologist named Diane Eyer published a daring challenge to a public myth that had been widely promulgated by the medical establishment: the notion of "infant bonding," which implies that people may be permanently impaired by a lack of physical contact with their biological mothers in the hours after birth.[28] Eyer's challenge was unusually bold because it took on not only some influential elders in the child development scene but also some deeply held orthodoxies within contemporary culture. She frames one of the orthodoxies as "an ideology in which mothers are seen as the prime architects of their children's lives and are blamed for whatever problems befall them, not only in childhood but through their adult lives."[29]

Eyer's exposé of the bonding myth offers us a prime example of how easy it is to sell today's public on wildly imbalanced views that put adult behavior at the center of children's development while ignoring the strengths and contributions of the children. Ironically, such views end up making the same mistake as the child-centered imbalances discussed above: they overlook the crucial, growth-inducing interactions that spring from sound relationships between children and adults. Both child-centered and adult-centered beliefs—and especially the noisy opposition between them—divert our attention from the urgent task of improving the extent and quality of those key relationships.

The story that Eyer tells not only identifies a common misconception but also raises questions about how some institutions and experts may promulgate a bogus notion through the mass media. Equally disturbing, the tale shows how an ideological orthodoxy can lead otherwise intelligent people to accept ideas that are illogical, harmful, and readily disproven.

The notion of bonding originated with a poorly designed study of fourteen mothers, conducted by two pediatricians in the early 1970s.[30] The study reported that, when given some extra hours of physical contact with their infants, these mothers showed better parenting skills on a few measures (four out of seventy-five parenting measures, to be precise). The infants, too, showed some higher-than-average performances on a few tests. On the basis of these data—and some observations of goats from the ethological literature—the study concluded that there is a critical period right after birth, during which time mothers are biologically primed either to "bond" with their infants or to reject them—all with great consequences for the infants' subsequent development.

Soon pediatricians were off on speaking tours promoting the notion that mother-infant bonding was critical to development. As the notion spread through the medical and child-care professions, and eventually into the public domain, claims became more dramatic and more exaggerated. Children who failed to bond properly were destined for failure, for unhappy relationships of their own, for lives of violence. They could become drug users or child abusers. And it was not only in sensationalist news stories that such views were aired. Leading child experts jumped in with both feet. The pediatrician T. Berry Brazelton, a well-known provider of parenting advice whom many have called today's Dr. Spock, told Bill Moyers in a 1988 interview:

... if he [the child] doesn't have that [bonding] through infancy, it's hard to put it in later ... and these kids that never get it ... will become difficult in school, they'll never succeed in school; they'll make everybody angry; they'll become terrorists. ... [Moyers: And you think that goes back ... to this bonding period?] Yes.[31]

Dr. Brazelton, a brilliant researcher who himself has conducted seminal research in child development, may well have meant something more subtle by his statement than his words seem to indicate. Perhaps, for example, he was referring to the more extended time of attachment that indeed is critical for children's social development rather than to the mystical period of hours that are known to the field as bonding. Yet in the present climate, this distinguished pediatrician's widely heard statement could only contribute further to the message that adults may cripple children through brief absences. Needless to say, this is hardly a comforting message to parents who adopt children past the "bonding" period. How could they know whether their adopted child had "gotten it" or not in the child's first hours of contact with its biological parents? Children who had not "gotten it" apparently were starting off with severe emotional handicaps. This was a disquieting message too for mothers who were incapacitated by health problems during the period immediately after giving birth.

Yet according to Eyer, the medical profession reacted to the strident claims about bonding more with relief than with discomfort. Among other things, the exaggerated claims gave obstetricians and hospitals one more technique to add to their repertoire of expertise. Obstetrical procedures now would include a new set of birthing rituals designed to bring mother and infant into extended physical contact during the mother's hospital stay. These rituals provided a pseudoscientific justification for a profession already under siege for its unwieldy, expensive, and often error-riddled handling of childbirth.

In fact, the science of bonding was transparently weak from the start. Long before Bill Moyers interviewed Dr. Brazelton, and during the whole time that hospitals were proudly reforming their birthing procedures, serious scholars had poked holes in the research and rejected its implications out of hand.[32] The data supporting it were shown to be insubstantial and the processes supposedly accounting for it were shown to be implausible. Critical reviews of the bonding notion were widely available in top scientific journals, books about parenting, and widely read texts.[33] Even so, by the time of her 1992 treatise, Eyer finds the notion of bonding to be still so dear to so many interests that she calls it "impossible" to conceive of it being discarded.

Apart from its disquieting message to parents who adopt or have other uncertainties about the child's parental contact in the period after birth, what could be the harm of this seemingly benign notion? Certainly there is nothing at all wrong with parents cuddling with their children at any time, including the moments after birth. It would be wrong indeed to argue against any nurturant parent/child physical contact. My objections to the bonding notion intend no such thing and they should never be interpreted that way. The harm of the notion is simply that it creates a delusional smokescreen. Like all exaggerated claims and distortions that obscure the truth, the bogus notion leads us away from worthwhile efforts and into unfruitful ones. Most disturbingly, the notion ends up discrediting valuable ideas that have been loosely, and wrongly, associated with it.

The focus on bonding has stolen attention from the *real* essential need of all young children: regular participation in at least one secure, growth-inducing relationship. Such key relationships have been called *attachment* relations in psychological writings from a more serious and more substantial theoretical tradition than that represented by today's bonding craze. Within the fields of psychology and psychiatry, the distinguished "attachment" research tradition, with its valuable emphasis on sustained, long-term relationships between caregiver and child, has been unfairly damaged by controversies surrounding the far less credible notion of bonding.[34]

Relationships that build the foundations of children's development go far beyond moments of physical contact during allegedly "critical" periods after birth. In fact, they do not even rely on *particular* moments with the child's own biological mother. Rather, the child's relational needs are *nonspecific*. This is one of the many ways in which resiliency is built into our species. Guardians of all sorts can interact with children in high-quality ways that establish excellent interactional and communicational settings for their growth. In extreme cases, even young children themselves have been able to provide sufficient relational stimulation for one another's healthy development.[35] The point is that children need relationships that they can benefit from and that they can count on over time. A hug in the maternity ward is no silver bullet.

A similarly simplistic mentality has clouded the debate over maternal employment. Penelope Leach, Dr. Brazelton, and others have expressed concern about mothers "giving up" their small babies when they return to work.[36] The implication is that young children will be damaged without full-day contact with their mothers: this and no less is "every child's birthright," in the memorable phrase of one child psychologist.[37]

In fact, because of the important public policy implications of maternal employment and child care, this is an area where a great deal of research has been done.[38] We know from this research that young children do not suffer from being apart from their parents during the day, as long as they are in a nurturing, communicative environment and as long as they have a stable home to return to on evenings and weekends. The *quality* of children's relationships with their parents and guardians—as well as with other people in their lives—is far more important than is the extent of time that they spend around any one person, including their mothers. Yet heated arguments swirl around the desire of many mothers to take up serious careers. *Maternal deprivation* is held responsible for all the problems of youth today. Working mothers are induced into feelings of guilt by statements such as the following from Dr. Brazelton, who considers the "real issue" for mothers to be "when to return to work without endangering their baby's development":

> Although financial and career needs may be pressing, these women cannot ignore their new roles as mothers in making the decision. Both the baby's needs and their own longing to nurture well are critical to their peace of mind as they return to work. Denial is a defense against the pain of giving up a small baby.[39]

The real issue for mothers, and for all parents and citizens, is how to raise our young in a manner than imparts basic virtues such as competence, good values, personal and social responsibility, the capacity for sustained relationships, and the desire to believe in something beyond the self. This critical mission is ill-served by whipping working mothers into frenzies of guilt over false ideas concerning maternal deprivation. A mother's presence is valued by practically every young person, but it is only one part of the mix that goes into a child's character development. Isolating it as "the answer" to the child's healthy growth only diverts our attention from the essential elements of effective and responsible parenting.

Beyond love and care, one of these essential elements is discipline. Sadly, but perhaps predictably within the tenor of our times, discipline in the home has become a subject of hot controversy—rather than, as it once was, a matter of straightforward common sense. As with the issue of maternal child care, our public discussion of child discipline is adult-centered and simplistic. The same kind of oppositional thinking, replete with extreme and exaggerated positions, governs the debates. In the meantime, our sense of balance in understanding family discipline is lost, and young people are growing up without the benefits of steady, consistent guidelines for their behavior.

As a consequence, discipline in the home has become a vexing dilemma rather than an art that comes naturally to parents. It has become, in fact, a lost art. Stories about unruly, disrespectful, and unmanageable children dominate the conversations of adults everywhere. Families are torn with division over how to respond.

Almost daily, our newspaper advice columns are full of incidents such the following, drawn from the ever scrupulous "Miss Manners"[40]: Two sets of children, related as cousins, sat down to a holiday dinner. One set acted reasonably well, the other "came and went at will, taunted the other children for obeying their parents, interrupted to voice complaints and state food preferences, and returned adult attention with silence." It is not surprising that the parents of one set complained to the parents of the other set. What *was* surprising was which parents turned out to do the complaining. It was the parents of the *disruptive* ones, who told the other parents that they were cruelly repressing their children, stifling their spontaneous behavior, and so on. The seasoned Miss Manners claims not to have been surprised by this turn of events. But she admits to being "flabbergasted" when hearing that "the recipients of such outrageous remarks listen seriously and devote some time to asking themselves if they are, in fact, harming their children."

The parents of the well-behaved children could not have been induced into such soul-searching unless there were powerful cultural supports for the challenge that the other parents hurled at them. Beyond the adult-centered conceit that strict parental discipline could repress a child's vitality and spontaneity, the taunt reflects a general, culture-wide insecurity about discipline and control. Parents are insecure about whether they *can* control their children, about whether they *should* control their children, and about the consequences of whatever they choose to do or not to do. They worry and argue about the proper methods of discipline. Their insecurities are fed by a lack of consensus within the culture; and their anxieties are heightened by one area of common agreement, mistaken though it is: the belief that parents' actions in and of themselves have the sole power to shape childrens' character. This cloudy mix of insecurity, anxiety, and misconception has lead many into a state of parenting paralysis. In such a state, short-term crisis management substitutes for firm, predictable disciplinary practices. Before long, extreme solutions begin to take root and flourish.

On the one extreme, in recent years there has appeared a collection of childrearing books that passionately advocates physical punishment as a necessary ingredient in all child discipline.[41] The authors argue that children literally must be beaten into submission if they show signs of disobedience and disrespect for adult authority. Often these authors draw their inspiration from the Bible, which they believe not merely *allows* physical punishment but *requires* it.[42] They cite biblical passages such as the following: "He that spareth the rod hateth his son: but he that loveth him chasteneth him betimes" (Proverbs 13:24). "Withhold not correction from the child: for if thou beatest him with the rod, he shall not die" (Proverbs 23:13). Many who write about childrearing from a fundamentalist tradition have interpreted such messages as the literal word of God.

People, of course, have an absolute right to their religious views; and, in actuality, the disciplinary guidelines that many of these authors prescribe are controlled and relatively nonviolent. In *Growing Up God's Way*, for example, John Stormer gives advice about "how to spank" that begins with the injunction that spanking "should not be carried out in anger or with an attitude of getting even with a child."[43] He cautions against striking any part of the child's body other than the bottom and he elaborately describes procedures that avoid any lasting damage to that part of the anatomy. He advises parents to temper the spanking with prayer, love, and forgiveness as well as to "be reasonable in what you expect from your child."

Unfortunately, some parents who claim inspiration from such sources are, in practice, neither as moderate nor as careful as the advice would suggest. Philip Greven has documented a number of shocking incidents of child maltreatment that members of some religious sects have justified through biblical injunctions.[44] Children have been beaten for hours, even to the point of death, out of the belief that their "wills" must be broken before their souls can be saved. In such cases, the punishments not only have been harsh, but they also have been wholly out of touch with children's capacities to understand what they are being punished for. Often the child is too young even to realize that there is a connection between her own behavior and the maltreatment that ensues. Greven quotes from a chilling journalistic account of one such case, a small girl who had been punished for *four hours* by a man who was trying to live up to the prescriptions of his religious sect:

> . . . the little girl in the diapers would not receive her discipline. She cried and cried and [he] kept hitting her, trying to make her tears stop. "I wasn't sure of myself," he recalls, "so I kept calling [a fellow church member]. I'd say, "She's doing the same thing. I don't know what to do." He told me, "You spank her till she breaks."[45]

These kinds of practices are adult-centered to a horrifying extreme. They show little recognition of the child's thoughts or concern for the child's feelings. Their only effect can be to leave the child hurt and bewildered. Lacking any meaningful connections to the child's perspective, there is no way that such harsh practices can accomplish their avowed mission: to lead the child towards the adult's conception of socialized behavior. In order to accomplish this, as I shall discuss in Part III, adults must interact with children in ways that clearly communicate the messages that children need to grow up properly. Discipline is an important part of such interactions. *But it must be rational, and it must make sense to the child.* Clarity of communication is far more readily accomplished through calm disciplinary practices such as sending a child to his room, or temporarily removing some of the child's privileges, than through intemperate acts of corporal punishment.

This said, it is also important to avoid stereotyping common disciplinary practices, whether religiously driven or not, that are neither cruel nor violent. Greven and others who have written about physical punishment do little to distinguish between acts of real abuse on the one hand and the mildest tap on the bottom on the other.[46] This is painting with a very broad brush. Over 90 percent of American parents use some form of corporal punishment with their children on certain occasions.[47] This is not a disciplinary method that I would advocate. There are always wiser, safer, and more effective means of discipline such as withholding priviliges. But what purpose does it serve to stigmatize all these parents by grouping them with people who are truly abusive? Such broad-brush stereotyping only contributes to the polarization that is fragmenting our society and weakening the sense of solidarity that creates a culture's needed youth charter.

Like other imbalances that I have discussed throughout this chapter, this one also diverts our attention from the real problem. In this case, the problem is how to establish a program of discipline that facilitates children's development. I shall make the case in the last part of this book that the solution is, once again, an interactional one. Neither the laissez-faire permissiveness of child-centered approaches nor the harsh punitiveness of adult-centered ones can transmit anything of value to our children. Yet it seems easier to gravitate towards one extreme or the other than to find a common ground.

In trying to avoid the extremism of today's public discourse, many who raise children are lured into a state of unrealized contradiction, vacillating unpredictably between passivity and anger, between permissiveness and sudden harshness. In such a state, confusion supplants communication. The beneficial possibilities of interaction and communication become lost to both adult and child. Unfortunately, it is the fruitful interactional center that seems the most difficult ground to hold in the present epoch.

The Nature of the Child

Oppositions between child- and adult-centered approaches have fueled a number of misconceptions concerning the nature of children and their developmental needs. As I shall discuss in the following chapter, it is important that we understand the children's nature, especially with respect to their natural virtues. Not only is such understanding crucial for guiding our childrearing efforts, but it also can help us appraise and avoid the special risks of modern times. The false oppositions accomplish just the opposite. They lead us toward solutions that belie the child's true nature and that are therefore so remote from it that they place the child at further risk.

Because of false oppositions concerning the nature of the child, the educational world has become a political minefield. Educators who should be joining forces to reverse the appalling decline in children's school performances are instead engaging in battles tinged with ideology. Some educators shy away from fundamental issues entirely, fearing that they might awaken the storms of controversy.

None of the controversies could long sustain themselves if a more reasonable view of children's nature prevailed. The raging debates in education rest on views of children's learning that are so simplistic that they defy common sense. Any parent or teacher ought to know better, and probably would if not blinded by the ideologically driven polarities. It is a testament to the deceptive potential of false oppositions that some of the controversies have come to dominate our educational scene, much to the disservice of the students whom we are supposedly trying to educate.

Teaching children to read has become a battleground between those who promote a "whole language" approach and those who favor breaking words down into their phonic units. The hostility between the camps has been such that there is little dialogue between them. Rather, they exchange accusations implying that the other's approach can permanently damage a child's ability and will to read. Some particularly fierce advocates have convinced lawmakers to step in on their side: bills demanding that public schools employ a phonics or a whole language approach have cleared state legislatures in recent times. It is, of course, highly unusual for legislators to intervene in schools at the level of pedagogical policy. Are the stakes really that high? They only seem so if we are lured into believing that children learn in one way, and one way only. But this belief is untenable for at least two reasons. First, all learners rely on multiple processes to gain skill and knowledge. Children are no exception. The more avenues that we offer them into learning, the more likely it is that they will find a way to take the journey. *Both* whole language and phonics provide avenues into reading, and any sensible teacher makes both available to her students. The second reason is that there are profound individual differences among children. Some may take to one style of teaching, others to a radically divergent style. Again, this argues strongly for joining the two strategies rather than opposing them.

There are a number of similar controversies that cluster around the opposition between those who would take a synthetic approach to instruction (emphasizing unity and integration) and those who would take an analytic one (breaking subject matter into smaller units to be mastered). The opposition may follow similar lines to the child- and adult-centered polarity that I have discussed throughout this chapter, although this may be oversimplifying the matter to some extent. It certainly follows along the lines of viewing school as a place for expression *versus* achievement; as a place for fun *versus* serious and rigorous effort.

Again, everything we know about children tells us that they need both options in order to thrive. Without the opportunity to exercise their creative energies, they will soon lose interest in the materials that schools present to them. But this does not mean that they will fall apart when asked to achieve something that demands hard work. The "hurried child" notion notwithstanding, it is not in children's natures to find challenge stressful, as long as they are given support while facing the challenge. In fact, what children find far more stressful is the expectational vacuum created by a lack of challenge. This is the real risk for today's children—nothing to strive for, a dispiriting parallel to the sense of "nothing to believe in" that I discussed in the previous chapter. Children are natural strivers, but they need to find settings where they are both engaged and challenged. In such settings, both fun and rigor may play a part.

In describing false oppositions arising out of the child/adult-centered polarity, I have spoken loosely of ideological leanings in one direction or the other. Neither a child- nor an adult-centered bias is, strictly speaking, an ideological position, although for some it may be part of a more extensive world view. Nor does either represent a systematic political position, though politicians do play off them for their gain. In education today, however, there are some controversies that constitute real political issues. For example, there is a long-standing debate about whether schools should aim to foster equity or excellence within the student population. Apparently, advocates of each side cannot imagine schools doing both, since, in their view, creating programs of worth for slower students precludes spurring gifted students to make the most of their potential. This is a destructive fight that has captured the energies of well-intentioned educators for many years. It is also another false opposition. We can and must do both: school programs that attempt one without the other inevitably fail on *both* counts.

In recent years, the loudest political contention on the educational scene has revolved around our societal choice between diversity and unity. Should schools encourage students to maintain their own cultural identities, even to the point of adapting the curriculum to this effort; or should they aim to provide a "one best" education for all, in the hopes of not only educating students well but also promoting national unity? More ink has been spilled over this one than on all the other debates combined. Invectives of all sorts have been hurled by one side or the other: "racist," "sexist," "fascist," "liberal," "leftist," and, of course, a new one thought up explicitly for this purpose: "politically correct." The front lines of this particular culture war have been our colleges and universities. Yet there have been reverberations at earlier grade levels as well. It is these that I shall comment on here. Anyone working in our schools today is likely to encounter these reverberations sooner or later.

My own most memorable first-hand encounter with them was during an educational effort that I organized in a multi-ethnic urban community filled with recent immigrants. The teams of teachers and researchers were always looking for good writing topics that could engage students' interest as well as open up basic issues for instruction and discussion. In addition, a school-wide priority that year was the subject of citizenship: what it meant, its rights and responsibilities, the societal institutions that depend on it and protect it, how it historically came about in our democracy, and so on. Naturally this would be presented differently to children at different grades—this was an elementary school—but the idea was that all children could learn something about citizenship in our society.

One suggestion that I had for the school was to ask children in all the grades to write an essay on "What it means for me to be a citizen of the United States." I knew that this was a question about which all the children would have something to say—the younger ones, perhaps, about geography, food, or sports; the older ones about history, society, culture, government, and perhaps even their own future prospects as American citizens. Whatever the children wrote, it would provide many opportunities for instructive discussions, both with teachers and peers. I expected that the newly arrived immigrant children would find the task especially interesting, and that it could offer them things to talk about with children from the more established families.

The suggestion did not get very far. Whatever the merits (or demerits) of the idea, the actual reason that it went untried was surprising to me, and informative. Many teachers said that it would be fine with them, but it would raise hackles with some of the other, more militant teachers, as well as with some of the more vigilant parents. Why would such a benign project raise hackles, I naively asked? *Because everyone in the community had become so sensitive about* any *cultural issue, and everyone wanted to avoid trouble.* Moreover, there was a community-wide fear that the children would be somehow "brainwashed" if the school introduced any culturally sensitive issue. It would do little good, I was advised, to inform parents that it is not in children's nature to be so readily brainwashed.

The community, in short, had paralyzed itself over the culture wars and over a widespread misconception about the nature of the child. The fear ran so deep that teachers were afraid to ask their students what their national identity meant to them. A rich and vital source of children's personal, social, and historical awareness was thus ruled off limits for school discussion. American citizenship for this school would be studied only through dry and distant civics lessons. Connecting to the child's lived experience had become too risky in the present political climate.

Education and politics simply do not mix. Every time that a political issue has found its way into the schools, or, reciprocally, that an educational issue has become politicized, the mission of schooling has suffered. Precious time and energy have been diverted and complex ideas have been reduced to slogans. Political straw men have been created; and promising new solutions have been misrepresented and discredited.

In the course of these polarizing quarrels, misconceptions about children have proliferated. The impoverished and superficial nature of modern political debate provides fertile ground for misconceptions to spread. In addition, many of the misconceptions that I have discussed are highly compatible with the interests of institutions that gain their public support by promoting one-sided explanations of social problems. Many who work within these institutions have felt little professional incentive to bridge the false oppositions or to puncture the misconceptions that have defined our recent public discourse about youth. Under such conditions, it does not take long for misconceptions to become entrenched in widely shared public myth. This is where we stand today; and this is why now we must make special efforts to uncover the entrenched myths and to expose them to the fresh air of truth.

Part III
The Response

6

The Natural Virtues

Some remarkably banal metaphors for children's development were advanced by the behaviorists who dominated academic psychology until the latter part of this century. When I was a beginning student, I remember a lecture by a prominent Skinnerian who compared a child at birth to a lump of clay.[1] The idea was that, from birth onwards, the child's behavior is molded into socially acceptable "shape" by feedback from various environmental forces, including the child's parents—in much the same manner as a sculptor shapes a lump of clay into something that appears meaningful to those who look at it.

Let us pretend for a moment that the oldtime behaviorist metaphor is entirely adequate: that children *are* just like lumps of clay to be shaped into civilized persons. Even if this *were* so—even if this mushy metaphor were a wholly accurate descriptor of the child's natural endowment—it would *still* be the case that even clay has certain fundamental characteristics. And it would still be the case that anyone who molds clay would need to know something about the nature of those characteristics. If a sculptor got it wrong—if he assumed, for example, that clay could be worked like stone or like wood—he would end up with nothing but a mess on his hands. No matter how restricted a view we have of a child's natural characteristics, it is still essential that we understand them correctly if we are to provide the optimal settings for their growth.

Now, after decades of scientific research with infants and young children, we know that the behaviorist metaphor is not at all adequate. Children come into this world far more formed than any imaginable lump of clay. Moreover, they are ready to interact with their social worlds; and they do not receive stimulation passively. Children actively interpret *all* the feedback that they receive from the environment. In fact, they play a large part in selecting the feedback that they will react to. Every parent who buys her infant an expensive toy only to find that the child is more fascinated by an old keychain soon discovers the power of children's own preferences.

Psychological science in recent years has given us a rich and enlarged view of the child's natural constitution. If the environment were to be thought of as a sculptor, it would have at the outset a formidable piece of art to work with.

In the present chapter, my focus is on the child's—every child's—native endowment. My intention here is to describe the considerable natural virtues that children, and the people who wish to promote their development, have to work with. I use the term "virtues" in a classic sense, to mean strengths. Yet I am of course cognizant of the word's moral connotation, and I wish to draw on that meaning as well. The main point that I shall make in this chapter is that children are born far stronger, far more adaptive, and far more disposed towards developing moral character than our present-day thinking and practices have given them credit for. It would aid our childrearing efforts immensely if we would see the child's natural virtues for what they are.

Not many generations ago, it was legend among grandmothers that "kids are resilient." This was the comforting bit of wisdom that grandmothers typically offered their own children, who, still green at parenting, may have been worrying excessively about some physical or emotional hazard facing the young. Age, experience, and emotional distance had taught the grandmother how sturdy young children can be.

As yesterday's parents turn into today's grandparents, one hears less and less of such reassuring advice. With each succeeding generation, the culture has drifted further away from the older view of children (and of the species in general) as hardy and resilient. In its place has arisen a view of human nature as fragile, easily damaged, and unlikely to recover from insult or injury. Parents seem more in search of messages that heighten their anxieties than advice that could reassure them about the well-being of their children. If there are still grandmothers who recall remnants of the old wisdom, their words must be falling on deaf ears, dismissed as out of touch. The predominant cultural conceptions have made their insights obsolete.

In fact, this is just one more instance of modern misconceptions replacing some sounder intuitions of earlier times. As I noted in Chapter 5, the view of children as delicate and fragile is part of the modern family's shift towards a child-centered orientation. As with other aspects of the shift, social historians have attributed this conceptual change to the increased affluence and smaller size of modern families.[2] No longer seen as economic commodities, children are seen as beyond price, indeed priceless. While in many ways, as I have said, this is a proper and laudatory change, when combined with a lack of purpose it can promote an unwholesome sense of preciousness with respect to young children. (One recent book, in fact, complained about what it called the "too-precious child" syndrome among many of today's families.)[3] A sense of preciousness can lead in turn to exaggerated concerns over children's health, safety, and emotional well-being. It is not that parents are mistaken to be concerned about such things: parents' first responsibility is to protect their children, and every child deserves a safe and nurturing home. But such concerns must be realistically targeted at children's actual vulnerabilities. When they are not, protection turns into overprotection, and children are robbed of the chance to develop their own protective skills. This is why it is so important to start with an accurate view of children's natural strengths.

A compilation of the dispositions and abilities that children are born with would take a book in itself, and the list is growing longer with every foray into the infant labs.[4] The compilation would include many adaptive reflexes, social sensitivities, emotional response systems, linguistic predispositions, and incipient cognitive awarenesses. For the present, I shall begin by noting four inherent characteristics that promote the child's adaptation to a wide range of circumstances. I note these particular characteristics because, despite their centrality to the everyday functioning of all children, they have been widely discounted by adults in recent times. Then I shall discuss the moral virtues and sensitivities that all children enter the world with. I shall make the case that these virtues and sensitivities establish ready-made building blocks for the further development of children's moral character.

Natural Dispositions for Adaptation and Learning

1. *Children thrive on challenges*. Children are always in search of opportunities to gain skills and to prove themselves. They are motivated by a "drive for competence," just as they are by a drive for sustenance. When provided with challenges that fully test their abilities, children respond with energy and enthusiasm. When denied such challenges, children become insecure and apathetic. Ironically, sheltering children from "stressful" demands such as meeting high standards of school achievement creates a truly stressful condition for them. It frustrates their natural desires to wholly express their talents.

2. *Children are curious about the mysteries of life and are capable of understanding serious discussion about grave matters*. Even death itself is more fascinating than troubling to most children. In fact, children become less troubled by frank and open discussions of death than by the hushed, secretive posture that many adults believe to be protective of children's sensibilities. When concerned professionals arrange special counseling sessions for children in the wake of public or private disasters, they often become surprised at what they consider to be children's cavalier attitudes to the event. Yet the fact is that children are *less* likely to be disturbed by a calamity than are adults, partly because children are so psychologically adaptable. Rather than emotional counseling, children require thoughtful and honest answers. It is their curiosity and not their affective comfort that most motivates them. Censoring the truth from children, or even just shading it, has the opposite effect as intended: it makes children *more* afraid of the unknown, *and unnaturally so*. Children are attracted to rather than threatened by news about the real world. Indeed, this disposition is part of every child's adaptational inheritance.

3. *Children adjust quickly to change and are not readily traumatized*. When used to indicate psychological damage, the term "traumatic" is one of the most overworked words in the language. In the literal sense, the term "trauma" refers to a permanent impairment resulting from a single injury. Certainly this occurs with some frequency following physical insult, as when a blow to the head causes irreversible brain damage. Real psychological traumata are rare, and they are especially so in children. I know of no cases of a childhood psychological trauma following, for example, a family outburst, normal death or illness, a newscast of any sort, a motion picture or television show, a problem with a friend, or for that matter *any* event in the broad range of most families' experi-

ences. Of course even children are not infinitely resilient. In the clinical literature, there have been some documented cases of genuine childhood traumata. These usually have occurred after horrific events such as a child's discovery of a parent who had just committed suicide. But in the vast majority of incidents, children recover quickly after an upsetting event. Many times, a child develops new strengths in the wake of an emotionally difficult experience, especially when the child has access to a caring adult's support and guidance during the troublesome period. The medical adage that a bone is strongest at a place where it was broken has its parallel in psychological development as well.

4. *Children are active interpreters of their own experience*. Children make sense out the world in their own way—a way that is both incisive and stubbornly resistant to either manipulation or deception. This may be the characteristic of children that adults understand the least. Most adults seem to hold a behaviorist view of the child as a passive learner— a view that has been roundly discredited in psychological science. Children do not respond unselectively to environmental pressures; nor do influences register on them like an image on camera film. Rather, children enter into every new situation with their own dispositions and histories; and as a consequence they shape the situation, and their experiences in it, as much as the situation shapes them. This means that children are not susceptible to instant molding by adverse influences such as "peer pressure," rock and roll, or unsavory TV programming. If children misbehave after exposure to such influences, the roots of their misbehavior extend a long way back into the child's personal and family history.[5] Nor will removing dissolute friends or unwholesome entertainment provide quick fixes to any problem. Children will change their behavior only when doing so makes sense to them. Every child has a world view of his own, and it must be seriously engaged if it is to be influenced.

There is a reason that I have begun with these four dispositions from the entire bountiful repertoire of natural strengths and abilities that children are born with. The reason is twofold. First, these particular dispositions often are disregarded in today's popular views of children. Second, by disregarding these particular dispositions, it becomes possible for adults to dismiss the task of fostering personal and social responsibility in the young as being age-inappropriate and therefore off course. If we believe that children are stressed out rather than turned on by challenges, it seems dangerous to urge them to achieve. If we believe that children are threatened by exposure to life's truths, it seems proper to refrain from discussing grave matters with them. If we believe that children are easily traumatized, we must shield them from change and treat their feelings gingerly. If we believe that children are readily molded by every new influence that comes along, we should keep them away from everyone that we do not wholly approve of. In general, if children are deemed incompetent and fragile, it seems cruel to ask them to assume any responsibility for their own lives, let alone asking them to assume responsibility for helping others.

All of this well-intended vigilance creates a protective bubble that prevents children from exercising their own adaptive skills and discourages them from developing new ones. Even more destructively, it sends to children the implicit message that they are incapable of venturing into the world and taking on responsibilities of any sort. Instead, children receive the message that they are to confine their activities to the dreamy and playful world that many adults imagine childhood to be.[6] As I shall discuss in Chapter 8, too many parents today, from both middle-class and disadvantaged communities, unintentionally communicate these debilitating messages to their children

One wonders why today's parents are so drawn to such messages. It is more gratifying to think of children as helpless and needy than as sturdy and competent? Is it easier, and less time consuming, to shelter a child from the world than to help the child adapt to it? Is it simpler to provide total service to a child (especially in today's small families) than to require a child's contribution? Does it feel safer to micromanage the child's social world than to provide the child with support and guidance as the child makes her own way in it?

Whatever the reasons from the parents' point of view, as far as children are concerned, a message implying that they are infinitely dependent is *not* a comforting one. Children thirst for chances to establish their own competence.[7] They avidly seek real responsibility and are gratified when adults give it to them. When an adult sets an expectation of responsibility in the context of supportive guidance, a child is provided with an invaluable opportunity for self-enhancement. Children intuitively recognize this. As a consequence, they become energized when adults provide an opportunity for responsibility and demoralized when adults withhold it from them.

In Chapter 5, I noted some misconceptions that have followed from an imbalanced reading of Piaget by some followers who advocate a one-sided "constructivism."[8] Among the fallacies of the extreme constructivism in many educational circles today is the belief that children are wholly limited by their "stage" of development. According to this oversimplified view, adults must gear their guidance and instruction precisely to the child's stage. Otherwise, the adult's communication will be "age-inappropriate," perhaps putting too much pressure on, or at the very least confusing the child. This is a highly static view of development, and an implausible one at that.[9] If everything presented to children were strictly held to an age-appropriate standard, children would have access only to things that they already knew about. Nor is it even possible to fine-tune a message so that it comes in at exactly the level of a child's ability (or just above, as some constructivist educators have suggested).[10]

Fortunately, children's minds do not need to be treated that delicately. If they did, in fact, few children throughout the ages would have learned much of anything about the world. A child's natural capacity to learn is robust enough, and the child's desire persistent enough, to plow ahead even when most of what she hears is above her head. There is almost always something in an experience that a child can grasp. The process of doing so is what moves a child forward. The decision to withhold such opportunities from children is a serious error stemming from a misconception about the nature of children's developmental capacities.

The Moral Virtues

There has been a refreshing new look at human nature among philosophers and social scientists recently. The "profoundly self-interested" person who rationally sizes up what is best for oneself in every situation is no longer the unchallenged prototype of humankind.[11] Rather, as James Q. Wilson's recent treatise put it, we now know that there is a "moral sense" intrinsic to our species.[12] I have made much the same point in *The Moral Child*, my own integration of scientific findings on children's moral capacities. While the child's moral sense is by no means dominant on every occasion, it is as much a part of the child's natural way of responding to the world as is any of the child's other inclinations, dispositions, or drives. It cannot be stamped out or subjugated for long.

Even within economics—that last bastion of a "rational choice" theory that assumes self-interest as a bottom line—there have been recent stirrings of a nobler vision. Amitai Etzioni's influential proposal for a "new economics" was titled *The Moral Dimension*.[13] In it, Etzioni persuasively argues that no human decision making can be fully understood if we ignore the moral sensibilities that inevitably inform all social choices, including monetary and business decisions. Etzioni's polemic has found an enthusiastic audience, even among hard-core econometricians. In the wake of the excessively rationalistic Enlightenment theory, scholars now are ready to consider that moral sentiments make up a core part of who we are, of how we think, how we feel, and how we act, in every sphere of life.

All of this is true at the beginning of life, at least in germinal form. The seeds of the moral sense are sown at conception, and its roots are firmly established at birth. Every infant enters this world prepared to respond socially, and in a moral manner, to others. Every child has the capacity to acquire moral character. The necessary emotional response systems, budding cognitive awareness, and personal dispositions are there from the start. Although, unfortunately, not every child grows into a responsible and caring person, the potential to do so is native to every member of the species.

This is just one of many reasons why it is such a tragic waste when a young person drifts into a condition of amoral apathy—or, worse, into a frenzy of antisocial activity. When an entire generation shows signs of moving in such directions, one must look for the cultural forces that are leading them astray. And one must do what one can to reverse the cultural drift. Natural dispositions, however robust, are not in themselves enough to ensure moral character. In forming a person's mature moral sense, culture and nature work together from the time of birth, in multiple ways that I shall discuss in the following chapters.[14] When vast numbers of young people take to aberrant or attenuated moral pathways in the course of their development, we can be sure that the operative cultural influences are not rousing the full potential of the species.

Drawing on state-of-the-art research in the social sciences, James Q. Wilson recently made a compelling case for the moral potential inherent in all humans.[15] Wilson identifies four "sentiments" that provide an early basis for moral growth: sympathy, fairness, self-control, and duty. Wilson points out that signs of these sentiments appear so universally in very young children that they may be assumed to be natural. I have read the data in the same way that Wilson has, and, as he correctly noted, I came to many of the same conclusions in *The Moral Child*. I believe that Wilson is fundamentally correct in his assertions about human nature.

But Wilson has made his case on more limited grounds than is necessary. Each of the four sentiments that he identifies is representative of an entire *class* of emotions, intuitions, and regulatory systems that are present at birth and that predispose children toward moral awareness. Sympathy is one of many early moral emotions; fairness is one of many early moral concepts; and self-control and duty are part of entire personal and social regulatory systems that spring from inborn adaptive processes.

Studies in child development have discovered that the roots of a child's moral sense are long and extensive. In psychological terms, there are at least four overlapping processes that ensure moral awareness from an early age: moral emotions, moral judgment, social cognition, and self-understanding. These processes roughly coincide with Wilson's four sentiments, but they represent far broader classes of psychological phenomena.

Moral emotions refer to one's affective reactions to moral encounters, including reactions such as empathy, fear, and guilt.[16] Moral judgment refers to one's manner of determining prescriptive choices about social conduct and one's means of evaluating matters of justice, care, truthfulness, responsibility, and ethical duty.[17] Social cognition refers to one's conceptions of the other, of the social world, and of one's means of gaining access to information about social interactions and social relationships.[18] Self-understanding refers to one's conceptions of the past, present, and future self, including all the multiple aspects of self-control and self-regulation.[19]

To a greater or lesser extent, each of these processes is active at birth and develops over the life course. I say "to a greater or lesser extent" because some processes begin at a stronger state of readiness than others and some make more dramatic progress during the course of development than do others. Each of the processes plays a unique role in disposing young people towards prosocial and away from antisocial engagements. They also work in synchrony, combining with one another in ways that increase one another's effectiveness. The four processes continuously interpenetrate all throughout the course of development, spurring each other's growth. Just as importantly, they provide *redundancy* to the moral system. Where one process fails, another intercedes to ensure the moral act.

First among the inborn proclivities towards prosocial behavior is a cluster of emotional reactions known as *empathy* and *sympathy*. These interpersonal feeling states link a child to others through a sense of shared responding. In the course of empathic and sympathetic reactions, the child's own emotional comfort is affected, either positively or negatively, by the child's perception of another person's well-being. This emotional effect provides the child with a motivated reason to care about another person's welfare, to aid the other, and to keep the other from harm's way.[20] It also gives the child an affectively charged reason to avoid hurting the other through violent acts of the child's own.

Although related, empathy and sympathy are different in important ways. Nancy Eisenberg has proposed the following distinctions between the two constructs:

> . . . we define *empathy* as the sharing of the perceived emotion of the other. Specifically, it is an affective state that stems from the apprehension of another's emotional state or condition and that is congruent and quite similar to the perceived state of the other. . . . *Sympathy* . . . we define as an emotional response, stemming from another's emotional state or condition, that is not identical to the other's emotion but consists of feelings of sorrow or concern for the other's welfare.[21]

Such a distinction suggests that empathy and sympathy each bring their own influence to bear on children's social conduct. In empathy, a child shares another's feelings; yet the child's primary concern may remain with the self. The child, for example, may resent those who cause him to feel the same unpleasant things that they are feeling. In such cases, empathy would not necessarily trigger behavior that is other-oriented: a plausible alternative response could be to disassociate the self from the other and to stop empathizing. Empathy may provide the emotional substance behind a desire to care for another, but it does not in itself fully establish that desire. Sympathy, on the other hand, implies a direct concern for the other and not an absolute sharing of feelings. This means that sympathy inevitably has an altruistic orientation. Its affective demands can be satisfied only through prosocial action or through resistance to antisocial action. While sympathy may at times draw upon empathy for its emotional substance and charge, of the two emotions it is the one more strongly directed towards helping and not harming the other.

The developmental roots of empathy and sympathy begin very early in life. Although it is a matter of speculation (and, to some extent, semantics) whether *true* empathy or sympathy can be found in newborns, psychologists have identified reactions that certainly represent early precursors.[22] One of the first such reactions is an infant crying response that Piaget called "contagion."[23] In nurseries and neonatal wards, two- or three-day-old infants have been observed crying at the sounds of other infants' crying.[24] Without any physical pain of their own, therefore, infants emit matched vocal signs at the sound of another's distress. Contagious crying simply may be caused by the infant's perceptual confusion of itself with others in combination with the infant's tendency to reproduce its own behavior. A circular pattern may be triggered, in which the infant repeats the crying response that it mistakenly takes as its own. Still, even if only attributable to this sort of egocentric confusion, contagious crying indicates an initial disposition towards spontaneously responding with a sign of distress to another's discomfort. At the very least, this disposition represents a precursor to both empathy and sympathy.

There are a number of other emotional proclivities appearing early in life that contribute to a child's prosocial tendencies. Jerome Kagan has identified five categories of "moral emotions" that he assumes to be native to our species.[25] *Empathy* is one (Kagan does not differentiate it from sympathy). The other four are: *fear* of punishment or disapproval; *guilt*; *"ennui"* from oversatiation of desire; and *anxiety* over inconsistency between one's beliefs and one's actions. Kagan cites evidence for the universality of these emotional reactions. If he is right—and I am convinced that he is—this means that every child enters the world with an arsenal of feelings that discourage the child from harming others.

We could add still other early emotional reactions to Kagan's list. *Shame* is an early deterrent to antisocial conduct as well as an inevitable forerunner to the even more powerful force of guilt.[26] *Guilt* itself is a fundamental early moral emotion, and it has several important variations, including an *interpersonal* form that is especially directed toward regulating the moral quality of social relationships.[27] Other moral emotions that have been reliably observed in young children include *outrage* over unfairness, *contempt* for the misconduct of others, *pride* for the good conduct of the self, and *horror* over observed violent outbursts.[28]

With the right kinds of social experience and guidance, early moral emotions develop into powerful systems of moral action. Empathy provides a good example of how inborn emotional responses can combine with social experience and cognitive growth to produce a disposition to act in a prosocial manner. As with all the other moral emotions, the child's capacity for empathic responding is broadened and transformed through actual social experience. When children turn their empathic impulses into deeds, they gain practice in helping others. Often they may receive guidance as well, particularly when a parent or other mentor provides feedback to them about the effectiveness of their attempts to help. Over time, practice and guidance turn the child's random empathic impulse into a consistent mode of behaving kindly towards those in need.[29] Effective action—such as helping others in appropriate ways—becomes linked to the natural emotional response. What is more, the emotional response itself becomes broadened to include those whom the child may have never met, such as starving children in distant countries. All of this also requires the growth of cognitive skills such as understanding the problems of different people and knowing how best to help them. The main cognitive skill that supports empathic responding is called "social perspective taking"; or more colloquially, taking the role of the other.[30]

Because social experience and cognitive growth are essential in transforming the early emotional response into an effective and reliable system of moral action, there is great variation among children in the degree to which the moral emotion ultimately prevails in their social behavior. Again, empathy provides a clear illustration of this point. Some children become able emotionally and cognitively to share other perspectives with great sensitivity. Some seem unwilling or unable to do so; and others do so in erratic or distorted ways. Young delinquents have been observed to show surprise at the notion that they should care at all about the harm they cause others. In cases where violent youngsters do express empathic sentiments, these sentiments are often wildly misplaced. One youth with a long history of mayhem was heard worrying about the pain that pine trees might feel when they are cut down to make Christmas trees.[31] Such failures or distortions of empathy develop long after birth. Although the scientific jury is still out on what causes them, they are most likely attributable to later intellectual and social experience rather than to congenital emotional deficits.

Beyond their natural emotional response systems, children enter the world *prepared to learn* about other people, about themselves, and about how to conduct relationships with others. In the normal course of development, young people develop during childhood and adolescence a strong understanding of the social world and their place in it. They understand the properties of other persons, the workings of interpersonal relationships such as friendship and authority, and the complexities of societal institutions. They can analyze the connections and disconnections between their own perspectives and the perspectives of others. Perhaps most significantly, they can use their keen social understanding to guide their communication, conduct, and feelings toward others.

Infants are born well-prepared to enter a world in which social relationships are critical for survival. Several recent studies have confirmed the newborn's impressive ability to coordinate its attention and actions with the activities of others. The intricate interactions that occur between infant and mother provide a clear indication that infants begin life with the responsiveness necessary for sustaining meaningful relations with others.[32] Infants also are able to skillfully coordinate their activity with others, displaying a complex, self-aware, and adaptive form of social understanding that scientists have called "intersubjectivity."[33] Research conducted in the Scottish labs of child psychologist Colwyn Trevarthen has shown that infants know when their mothers' actions are (and are not) synchronized with their own.[34] Significantly, infants show distress in the absence of good coordination. This shows both an acute awareness of interactional norms and a sensitivity to the vicissitudes of attachment relationships.

Young infants also show a desire to accomplish a number of social goals. These include a desire to maintain proximity with the caretaker, to maintain a sense of security, and regulate their emotions.[35] They show a need to succeed in social interaction—to discern the rules governing social life and to act appropriately—along with an intrinsic interest in the persons with whom they are interacting.[36] All these natural desires drive the infant's efforts to understand the social world starting at the time of birth.

Beginning with a natural interest in other persons and a natural desire to succeed in social interaction, a young person acquires more advanced social understanding throughout the entire period from infancy through adolescence. All of the advances in social understanding build upon important awarenesses that are present either at birth or very early in infancy. We are long past the days when psychologists believed that infants enter the world in a state of social isolation or ego-centric autism. The socially sensitive nature of newborn behavior has been established without question.[37] Advances in children's social and moral understanding have fertile soil in which to grow. Some advances result from the accumulation of knowledge and experience, whereas others result from periodic reorganizations in the young person's conceptual orientation to the world.

In the moral domain, developmental psychologists have stressed three conceptual systems, closely linked to behavior, that advance rapidly in the childhood and adolescent years: (1) care for the welfare of others; (2) understanding of justice; and (3) respect for rules.[38] All three make their appearance early in life but depend upon later development for their full elaboration. As I have shown above, moral emotions such as empathy and sympathy orient very young children toward care, and the subsequent growth of social-cognitive skills enables young people to care for others in effective and responsible ways. The same developmental principles apply to the child's emerging concerns for justice and social rules.

Very young children have some awareness of rules. During infancy and toddlerhood, children invent repetitious patterns of playful behavior that verge on becoming "regularities."[39] These have no moral significance except as developmental precursors to games with social rules, because they are not yet social and do not carry with them any sense of obligation. For example, a two-year-old might roll a rubber ball across the room in a repeated pattern, but without the sense that there is anything necessary or obligatory about the pattern. Very young children also observe regularities in their social environment, ranging from dress codes to modes of conduct.[40] They will follow the directions of adults who enforce such regularities upon the child's own behavior, but again without their own understanding of why the rules are important and without any internalized respect of their own for them.

During childhood, playful regularities become transformed into collective rules, usually in the form of household codes and conventions, organized games in the family and peer group, and school regulations. No longer subject to the child's momentary whims, social rules are stable and obligatory. In orderly family and community environments, rules are clearly communicated, uniformly applied, and consistently enforced.

Learning to submit to social rules is an important milestone in the young child's moral development. From this experience grows an awareness of the obligation to respect the rights of others and the rights of society in general. From this experience also grows a habitual respect for the social order. The "good habits" learned from consistent applications of social rules are at least as important for the young person's conduct as the conceptual awareness of the rules themselves. Ideally, habits and reflection go hand in hand in the course of moral development, although this is not always the case. As I shall discuss in the following chapter, environments that do not present children with firm rules and other shared expectations fail to provide children with either or both of the essential moral capacities: good habits and reflective awareness.

Consistent rules, fairly administered, help awaken a child's sense of justice. Other common experiences in early childhood also nurture justice concepts and concerns. Toddlers share toys with playmates, divide snacks, and learn to take turns with swings and bikes.[41] Sharing and turn taking both contribute to the child's ability to resolve potential conflicts peacefully. For most young people, these early activities will develop into a full-blown sense of distributive justice by the beginning of adolescence.[42] As with the young child's first rule-following acts, early sharing and turn taking are rarely accompanied by a sense of moral compulsion; but they lay the groundwork for an emerging dedication to resolving conflicts through fairness rather than force.

Again, the child's experience within key social relationships is critical in determining the course that development takes. Social rules for most children are manifestations of adult authority, albeit impersonal and generalized ones. Fairness, too, is a common admonishment of adult authority, as are truthfulness, courtesy, and a host of other socially desirable virtues. In all these ways, the role of adult authority for children's moral growth is central and indisputable. At the same time, peer relations also play a crucial role in the formation of children's moral orientation. Rule following, sharing, cooperation, and truthfulness all develop during peer engagements that in many instances are wholly separate from the world of parents or teachers.

In all areas of the child's social and moral awareness, the quality of a child's social experience determines the direction that the child's natural propensity for learning will take. The developmental effect of social relationships builds over the years, in either positive or negative ways.[43] Early adaptive experience can orient a child towards further beneficial social engagements and can provide the child with skills needed to conduct these engagements in a productive manner. Conversely, early maladaptive experience can distort one's later choices and poison the climate of one's future relationships. In this sense, one's personal development at any point in life may be described as the history of one's social relationships; and the child's moral orientation is a product of this history, for good or for ill.

Beyond social and moral understanding, the child's self-understanding plays a special role in promoting positive social conduct, both because it provides its own incentives and because it acts as an important mediator between moral judgment and moral conduct. For the same reasons, a strong and mature sense of self can deter antisocial activities, including violence. Self-understanding, like the other components of a child's early repertoire of skills, starts to develop early. By the middle of the first year of life, infants show awareness that they are distinct from others and that they have a personal continuity over time.[44] Between eighteen and twenty-four months of age, infants develop knowledge of their own physical and active characteristics. Moreover, recent research on "social referencing" suggests that infants may be aware of their own emotional states.[45] During childhood and adolescence, self-understanding grows in multiple ways.[46] Children develop an increasing sense of their own agency, their personal continuity over time and their distinctness from others, and their own objective characteristics. Some similar developmental patterns cut across all these dimensions. Early in childhood, the self is understood as a collection of separate, and unrelated, surface characteristics. In middle and late childhood, the self is understood through comparison with others. Adolescence brings an understanding of the interpersonal implications of particular features of the self: the self is viewed largely in terms of its real or potential effect on other people. By late adolescence, many young people organize their sense of self around a personal philosophy and a related set of plans for the future.

In the course of development, moral beliefs can play an increasingly central role in the definition of self. By middle childhood, there is normally an awareness not only of right and wrong but of one's own *personal responsibility* to promote the right and combat the wrong. Studies of children between the ages of four and eight have shown that younger children know full well that it is wrong to steal, lie, and hurt others, but they do not assume that doing such things will cause the perpetrator personal distress.[47] In contrast, older children in this age range accept that one should feel bad when one has violated a serious moral standard. This emotional change, I believe, can only be explained by a developmental shift in the children's notions of how morality and the self are connected. The younger children see nothing more than an indirect or peripheral connection, whereas the older children assume an emotionally vital one. The latter perspective goes hand in hand with an increasing sense of personal responsibility.

By the time of late adolescence, a young person has acquired the potential to integrate her sense of self around moral concerns. As a consequence, some young people become increasingly reflective about their moral purposes in life. This sense of purpose can fuel the encouraging belief that one's personal talents, interests, and commitments can contribute to society; and this belief in turn can provide a basis for positive social participation and hope for the future.

Not all young persons, however, link personal commitment and moral beliefs to the self. The development of self can take many paths, and persons vary widely in the extent to which they look to their commitments and convictions in defining their personal identities. For some, moral values are central to their self-understanding as early as childhood; for others, morality may always remain peripheral to who they think they are.[48]

Of course, such a difference affects the extent to which a person ultimately takes moral concerns seriously and translate her values into action. Studies of persons who show high levels of active moral commitment during their lives have found that such persons make little distinction between their moral and personal selves.[49] They identify themselves very closely with their moral goals and believe that if they were to forsake such goals they would not remain the same person. This stands in sharp contrast to those for whom moral concerns are compartmentalized, isolated from other primary self concerns such as material well-being, physical attractiveness, career success, or social status. As one reviewer of the literature on moral judgment and conduct relations has concluded: "Being moral, being a good person, being fair and just in a general sense, may be, but need not be, a part of an individual's essential self."[50]

The manner in which any person, young or old, integrates moral and self concerns is at least as important in determining the person's moral conduct as the nature of the person's moral understanding.[51] Differences among people in how central morality is to their self-concepts may be detected as early as adolescence. In one recent longitudinal study, a few adolescents held their moral beliefs to be central to their self-identities, and they maintained this conviction over the four-year course of the study.[52] The majority, however, segregated their moral concerns from their self concerns and showed little change in this dimension even by the time of late adolescence.

This is clearly a matter for concern, because there are both theoretical and empirical reasons to believe that the centrality of morality to self may be the single most powerful determiner of concordance between moral judgment and conduct.[53] Persons whose self-concept is organized around their moral beliefs are highly likely to translate those beliefs into action consistently throughout their lives.[54] Such persons tend to sustain a far higher level of moral commitment in their actual conduct than those who may reason well about morality but who consider it to be less pivotal for who they are. In their own statements, such people often maintain that they have no choice but to actively pursue their moral commitments, since their most fundamental life goals are determined by their moral convictions. They see little if any separation between their personal and their moral goals. In this regard, highly moral people demonstrate what Anne Colby and I have found to be a "uniting of self and morality."[55]

Natural dispositions cannot provide this unity, or for that matter any integration at all between morality and self. Nature provides the building blocks but not the architecture. Cultural influence and personal development inevitably determine the shape and direction of a child's moral character. Only through a developmental process that is rich in the right kinds of social influence can a young person find stable ways to integrate moral and personal goals. It is especially important, in a culture that elevates self-enhancement as a priority in and of itself, to provide young people with experiences and instruction that establish strong links between self and morality. Only in this way can the moral potential of children's natural virtues be realized.

7

A Framework of Guidance for Children's Intellectual and Moral Growth

In Part I of this book, I made the case that many young people today are in desperate need of guidance—not just any guidance, but responsible, effective, inspiring guidance that could help them attain the high intellectual and moral potential that young people through the ages have shown. In Part II, I suggested some reasons why our contemporary culture has failed to give young people the guidance that they need to reach their full potential. Among other things, I showed how we have become preoccupied by false and fruitless oppositions about children's developmental needs. As a result of such preoccupations, our childrearing and educational practices drift without coherence or direction.

In the opening chapter of Part III, I have described natural dispositions that prepare the ground for the child's development of competence and character. These "natural virtues" offer sound starting points for childrearing. I argued that society has been underestimating the child's natural strengths in recent years—yet another stream of modern misconception—and that this error seriously undermines the age-old adult mission of helping children realize their full potential. In order to offer children the kind of constructive social influence that enables them to build character and competence, we must work with children's natural characteristics as they really are and not as some romanticized myths would have them be.

This leaves the question how to offer children constructive social influence that will help them make the most of their natural strengths. The remaining four chapters of this book address this question. The present chapter does so in a general and theoretical manner; and the following three chapters do so in the particular settings of home, school, and community. In a sentence, the present chapter is about the lengthy and intricate developmental process that child psychologists have called "socialization." I shall introduce a view of socialization that is somewhat different from the one that may be found in most child psychology textbooks—and that is very different from the views that are prevalent in today's childrearing manuals.

The purpose of this chapter is to lay out a general framework for how we may provide the most effective guidance for today's young people while they are still in their formative years. Some of the developmental theory in this chapter may seem a bit abstract for readers who are more interested in youth behavior than in psychological processes. For those readers, the remaining three chapters of the book are meant to explicate specific ways in which the general framework may be played out in the family, the school, in the community.

Building Bridges Between Generations

The metaphor that will run throughout this chapter is that socialization is a bridge-building process linking the child's spontaneous experiences to the ideas and values that adults must transmit. To continue with the metaphor, the bridges must be capable of bearing two-way traffic. But the bridges also must contain signals that direct the eventual flow of the "traffic"—that is, the child's behavior—towards the mature adult vision of competence and character. Bridge building of this sort is an *interactional* approach that avoids the false oppositions that I have outlined in previous chapters. My claim in the present chapter is that this bridge-building approach is the only viable means of providing guidance for the legions of disaffected, demoralized, and directionless young people growing up in today's world.

The main task of socialization is to impart the invaluable tools of a culture to its young people. The tools may include knowledge, skills, habits, attitudes, values, practices, understandings, and a host of other mental and behavioral products of learning. Adults, by and large, have such tools in their grasp. Young people, for the most part, do not. Most adults who come in contact with the young perceive it to be their role to act as agents of the culture and to transmit it to the young. Adults generally try to communicate the culture to the young, and they in turn expect that young people will try to learn it.

In reality, though, young people do not always absorb the culture as readily as adults might expect. For one thing, even young children have their own perspectives on the world, and these perspectives can be remarkably sturdy and well formed. As I noted in the previous chapter, it is a mistake to consider children to be like lumps of clay, like blank slates, or like any other passive, undefined objects. From the earliest ages, children function exquisitely as well-formed, adaptive individuals with distinct characteristics.

Initially, the main source of children's characteristics lies in their natural dispositions. Later, as children acquire their own histories of social experience, they develop a "second nature": that is, an organized cluster of robust dispositions that continues to change over time and that determines the child's personal responses to the world.[1] A child's second nature works in the same manner as the child's original one, establishing in the child a strong individual perspective that actively interprets all of the child's transactions with the outside world. Any socialization attempt by a parent or other adult inevitably is filtered through the child's individual perspective.

The robustness of the child's own perspective presents both a problem and an opportunity for those who wish to socialize the child. The problem is that, since children interpret the world in their own way, they may be unwilling or unable to absorb the socializing influences. Children may resist the external influences if the influences do not suit them; children may not understand the external influences if the influences are beyond their experience; or children may distort the influences by confusing them with other, dissimilar messages. The opportunity for socialization is that a child's well-formed and active perspective provides a firm foundation for further cultural learning. Just as the child's second nature builds on a platform of the child's natural virtues, every socializing influence builds on a platform of the child's spontaneous perspective, which itself provides substantial knowledge, awareness, feelings, goals, and other substantial materials for the construction.

Any encounter between a child and a socializing adult may be problematic, or it may be propitious, depending upon how well the encounter engages the child's own perspective. Problematic encounters occur when adults fail to coordinate their messages with the child's knowledge, goals, and feelings. The two types of imbalances that I discussed in Chapter 5 create poor coordinations of perspectives. The child-centered imbalances create poor coordination by failing to provide children with challenging new ideas or the guidance that children need. The adult-centered imbalances create poor coordination by failing to engage children's own goals in any meaningful way. For an effective socialization encounter, an adult first must build a bridge to the child's perspective and then lead the child in a positive new direction.

When stated so plainly, this seems like an obvious and noncontroversial principle; at least to me, it sounds like common sense. Yet this view is rarely represented among the polarized childrearing positions that we have become accustomed to hearing. Instead, we hear one version after another of the empty opposition between extreme nativism on the one hand and extreme environmentalism on the other—between, on the one hand, laissez-faire, child-centered views which claim that children grow best when left alone and, on the other hand, rigid, adult-centered views which assume that children will respond attentively to anything that we say. The elementary notion that children learn by *interacting* with those who have a purpose and a direction to offer them has been the most elusive idea of all among today's overheated polemics.[2]

Bridge building, as I have used the phrase, is simply a metaphor for communication that provides a direction for the younger generation. Socialization means nothing more (or less) than communicating skills, information, and, most centrally, goals. Recent studies tell us something about how this is accomplished as well as how it is not accomplished. For one thing, we know that it cannot be done as easily or as directly as some impatient public figures have assumed. Lecturing is practically useless; and one cannot simply send stern directives to young people outlining what one expects of them. Rather, the process entails an intricate process of direction, support, collaboration, and negotiation. In developmental studies, this process has been called "authoritative childrearing," "induction," "scaffolding," "guided participation," and, my own term, "respectful engagement."[3] Each of these terms emphasizes a slightly different aspect of the interactive process. Here I shall focus on what I consider to be the process's core component: *the transformation of children's goals through guiding social influence.*

Children enter into every social encounter with their own goals. The child's agenda may be to seek nurturance, to gain a desired commodity, to converse, or simply to play. Adults, too, have goals in all of their social encounters. In an encounter with a child, an adult's agenda may coincide with the child's goals, but likely it will include socialization goals as well. That is to say, an adult's agenda in interacting with a child usually includes goals such as introducing new ideas, skills, and goals to the child.

If adults are to accomplish their socialization goals, they cannot ignore children's own goals for social encounters. But neither can adults allow the encounters to rest there. Only by recognizing children's agendas while never losing sight of their own can adults communicate new purposes to children. Over an extended period of time, an adult proceeding in this manner will transmit an entire perspective on the world to the child. Such a perspective usually brings with it a new set of motivated goals as well as the intellectual and personal tools to carry them out.

Transformation of a child's goals through guiding social influence is a gradual process that always takes place in a context of mutual engagement. To achieve such engagement, it is necessary that the adult's goals initially match the child's, at least in part. At the outset, adult and child must share some agenda, even if the adult also has other purposes in mind. This may require some accommodation on the part of the adult.

For example, a mother wants her two-year-old son to learn table manners. She starts by getting him to handle a fork and spoon, and he joins in eagerly in a spirit of play. In its initial phases, the child's use of silverware bears little resemblance to table manners. It is erratic, rambunctious, incompetent, and it ends up making more of a mess than if the boy used his fingers. The mother bears with him, perhaps joining in the spirit of playfulness, or at least putting up with it. Eventually, using assistance, demonstrations, admonishments, and constant cajoling, the mother guides her son's playful behavior into an organized system of tidy eating. This system of tidy eating is accompanied by a whole perspective on table manners and their societal implications. The boy, for example, may devalue the offensive behavior of those who eat sloppily ("What a pig Freddy is!"), and he eventually may come to disassociate himself from such persons. Once the boy assumes such a perspective on his own, it requires less and less reinforcement from the mother. Psychologists have used the metaphor of "scaffolding" to capture the gradually reduced need for adult support during the extended period that it takes for a developmental transformation of the child's goals.[4]

Table manners are but one example of a socialization product. In comparison with all the other habits, attitudes, and goals that are formed through social influence, table manners are a relatively trivial product. But virtually every advanced intellectual insight, and virtually every mature moral response, owes some debt to a socially induced transformation of the child's goals. If the child's natural dispositions are to become an effective instrument of intellectual and moral achievement, they must be extended, amplified, modified, and enriched through this kind of social influence. This is why socialization is so crucial both to the future of the child and to the society that the child will inherit.

The essential component of socialization is the right kind of communication. Every transformation of goals begins with a partially shared agenda, and a shared agenda cannot be established without the kinds of communicative bridge building that align the child's and the adult's initial goals. Without an initial match, there is no possibility that the adult can exert any lasting influence on the child's perspective. All guidance, therefore, must begin by building bridges to the child's inclinations, whether they be inclinations of nature or of "second nature." The most effective sort of bridge building starts by recognizing the child's own abilities and goals and then proceeds to draw these into the adult's framework of guidance.

Cognitive psychologists have described this sort of bridge building as a process in which "experts" establish "cognitive apprenticeships" with learners.[5] The adult (or "expert") teaches the child (or the "novice") new intellectual skills by collaborating with the child on a task such as, for example, a challenging science project. The adult converses with the child about the task and makes note of the child's spontaneous way of approaching it. Together adult and child try out solutions that begin with the child's strategy. At the same time, the adult demonstrates—or "models"—other ways of solving the task. These other ways of solving the task must be strategies that share some characteristics of the child's approach, but the new ways must go beyond the child's approach in power and effectiveness. As long as the new ways do not depart too radically from the child's own approach, the child can observe them, understand them, and join the adult in using them. It is through such processes of modeling and collaboration that the child acquires new insight and skill.

Anthropologists in recent years have discovered that this kind of instruction is used widely in many of the world's traditional cultures, typically with great effectiveness.[6] Mayan mothers, for example, teach their daughters sophisticated cooking skills through intricate apprenticeships that may extend for years. At first, when the daughter is very young, mother and child join in playful games with foodstuff, such as rolling and patting tortilla dough. Soon the child is making her own rough tortillas. The mother refines these into well-shaped ones and bakes them in the oven. The child observes, participates, and practices, all the while receiving finely tuned guidance from her mother. When the daughter is ready, the mother lets her try her creations in the oven, under supervision that is initially watchful but later more relaxed. By the end of childhood, the daughter is an accomplished cook, able to fully use all the culinary tools and know-how of the culture.

In my writings on children's moral development, I have called bridge building of this sort "respectful engagement."[7] The elements of respectful engagement are: (1) creating a dialogue or a project in which the adult and the child share a common interest; (2) structuring the dialogue or the project in ways that introduce the adult's intellectual or moral agenda to the child; (3) encouraging the child to participate actively in the dialogue or venture and allowing the child's free expression of beliefs (however wrong these beliefs may seem); and (4) expressing, in ways that the child can comprehend, the adult's own perspective. All four conditions are necessary if the adult is to have a lasting, constructive influence on the child's perspective.

For effective moral instruction, adults must confront children with basic moral principles that are clearly stated and sincerely held. Principles such as fairness, kindness, honesty, and social responsibility cannot be compromised. When adults unambivalently express their conviction in such principles, they "model" for children a firm respect for moral values. This encourages children to orient towards their own natural moral feelings and to develop an even more enhanced moral sense. At the same time, this kind of guidance also increases children's respect for authority.

As a bridge-building enterprise that relies on open communication, "respectful engagement" establishes a climate of tolerance for divergent opinions. Tolerance in instructional dialogues need not imply, as some have wrongly deduced, that adults should practice values neutrality while discussing ethical issues with the young. In fact, displays of values neutrality from adults have an opposite effect to that intended. By failing to confront children with real beliefs, genuinely held, such displays engender in children an attitude of passive indifference—and even cynicism—towards the enterprise of moral choice. Why should a child bother working through a moral problem, or risk taking a stand, when the child's moral mentor refrains from doing so?

Like all socialization practices, moral instruction must touch children's goals as well as their beliefs, skills, and feelings. As I have discussed above, influencing the child's goals means sharing the child's agenda while at the same time moving it in a new direction. This can only take place when an adult assumes a role of leadership in relation to the child. The leadership, of course, cannot be in the form of an arbitrary, tyrannical force that the child perceives as external to the child's own beliefs and dispositions. In order to have a lasting, positive influence on the child's perspective, the adult must exert leadership within a participatory, collaborative relationship.

In a similar vein, child psychologists have learned to distinguish between *authoritative* and *authoritarian* parent/child relationships.[8] In an authoritative relationship, the parent communicates firm, consistent, and clear expectations to the child in the context of open, two-way dialogues. In an authoritarian relationship, the adult communicates little more to the child than arbitrary power, expecting the child to listen and behave without any input of the child's own. Research has demonstrated that *authoritative* relationships lead the child towards genuine competence and responsibility, whereas *authoritarian* ones cause the child to behave well only as long as the adult is looking.[9]

Ironically, the results of *authoritarian* parenting are in some ways similar to those of *permissive* parenting, even though the two styles look diverse on the surface. In both cases, children come away without opportunities to learn stable, internalized means of control—in authoritarian relationships due to the lack of reason or consistency in the parents' rules, in the permissive ones due to the lack of any rules to begin with. As a result, neither type of relationship offers children compelling standards that they can take on as their own to guide them through life. In contrast, *authoritative* relationships combine consistent standards with rational explanations about the purpose of the standards. The parent not only expects the child to act according to such standards but also communicates with the child about why this is so. In the long run, children naturally find this combination compelling.

Relationships that are collaborative, guiding, and openly communicative in nature help children acquire the skills and knowledge that they will need to ensure both their own and the culture's survival. Rudimentary as well as complex skills both may be passed along in this way: the process of generational transmission relies on the identical principles of communication and socialization whether the achievement be cooking or literacy. There must be an initial match of interests between adult and child. This does not mean capitulation to the child's agenda but rather commitment to an agenda that is mutually negotiated and temporarily shared. With persistent guidance, the child's own agenda eventually will develop in the direction of greater skill and wisdom. In many ways, but not all, the child's new ideas will emulate the elder's perspective. Not all, because new generations do find ways to progress beyond the old ones.

The paradox of socialization is that, through guidance, children learn to find their own voice. This occurs in the moral arena as well as in the intellectual sphere. Respectful engagement and other forms of guided collaboration help children develop not only a strong moral orientation but also a deep understanding of everyday moral issues. The child learns how to find the moral issue in an ambiguous situation, how to apply basic moral values to unfamiliar problems, and how to create moral solutions when there is no one around to give direction. The only way to master these key challenges is to develop an ability to interpret, understand, and manage moral problems. This requires a certain degree of autonomous thinking and reflection on the part of the child. Effective socialization encourages children *both* to respect moral authority *and* to learn to think on their own; to enhance their moral feelings *as well as* their moral beliefs; to respond habitually to moral concerns *and* to reason well about moral problems.

Among moral educators in recent years, there has been a heated debate between those who would train children to have good habits and those who would encourage children to develop the capacity for moral reasoning and reflection.[10] The debate has been roughly along conservative/liberal lines. Perhaps predictably, conservatives fear that too much reasoning and reflection will stifle the moral response and erode respect for authority, whereas liberals fear that too much emphasis on habit will turn children into blind followers or morally obtuse automatons.[11] As I discuss in the final section of this chapter, I see this as yet another unfortunate opposition. At least in this particular case, though, I can understand the distinction that the opposition is based upon: because acquiring the capacity for one does not in fact ensure the capacity for the other. Yet I would find it lamentable to be forced to choose between the two in raising future generations.

Constructing the Whole Child

Promoting both habit and reflection is but one of many ways that sound socialization practices aim at what loosely has been called "the whole child." In education circles today, some unanalyzed rhetoric about "whole child" approaches has borne its own share of myth and misconception; but the general perspective does represent a valuable move towards a more unified and comprehensive position on children's developmental needs. In order to advance the beneficial components of this position, it is crucial for us accurately to define "the whole child" and to identify the sorts of socialization practices that take this integrated and comprehensive vision as their goal.

At its most general level, a "whole child" approach to childrearing means fostering both intellectual and moral growth in young people. Socialization must assume the twin goals of competence and character: one without the other will not do. If a child attains skills without a clear sense of values, the child will either misuse those skills or fail to find any sustaining purpose for them.[12] If a child acquires values without skills, the child's good intentions will amount to nothing more than ineffectual gestures. Instructional practices that divorce intellectual from moral concerns—whether these practices take place in the home, in the school, or in the community—always risk such imbalances. Only socialization practices that take a comprehensive approach to children's development can impart the elements of competence and character and, just as importantly, join them together.

What are the elements of competence and character, and how may our socialization practices advance them both, in an integrated fashion? Here again, we must start by resisting simplified polarizations of disparate capacities. On the competence side, socialization must impart intellectual skills and knowledge *as well as* learning dispositions; creativ-

ity *as well as* disciplined and rigorous thinking; a proficiency with cooperation *as well as* a facility for competition. On the character side, as I
discuss below, it is essential to unite habit and reflection. Too often in
today's cultural disputes, disparate capacities such as these have been
seen as alternative *choices* that parents and educators must decide
between. This is another instance of the destructive oppositional thinking that I discussed in Chapters 4 and 5. It is not only possible but necessary for our socialization practices to aim at both sides of these supposed oppositions.[13] Rather than viewing these as polarities, we should
view them as dualities that should complement and strengthen each
other in the course of development. None of the elements of competence and character is one-dimensional, as some of our more divisive
educational debates might suggest.

Advocates of "cultural literacy" are correct in assuming that children
need to learn facts in order to solve problems properly, to communicate
effectively with others, and to make their way around in the world.[14]
But true competence requires knowing which facts to focus on. It
requires the ability to sort fact from fiction and to reason well about
them both. In short, it requires thinking skills as well as factual knowledge. It is one of the most absurd errors of the modern era that some
educational critics have placed these in opposition to one another.

In a similar vein, it is untenable to separate creativity from rigorous
and disciplined thinking, as some other educational critics have
attempted to do.[15] Children have formidable creative tendencies and
certainly should be encouraged to exercise them: it is a waste of human
talent to allow schooling to become associated in a child's mind with
nothing more fruitful than rote memorization. But any achievement,
no matter how creative, requires a certain amount of disciplined effort.
It also entails its share of drudgery and frustration. If it is to have any
value, creative work does require *work*, for children as much as for
adults. In order to develop their creative talents, children must learn to
work seriously at them. Even very young children benefit from the kind
of balanced instructional atmosphere that promotes creativity and discipline jointly.

A well-balanced instructional program builds competence in young
people by avoiding sterile oppositions and by aiming at the child's
entire range of capacities and interests. This is what is meant (or at least
what should be meant) by a "whole child" approach to education. Children come away from balanced instructional experiences not only with

specific skills and knowledge but also with enduring dispositions that spur further learning.[16] Such dispositions include the capacities for critical and creative thinking, the attitude of curiosity and open-mindedness, the tendency to approach problems systematically, and the ability to learn from a variety of social settings, including ones that emphasis cooperation as well as ones that emphasize competition. Dispositions to learn are central in the lifelong growth of competence. They are at least as important a product of early education as any skills or knowledge that the child may acquire. In Chapter 9, I shall discuss the key learning dispositions and how we may promote them in our children.

The most contentious debates on children's competence have taken place in the area of educational policy, no doubt because there is so much dissatisfaction about the quality and performance of the modern school. Although Americans have come to believe that it is the U.S. schools in particular that are underperforming, in truth the present-day dissatisfaction extends worldwide. The universal problem is that a nineteenth-century model of schooling still holds a virtual monopoly over public schooling everywhere, even as we enter the twenty-first century. This nineteenth-century model is out of touch with vast populations of today's youth, and it badly needs reforming. I shall return in Chapter 9 to a more detailed discussion of our schools and how we may reform them so that they may contribute more constructively to children's development. For now, I shall simply note that such reforms must be guided by the same socialization principles that I have discussed throughout this chapter. Like all aspects of childrearing, building a child's competence in schools relies on communicating new goals and skills to the child. Moreover, cross-generational communication in any setting, including the school, is always a matter of building bridges between the adult's agenda and the child's own interests.

In order to build skills and understanding in the child, educators must bridge the gap between, on the one hand, the spontaneous interests, ideas, values, and goals that children develop early in life and, on the other hand, the knowledge that schools are in business to impart. In those happy cases where children readily make a productive transition to school, the link has a sense of inevitability about it. After all, school offers children an opportunity to enhance their competence. Children who are prepared to recognize this opportunity will engage themselves fully in schooling, for children are always looking for new ways to acquire competence. But many children never come to see the connection between what schools have to offer and what they themselves can—or want to—do. For such children, the gap between their spontaneous interests and the school's agenda is simply too great. They see no purpose to the activity, so they become disengaged.

If such disengaged children were a tiny minority of the population, we might have a spirited discussion about what kinds of special efforts should be taken on their behalf. But, as I have shown in Chapter 1, they are everywhere in today's society—most noticeably, but by no means exclusively, in the less affluent parts. *The challenge of educating our disengaged children is an integral part of the effort to educate all children, and it requires identical pedagogical principles.*

In rising to this challenge, educators must address both sides of the schooling gap. They must find ways of capturing children's spontaneous interests while at the same time providing children with essential skills, powerful ideas, and the thirst for further knowledge. Academic programs must be set in relation to where students have been as well as to where they should be heading. In the elementary years, programs must build upon the children's unschooled interests and skills, and they must lead to the sorts of understandings that will prepare children for learning within rigorous academic disciplines.

It is this kind of two-way bridge-building—extending backwards from the child's prior abilities and forwards to understanding within the academic disciplines—that is most needed in today's schools. As I shall discuss in Chapter 9, the oppositional ethos of many current school reform efforts has mitigated against just this bridge-building sort of effort. When reformers argue about the virtues of play *versus* drill, phonetics *versus* whole language, encoding *versus* comprehension, self-esteem *versus* mastery, or school-as-fun *versus* school-as-work, they are standing on one side of the gap and placing their opponents on the other. If we are to help all our children realize their full academic potentials, we must design school programs that build bridges across such gaps.

Socialization for Character: The Joining of Habit and Reflection

Socialization practices that focus on the character side of children's development must foster good habits as well as the capacity for careful reflection. We must not allow ourselves to become distracted by those who would polarize the two. It is indeed true that habit and reflection are two distinct psychological systems, with distinct developmental roots.[17] In order to integrate the two systems, we must recognize the differences between them; but in no way does this imply that we should set the two in opposition.

Habit is deeply embedded in the child's emotional and behavioral reflex system, whereas reflection derives from cognitive schemes of abstraction and is closely linked to the child's intellectual competence. Habits are based upon natural dispositions that are bolstered over years of actual practice; whereas reflection derives from advances in insight that can be hypothetical or speculative. Habit grows on the plane of action, whereas reflection grows on the plane of consciousness. Habit is automatic, whereas reflection is subject to decision (and indecision). Habit is spontaneous and embedded in one's immediate experience; whereas reflection draws on notions that are distant in time and place from the situation that one finds oneself in.

Both habit and reflection can be sources of moral action, though of very different kinds. Habit rules over the vast territories of moral behavior that most of us simply assume. In general, the vast majority of human social life is harmonious and well-regulated, beginning early in childhood. Children do not routinely rob, kill, or lie: such behaviors are exceptional even among troubled populations. The reason that children normally do not deviate from our social norms is that they acquire, through nature and practice, habitual patterns of emotional and behavioral responding. For most children most of the time, such patterns trigger prosocial acts such as helping or sharing and prevent antisocial responses such as violence or theft.

But on some occasions, children's normal patterns of behavior fall short of the situation's demands. Conditions change, and unexpected new circumstances suddenly appear. Strong new temptations may arise. Old habits become tested, or they no longer apply. At such junctures, children must turn to reflection in order to appraise their alternatives. These periods of reflective awareness can be crucial during key turning points in life. The deliberative choices that they engender can lead children to whole new levels of moral awareness and commitment.

The best examples of this that I know come from a study that Anne Colby and I published recently on the development of moral commitment.[18] All of the twenty-three highly dedicated people that we profiled in the book had moments of transformative insight that changed the courses of their lives and made possible their lifelong dedications to moral goals. Often these moments of insight came early in life, and they were followed by a process of reflective awareness that produced new insights and choices all throughout their lives.

The impassioned civil rights leader Virginia Durr, for example, threw off her own habitual racism in a series of incidents that began when she turned seven. During Virginia's birthday party, a cousin insulted a black child that Virginia was fond of. Virginia protested vehemently. With her protest began a whole new critical perspective on the system of discrimination that Virginia had grown up with and had taken for granted. Later, when at college, she still struggled with her own disinclination to sit at the same dinner table with black students. It was not until she began working side by side with black women on joint political causes that Virginia was able fully to shed her early prejudicial views and adopt a wholehearted belief in racial equality. Virginia's perspective grew over decades of similar observations, experiences, and reflections. It came to fruition when, in middle adulthood, she became a leader in the struggle to give voting rights to all Americans.

New choices of action based upon self-conscious moral reflection are both important and noteworthy, because they often disrupt the prior flow of development. Still, they are relatively rare in the course of human life. Habitual responses, in contrast, generate moral actions frequently, in ways so common that they that usually go unnoticed. All the acts of moral commission and omission that we often take for granted—a mother watching over her child, a dedicated teacher helping her student, a man declining to steal from a beggar—represent moral acts that are commonly conducted through habitual emotional and behavioral processes. This is why the moral life is built on a foundation of habit; even though, as in the case of Virginia Durr, its design at times may be modified through flashes of reflective insight.

In our study of people with high levels of moral commitment, we found that they eventually come to carry out their commitments in a spontaneous and nonreflective manner, as if by force of habit.[19] There is quality of "automatic pilot" that defines even their most courageous acts. This orientation is in fact similar to the way that most people operate when carrying out commonplace moral acts. What is extraordinary about highly moral people is that they apply this habitual moral mode to the furthest reaches of their social visions. Their moral sensibilities are quickly engaged by any number of observations or incidents. When so engaged, their moral sensibilities immerse them wholly in their moral concerns. Such immersion is accompanied by feelings of great certainty and clarity of purpose. But it must be remembered that reflection played a key role in the initial formation of their strong—and eventually habitual—commitments.

Young people must learn to act right habitually, as a matter of course. The moral life is built primarily on good habits. It is important that young people learn to resist immoral temptations in the same automatic way that most people refrain, without hesitation, from robbing a helpless beggar or hurting their loved ones. But reflection, when grounded in good values, supports rather than deflects the habitual moral response. Moreover, reflection is one way to guard against that periodic human tendency to blindly stumble into horrendous moral mistakes. Only when habit and reflection marry does sustained moral commitment become possible.[20] It is such commitment, and no less, that we must aim for in our children. It is this goal that must drive our socialization practices.

Both reflection and habit are essential ingredients in the final mix that defines a child's moral character. This point for those concerned with the moral character of young people is not to weigh their importance but to find ways of advancing them both. It is not enough to promote reflection and habit on separate developmental tracks. We must help children find ways to integrate the disparate psychological systems that reflection and habit represent. For the main part of moral growth is not simply acquiring good habits *or* insightful reflectiveness; rather, it is developing the capacity to move easily between the two. This capacity requires a conscious awareness of one's own habits; and, even more importantly, it requires coherence between one's theoretical moral beliefs and one's deep-seated emotional and behavioral response systems.

Habitual moral conduct and moral reflection create the conditions for each other's further development. Reflection about moral concerns cannot create moral habits, but in the long run it can nurture them and guide them. Similarly, good habit can frame and lead reflection into morally worthwhile directions. As the two systems become increasingly coordinated, ever greater support becomes possible. This is why promoting coherence between the two can be so beneficial for a child's character development.

There is no single way to promote such coherence. To the contrary, only a variety of experiences can help children integrate moral habit and reflection and ultimately to develop their capacities for sustained moral commitment. Variety in moral experience is as important for the growth of character as balance in instruction is for the growth of competence. The variety may include direct engagement in moral activities such as serving others in need, observations of moral behavior on the part of others, discussions of moral issues with respected peers and adults, and reflections about the meaning of moral activity for one's own sense of identity and purpose in the world. Formal instruction in a religious or spiritual tradition also play a key part, as does guided awareness of transcendent moral concerns in the world at large. In Chapters 8 and 10, I shall set these principles in the context of children's development in the home and community.

The marrying of conscious moral reflection and habitual moral response makes possible an eventual uniting of self and morality. At the same time, and for the same reason, it also makes possible a turning away from the nihilistic elevation of self that is entrapping so many of our young people today.

The integration of habit and reflection joins together the various intellectual and active ways that one can respond to a moral event. The reflective judgment lends support and perspective to the habit, and the habitual reaction lends substance and shape to the reflection. This makes a powerful combination, one that is both effective and inspiring. This integration facilitates all the key developmental processes that I have discussed in this chapter: goal transformation, communication, and commitment. It facilitates these processes by creating coherent systems of action and reflection that both bolster and challenge the child's moral commitments. Neither habit nor reflection alone could accomplish this. Habitual action by itself would lead to stagnation; reflection without ingrained habits would lead to ambivalence or passivity. When the two combine, the child's moral commitments can be kept alive in the truest sense—that is, they not only endure but keep growing.

A coherent integration of reflection and action rests on a unifying system of belief that must be represented in all the cognitive and behavior systems that direct a young person's life choices. It must be represented at the level of habit, at the level of judgment, and at the level of reflective self-understanding. The system of belief must be so compelling that it both preserves the stable commitments and guides the dynamic transformations of each system. In the process, the child's continued moral growth is made possible.

8
Parenting

There is a disturbing sentiment that I often hear when I meet with parent groups. One mother phrased it this way: "Parents today are afraid of their children." She was not referring to physical threats but to a kind of emotional blackmail that her children subject her to whenever they have trouble getting their way. She has heard many parents today express similar concerns, as have I.

Children, of course, always have tried to use emotion-laden tactics such as temper tantrums to get their way. Sooner or later, parents in most times and places generally have learned that it is best for everyone's sake to hold the line. But holding the line requires a certain degree of cultural support as well as a sense of conviction that the child's interests are indeed well served by doing so. In a time when cultural supports have disintegrated for many parents, and when parents' convictions concerning childrens' best interests are marked with uncertainty, parents are more readily worn down by emotional pressure from their children. They become vulnerable both to their children's demands and to their own worries about not doing enough for them.

Emotional pressures on parents can take many forms. The most benign forms are self-induced. Many dedicated parents harbor fears of disappointing their children in one way or another, of harming them by being insensitive or inattentive, of not protecting them carefully enough from the world's dangers. Some of the fears have substance:

unfortunately, much of the modern world *has* become a dangerous place for children, and it is understandable when parents feel a nagging discomfort about their inability to change this distressing fact. Other fears spring from the child-centered sensibilities of modern culture rather than from objective conditions in the world. Some parents fear that they may be treating their children unfairly, and they may be damaging their children's friendships, if they hold their children to a higher standard of conduct than that to which their peers are subjected. Parents who are not affluent, as well as those who are, feel a pressure to provide their children with all the toys and fancy clothes that others around them have. These are thoroughly modern-world pressures that bear down especially hard on parents who desire the best for their children.

Another self-induced pressure with a distinctly contemporary flavor is the fear that one is not doing enough for a gifted child. In my work as director of a human development center, I often am called by parents seeking guidance about their childrearing concerns. Of all the problems that I hear about—sleep disorders, school troubles, depression, bedwetting, antisocial behavior, and so on—by far the most common is the "problem" of the child who seems exceptionally precocious to a parent. What can the parent do to nurture the child's special talent? What extra attention, stimulation, resources, must the parent provide? What sacrifices are needed from the child's family if the child's extraordinary gift is not to slip away? My response, without trying to be callous, is to suggest that early precocity is not always an indicator of budding genius. The development of talent is a story played out over many years of life. Some children move quickly and some move slowly at the beginning; parents who would help nurture their children's talents along must be in it for the long haul. When asked, I also respond that, yes, I am convinced that your child is gifted, just as is practically every other child whom I have encountered. The challenge, and joy, of raising children lies in discovering and bringing out each child's amazing talents. My sense, though, is that my message does not do much to dispense that feeling of undue burden that so many parents with "gifted children" feel today.

Not all of today's parental pressures are induced by the parent's own worries or sense of responsibility. For one thing, children's age-old outbursts are still very much with us; and it has been astonishing for me to observe so many parents of young children these days yielding to their children's tantrums without a second thought. Over the years, children who get away with their tantrums learn more subtle and more effective ways of exerting emotional pressure on parents. In fact, new ways are being invented all the time, with great ingenuity, and they often work. One of the more common tactics that I have heard about from several parents of teenagers is "going on strike." The child simply stops functioning—no school, no work, no activities outside the house. In some cases, the child may stop dressing or bathing. Naturally the parent becomes alarmed at what looks like pathological behavior, and therapeutic help may be sought. Often, though, the situation is quickly resolved when the child restates the demands that the parent has been denying—a new freedom, a change in school, a better living space, more personal resources—and the parent this time responds. Such a resolution may create a great sense of relief on the parent's part. The relief, however, may prove only temporary if the child has learned the message that one need not take "no" for an answer as long as one is willing to go to any extreme in pursuing one's wishes.

Getting a child to take "no" for an answer is difficult in a cultural setting where children are taught the primacy of their own feelings. Whatever a parent communicates on the home front, children in our society hear many versions of the message that their feelings come first. Our children are constantly encouraged to be self-assertive and promote their own desires, and they learn to do so with impressive persistence. They besiege their parents, and the parents often feel that they must give in.

As a parent of children growing up in our society today, I have experienced this feeling many times myself. On this or any other matter related to childrearing, I do not place myself in any elevated category of practice or behavior. Where my own parenting is concerned, I am sure that I have made all the usual mistakes. One incident that I remember with clarity occurred when my two oldest children were still in grade school. It was a weekend and I was in charge of them for lunch. They requested McDonald's because of a special promotion that they had heard about, but I could not bear the thought of another fast-food meal. I offered a number of alternatives that my children rejected summarily. Their badgering persisted, heightening in intensity. Finally, in desperation, I told them that McDonald's was closed that day because it was a weekend! They bought the story and we ate at home. But even as the words left my mouth, I was incredulous that I was saying such a thing. As I look back, I am even more stunned that I could have reached such a state. My response to my children violated practically every belief that I have about parental communications. First of all, my excuse was a lie. As with all lies, the truth would eventually out as soon as my children discovered that McDonald's actually *is* open for weekend business. At that point, both my credibility and my children's respect for the truth would be diminished. Moreover, my statement had given them the implicit message that, despite my better judgment, they would have gotten their way by badgering me if it weren't for the unfortunate fact that it was a weekend. I certainly had not taught them respect for my authority, nor how to take "no" for an answer gracefully. Rather, I played right in to their already-active beliefs that adults should never disappoint their wishes.

The late twentieth century has not been an easy time for parenting. Strains on family life run the gamut from the economic to the emotional. Few parents believe that they are providing their children with "enough"—whether the "enough" be goods, protection, instruction, or time. A large and growing number of parents are raising their children alone, with few social supports. Many of these scrape by from day to day in a state of perpetual deprivation. Other parents enjoy all the material benefits of today's middle-class affluent life, yet they still feel unable to provide as they wish for their children. They are assailed by demands to keep their children supplied with expensive products, clothes, toys, and services. At the same time, while valiantly trying to keep up with every such demand, many parents sense a vacuum, an incompleteness in their family lives. The spiritual lines that run from generation to generation, the lines that always have created connections and channels of communication between parent and child, feel like they are fraying in the uncertain winds of modern times.

Parents may look towards respected experts or institutions for direction, but they find little consensus. In fact, the experts and institutions have been so damaged by attacks that they are fast losing their credibility. The most prominent example of this is the withering criticism that has been launched at teachers and schools in the past decade. Although some of the criticism is certainly justified, as I shall discuss in the following chapter, the overall effect has been to erode the sense of confidence that parents once had in those responsible for their children's education. Parents are riven with doubts about how their children are being treated at school, and they are quick to express these doubts. No longer can solidarity between parents and teachers be assumed. In front of their children, parents will complain about how unfair a teacher is in the way she grades or disciplines, about the unreasonableness of her homework assignments, and even about the teacher's general competence. The inevitable result is a breakdown in both the parent's and the teacher's authority over the child, and with it a diminishing of the community's capacity to communicate clear and compelling standards to its children. For, as I note throughout this book, transmitting standards effectively requires the kind of community-wide "youth charter" that can only be built through a fundamental consensus among *all* the important people in a child's life.

As the credibility of institutions beyond the family diminishes, so too does the family's own credibility and authority. Parents are finding themselves assailed over their shortcomings as childrearers. Accused of neglect or indifference because of their work responsibilities outside the home, admonished by politicians who bandy slogans such as "family values," blamed for all their children's failings, parents have been placed roundly on the defensive. Whereas once the status of parenthood carried with it a legacy of automatic respect, now it is more likely to be viewed judgmentally, with a certain degree of suspicion. Neighbors freely criticize one another's parenting styles in family conversations. Advice columns and talk shows constantly present examples of irresponsible parenting, along with appropriate censure. In many parts of Europe and the United States, there are movements towards holding parents legally responsible for their children's misdeeds.[1] At the very time that parents feel that their ability to control their families is slipping away, they are faced with indignant criticism and societal pressure to assume more responsibility for the behavior of their young.

The loss of family control is both perceived and real. Perceived, first of all, because many parents have lost confidence in their moral authority (and this of course is true of teachers as well, as I shall discuss in the next chapter). Between the confusing cultural relativism of modern times and the disquieting cultural wars of the present epoch, adults in our society have become uncertain about what are the "right" prescriptions and proscriptions to impart to the young. Parents look to public discourse for direction and find only noisy, politicized argumentation. It is no help that the airwaves are filled with debates over false oppositions carried on by public figures seeking attention or political advantage. Nor is it helpful that the cultural tenet of the day suggests that children are incompetent, amoral, and fragile creatures who are not ready for serious moral instruction. Parents look to the childrearing experts for ways out of this morass and find little more than undigested reflections of the relativistic and permissive sentiments of modern culture.

Penelope Leach is among the most widely read of today's childrearing experts. Her book *Your Baby and Child from Birth to Age Five* has supplanted Dr. Spock as the first thing many young mothers read in preparation for their newborn babies.[2] Leach takes Spock's child-centered leanings to an extreme that would seem remarkable in another time and place. Leach's vision of parenting is that of a mother vigilantly watching her child for signs of readiness before introducing expectations, regulations, or demands of any sort. In Leach's world view, children are seen as immovable objects, grounded by the frightening forces of their irresistible wills. Sleeping and feeding patterns must follow the child's schedule, not the parent's. Toilet training is a "choice" that "is, and will remain, the child's."[3] Urging a child to become toilet trained is a losing cause, because children must do as they wish: "Don't try to force the child to sit on the potty. . . ." Leach writes. "The clearer you make it that you really want him to sit there, the less likely he is to want to. Since toilet training can only succeed through his voluntary cooperation, battles will mean certain failure."[4]

But the truly astonishing section of Leach's book comes when she discusses children's social behavior. For reasons that I cannot fathom, she removes preschool lying and stealing from the moral realm altogether. About lying, she writes: "Your child breaks his sister's doll by mistake. Faced with it he denies the whole incident. You are probably angrier with him for the lie than you are about the breakage. But what matters is that he should recognize the mistake he has made. Confessing is not nearly as important."[5] About stealing: "Obviously you want to be careful that your child does not appear to steal, because other people are likely to make such a song and dance about it. But don't make it a moral issue at this age."[6] Why in the world not, one must wonder? Is your child's moral growth not important to you?

Leach's approach to children's behavior seems a surefire way to remove from parents the little sense of control that they still are able to maintain on the family front. In a passage that makes me incredulous whenever I read it, Leach *defends* the childhood strategy of bargaining in the face of parental authority. If a child is "rather intelligent," she writes, the child will discover that he has "bargaining power" whenever a parent issues a directive. For example, when a parent asks the child to put on some clean clothes, the clever child might answer, "If I get clean cos you want me to will you get out my paints cos I want you to." Now if this child's demand may seem a bit outrageous to those of us who do not expect to pay a price every time we ask a child to do something that is for his own good, we are the ones who are being unreasonable in Leach's world. "Unfortunately," she writes, "parents often feel that this is in some way impudent. They have the right to tell him what to do and they don't want to concede him the same."[7]

"Conceding children the same" can lead to a real loss of family control that is even more dangerous than the perceived loss of control that has impaired so many parents' moral authority. Every adult I have known in recent years has witnessed alarming incidents of young people unmanaged or unmanageable, beyond anybody's sphere of influence. One hears such stories daily, through the media or among friends. Some stories tell of children who cannot or will not be controlled. They disrupt a train ride, a family occasion, a whole neighborhood, disregarding every threat or plea hurled at them.[8] Other stories tell of parents who refuse to control their children. There also are cases of parents who fear that their children someday will try to harm *them*, out of a disturbed sense of grievance, rebelliousness, or revenge. A frightening number of these cases erupt into the grisly events that one reads about in the daily news.

More often than not, however, the lack of control is threatening in a more removed and distant way. Often it is subtle enough to escape the full consciousness of the parent. Indeed, in such cases the parent may well be an unwitting co-conspirator in the child's misconduct. A friend observed the following incident recently:

A child and his father stood at the counter of a supermarket. While the father unloaded the groceries on the counter, the child grabbed a pen from the shirt pocket of the cashier. The cashier asked for the pen back. The child begged to keep it, saying that it was just the kind of pen he had been looking for. The cashier replied that he, too, really liked the pen. He said that he would like to have it back. The child began to cry. The child's father then offered to buy another pen for the cashier and reached for one that was on display at the store. The cashier politely refused, saying that he would be happier with his own pen back. At that point, the father became belligerent. He told the cashier that he was being selfish and had no concern for the child's feelings. To howls of protest from the child, the father tried to give the cashier his pen back. Embarrassed at the disturbance, the cashier gave in. He quietly accepted the replacement pen from the father.[9]

When told of the incident, I found it unsettling, not so much because it violated my assumptions about parental standards—I have become inured to this feeling—but because it carried with it such a strong shock of recognition. I realized that, in a variety of ways, I had witnessed similar episodes and have heard many others tell similar tales.

I remembered a large Thanksgiving dinner that I attended recently. Several families were invited, and it was decided beforehand that people would take turns reading special quotations or saying words of grace. Everyone came prepared to do so. The turkey, however, refused to cooperate—it was slow to cook—and so did the children. Before the dinner, they did so much fussing, whining, and complaining about their hunger that the hostess decided to dispense with the ceremonies and get some food on the table. During the dinner, a few brave adults tried to say their pieces anyway, but their words were drowned out by the din and generally ignored. The children all scattered as soon as they finished, so there was no hope of doing anything meaningful afterwards. The children's impatience, and their parents' acquiescence to it, had drained the event of the spiritual reasons that created the occasion to begin with. Of course this was hardly a unique incident. How often do families manage to make their holiday celebrations truly uplifting these days?

Mundane holidays are a disappointing but mild enough turn of events for today's families. There are far more worrisome signs of their children's lack of control. I have seen children upbraid their parents for not serving them well or quickly enough. I have observed children insulting, cursing, yelling at, even threatening their parents. When I mention such incidents to colleagues, they do not strike anyone as remarkable or surprising. I have visited communities where the shops and streets shut down after dark because everyone knows that nighttime "belongs" to the young. The parents in such places may have no knowledge of, let alone say over, the whereabouts of their children at *any* time of the day or night. In such places, I have known adults who are afraid to look young people in the eyes for fear that this will be taken as a sign of disrespect.

There are those who believe, with some justification, that current societal forces have undermined parenting—that it is impossible to be a good parent in a climate of community dissolution and spiritual void. How can parents give children direction when the culture around them sends out little more than a cacophony of disjointed and detrimental signals? As sociologist Amitai Etzioni has written:

> Many parents point to the great difficulty that they have in teaching their children right from wrong. They remind us that they are fighting a culture that bombards their kids with unwholesome messages. . . . A community that is more respectful of children would *make parenting a less taxing and more fulfilling experience.*[10]

Of course it also can be argued that the difficult social conditions themselves have been triggered, or at least aggravated, by the failure of parents to maintain solid families and provide guidance for the young. At the same time, parents have been misguided by a confusing cultural ethic that undermines their authority and discourages their attempts to offer sound directives to their children. The overly child-centered advice from today's experts has played an especially demoralizing role here for both parents and children. A psychologist who works with troubled mothers was quoted recently as saying, "The current standards for good mothering are . . . formidable, self-denying, elusive, changeable and contradictory. . . . The net result is a lot of exhausted, confused, guilt-ridden mothers." She goes on to say, "Spock and Leach are prescribing a kind of child care that is impossible to deliver—a mother is supposed to be empathic and permissive all the time. . . . [Mothers] should be there to tune into their kids all day long."[11]

In the end, of course, cultural decay and family disarray fuel one another. Both trends must be reversed if we are to create a more wholesome climate for raising children. Good parenting need not await transformations in the society at large. In every corner of the world today, as in societies throughout the ages, there are always instances of parents who are resisting the general cultural trends and are establishing superb families. Good parenting is possible in even the most difficult and dissipated circumstances. As for economic deprivation, there is no reason at all to believe that, in itself, it destroys the possibility of good parenting. During the Great Depression, there were plenty of struggling parents who maintained strong family order and raised their children to the highest standards.[12] Likewise for children who have been raised during periods of rapid immigration, when families arrived with little more than the clothes they wore on their backs.

I have focused throughout this book on the trends that I find most worrisome; but it is important not to overlook the many beacons of hope. In every community, no matter how alienated or troubled, there are parents who are creating model families, who are struggling valiantly against adversity, and who are prevailing. Even in our most troubled neighborhoods, there are parents who succeed in fostering the highest levels of competence and character in their children.[13] They guide themselves and their families towards timeless beliefs and purposes. They raise their children with methods that worked well in past epochs and that are still working today.

The childrearing methods that such parents employ stand as exemplars of the socialization principles that I outlined in Chapter 7. In that chapter, I presented socialization principles in a very broad manner, focusing on how standards and skills generally are communicated across generations. In the present chapter, I shall show how these general socialization principles apply to parenting in today's world. I shall begin by connecting these principles to some informative recent accounts of successful childrearing patterns. In the amalgam of these general principles and recent accounts, we can discover guidelines for the sorts of parenting that will spur children's intellectual and moral growth in today's society.[14]

As I argued in Chapter 7, socialization requires holding fast to dual goals: the child's and the adult's. In any encounter, both the child's and the parent's goals will be complex. The child's goals may include playing, gaining some desired object, seeking nurturance, or trying to learn something. The adult's goals may include having fun with the child, giving nurturance to the child, or accomplishing things that have little to do with the child. But the adult's goals are likely to include an additional component: trying to pass on to the child skills or standards that the child does not yet have. In order to do so, the adult must share some part of the child's goals while at the same time leading the child towards the skills and standards that comprise the adult's socialization agenda for the child. Only through this dual focus can adults promote enduring, positive change in their children's competence and character.

It is this dual focus that enables successful parents to be in touch with their children's contemporary interests while at the same time making sure that their children are guided by the parents' standards. And it is this dual focus that many adults find so difficult to maintain. This difficulty is the crux of both the child-centered and adult-centered imbalances that I noted in Chapter 5. Many parents today have found it easier to lose themselves in the child's immediate goals. Others have found it easier to ignore the child's perspective entirely and to demand allegiance to rigid and incomprehensible dictates. Yet permanent, constructive influence depends upon creating a dynamic interaction between the perspectives of child and adult.

This is the reason that *authoritative* parenting helps children develop what researchers have identified as "instrumental competence" and "personal and social responsibility"—the virtues that I have abbreviated as competence and character.[15] This is also the reason that *authoritarian* and *permissive* parenting both tend to leave children unprepared for such growth. These two styles fail in similar ways for opposite reasons. In the authoritarian style, children cannot find sustaining rationales for the rules that their parents impose (and sometimes they cannot even find the rules, since authoritarian commands often mutate in accord with a parent's erratic whims). In the permissive style, there are no firm external standards to begin with, so the child drifts without direction in a limitless fog of impulse. In both cases, the child ends up uninstructed and unguided.

Authoritative parenting works where the others fail because it builds a communicational bridge to the child while *at the same time* directing the child to the standards and skills of the adult. A similar principle lies behind the other effective socialization precepts that I have discussed, such as "respectful engagement." The common theme among these methods is that they all stress *both* communication and control, *both* respect for the child's perspective and commitment to the adult's standards.

In an analysis of contemporary patterns of parenting, psychologist Theodore Dix has observed three broad classes of parental goals: *empathic, socialization*, and *self* goals.[16] Parents who are oriented towards empathic goals focus on their children's feelings. Empathic goals include trying to make a child feel happy, comforting a child when in distress, assuaging a child's pain or hunger, and so on. As Dix describes them, empathic goals "are intended to achieve outcomes that children want."[17] Socialization goals are oriented towards children's learning and development. They include helping children acquire important knowledge and abilities, encouraging children to develop their prosocial tendencies, and requiring children to curb any antisocial inclinations that they may have. Dix writes that socialization goals "benefit children, but will not necessarily please them."[18] Self goals are oriented towards a parent's own needs and wishes. Such goals could include trying to get a child to bed on time so that the parent will have time to read a book, or wishing to take a child along on a shopping trip so that the parent can buy some clothes for herself. Self goals are aimed at benefiting the parent. In their transactions with their children, parents either may orient to one particular class of goals or they may combine the different classes of goals in various ways.[19]

The child's socialization suffers when a parent tends to pursue either empathic or self goals singlemindedly. If, as a routine matter, either the child's feelings or the parent's wishes become primary in a parent's relationship with her children, the kinds of imbalances that I described in Chapter 5 arise. An exclusive orientation towards the child's feelings encourages willfulness and self-absorption on the part of the child and discourages the child's development of self-control and respect for others. An exclusive orientation towards the parent's wishes creates an atmosphere of neglect and disengagement, ultimately leading to feelings of cynicism and worthlessness on the part of the child.

In a convoluted way, some parents who claim (and perhaps believe) that their primary goals revolve around their children actually are pursuing self-oriented goals in a strongly lopsided manner. Such parents identify entirely with their offspring, becoming heavily invested in their children's every move. They may see their children mainly as reflections of themselves, glorying in their children's accomplishments—and denying, defending, or excusing their children's missteps. Or they may merge their own interests with their children's in a blatantly self-serving manner—as, for example, the parent who avariciously pursues material goods without limit or scruple because his children supposedly "need" the best of everything. Parenting such as this, allegedly devoted to the child's welfare, is in actuality nothing more than an indirect form of egoism. The child's real needs, and in particular the child's needs for guidance, discipline, and socialization generally, become lost in the parent's self-centered desires. For the child, it would be less confusing and more ennobling to deal with honest assertions of such desire than with such parents' self-righteous and disingenuous claims of total dedication to the child's welfare.

There are many other ways in which either empathy or self goals may become separated from socialization goals during a parent/child relationship. As I noted in the second part of this book, modern cultural beliefs have drawn parents' attention to their children's inner wishes and feelings. Parents have been urged not to disturb "the magic years" with harsh reality or unsettling demands. Moreover, as discussed in Chapter 4, recent years have witnessed the burgeoning of a generalized worry over children's self-esteem, sometimes to the exclusion of concerns about their skills and values. Parents are faced with the omnipresent sense that experiences such as feeling bad, not having fun, facing frustration, enduring hardship or difficulty, all could permanently injure their children's self-esteem unless such negative feelings are rapidly alleviated. On the opposite side, many parents in contemporary society have little time or inclination to attend to their children's feelings at all. These parents' lives are so filled with pressure, anxiety, or their own forms of self-absorption that there is little room in their minds for anything beyond an orientation to their own goals.

In either case—an imbalance towards empathic goals or an imbalance towards self goals—the parent very likely still has socialization goals for her children. Practically all parents do. Yet in relationships where either empathic or self goals dominate, socialization goals become removed from most of the everyday transactions between parent and child. Instead, the transactions focus solely on the child's or the parent's immediate wishes, and they ignore the child's developmental needs. Concerns about the child's socialization still arise; but they arise suddenly, in a disruptive manner, and in contexts that are neither engaging nor instructive for the child.

The parent may hear a neighbor complain about the child's unruly behavior. Or the parent may read a teacher's report about the child's lack of good work habits. At such times, all that parents can do is express concern (loudly or softly) about the child's failings. The parent has no useful context for connecting the complaint to instructive activities that could help the child do better. Such occasions could be found, of course, in the usual transactions that go on daily between parent and child. But if the transactions continue to be dominated by either the child's immediate feelings or the parent's immediate desires, they will not be available for serving the long-range agenda of socializing the child.

Although a parent's empathic and self goals can be problematic when they remain isolated from socialization goals, both *can* contribute importantly to a child's socialization when deployed in the right way. A parent's emphatic goals can open invaluable channels of communication between parent and child. A parent's self goals, when responsibly modulated in concert with the parent's overall childrearing mission, can help to orient a child away from pure egocentrism and towards the needs of someone else.

In his own account of what he calls "parenting on behalf of the child," Dix shows how a parent's empathic goals may be used in service of communication and socialization. We may see in Dix's analysis crucial elements of the bridge-building process that I have indicated as the heart of socialization. Empathic goals will cause a parent to pay close attention to a child's expressions of thought and feeling. The parent will listen carefully to the child's ideas, watch for the child's reactions to events, and respond actively to the child's requests. This does not mean that the parent does whatever the child wants, but rather that the parent shows concern and responsiveness. Encouraged by such responsiveness, the child learns to speak freely and openly to the parent. The child also senses that the parent is sharing the child's goals—an essential first step in the bridge-building process that I have described. At the same time, the child becomes increasingly receptive to the parent's own agenda, which hopefully includes the ultimate aim of socializing the child.

In Dix's terms, the parent's empathy has contributed to the child's socialization in five ways: (1) It has strengthened the child's trust in the parent/child relationship, thus increasing the child's receptivity to the parent's input. (2) It has decreased the possibility of conflict between parent and child, thus preventing disruptions in their communication with one another. (3) It has encouraged children to develop their social and communication skills, thus enabling them to benefit from interpersonal relationships generally. (4) It has enhanced the child's sense of competence and control, since the parent and the child together often do achieve shared goals that otherwise would be beyond the child's reach. (5) It has bolstered the child's own attempts to acquire skills and standards through pursuits that are both engaging and socializing.

This last point is especially significant, for it gets to the most natural link between empathic and socialization goals. As I noted in Chapter 7, children naturally seek to develop competence and character. This is a fundamental part of their everyday goals (although by no means the whole part). Socialization does not come entirely from the outside: in many ways, children desire precisely the same skills and standards that parents wish to transmit to them. Of course children often need support and guidance to do so, and at times they may not understand the purpose of a critical parental requirement or injunction. But nevertheless it is a mistake to consider socialization as an external demand that parents foist upon children against their wills. When a parent truly empathizes with a child's goals, the parent will understand that the child seeks not only immediate pleasure but also long-term growth. On their own, children gravitate toward activities that improve their abilities. They seek occasions where they can learn and practice athletic, artistic, social, and academic skills. Perhaps unbeknownst to many adults, a major part of children's intellectual and moral growth takes place during children's play with peers.[20] It is important for parents to support such peer socialization activities. For this reason alone, parental empathy is essential for effective socialization.

Empathy alone, however, is not enough. I have noted above the risks of child-centered imbalances that may accompany a parent's unreconstructed empathy for the child's immediate expressions of pleasure or discomfort. Dix, too, is clear about such risks. He writes:

> It is important to stress that, although empathic caregiving usually benefits children, this is not always the case. Were parents to act as their children want, their parenting would be shortsighted and indulgent. Parents who put trivial child needs above important parent needs undermine their own well-being and thus, indirectly, their child's as well. Furthermore, to socialize sharing, helping, and other prosocial behaviors, parents must impose rules that require children to act in ways that they do not want to act.[21]

It is when parents combine their empathic goals with other purposes that they serve to socialize the child. This is even true when the other purposes derive simply from the parents' own needs. Parents have other pursuits in life beyond parenting—work, recreation, education, friendships, and so on. Directly telling a child about such interests does not wound the child's self-esteem, despite many parents' hesitancy to do so for that reason.[22] To the contrary, when a parent honestly asserts her own needs to a child *in an empathic manner*, it builds both the child's self-regard and the child's trust in the parent/child relationship. It does so because such a statement treats the child with respect, as someone who can understand and perhaps even help with the parent's needs.

When parents express their own self goals openly, this also can bring children outside themselves. The expression gives children the message that there are other people in the world with needs that must be considered alongside the child's. Perhaps incredibly, many children today are not as aware of this as they should be. A parent's assertion of her own needs also may evoke cooperation, help, and a sense of service from the child, contributing to the child's development of social responsibility. Equally importantly, such an assertion is honest. In contrast, when parents try to disguise their own goals, proclaiming that everything they do entirely follows the child's interests, children eventually see through the pretensions. They will come to consider such statements disingenuous as well as condescending.

Of even more direct consequence for a child's development is a parent's integration of empathic with *socialization* goals. This is what makes possible a parent's enduring influence on the child's intellectual and moral growth. Unfortunately, this is also where parents have been most troubled and confused in recent times. Many parents have been caught on one or the other pole of the false oppositions that I discussed in Part II of this book. Many others have been thrown off by the severe imbalances in the contemporary culture's predominant views about children.

Nowhere is there greater confusion than that which surrounds the stormy topic of discipline. It is here that the integration of empathic and socialization goals is most critical for the child's long-term growth. It is here that many children are most urgently in need of sound parenting. Discipline is at the heart of socialization, one of its most essential components. Yet on the subject of discipline, today's public discourse has failed utterly. Controversy has replaced common sense in our childrearing books and manuals. Dogma and oppositional thinking has replaced clear understanding of children's developmental needs. I believe that this is a major cause of the decline in today's youth that I chronicled in Part I.

As an example of the confusion, let us examine the enormously influential writings of Thomas Gordon, founder of the Parent Effectiveness Training program and president of a corporation that markets advice to a large number of parents worldwide. My intention is not to excoriate Dr. Gordon nor to dispute everything that PET stands for. As I shall note below, I find some PET principles to be useful and important. But on the crucial subject of discipline, Gordon's writings reflect many of the same misconceptions and false oppositions that have been misleading today's parents in their efforts to raise competent and responsible children.

Gordon's advice is that children should learn *self*-discipline rather than a deferral to external control.[23] He writes that parents should try to influence children but not try to control them. In describing parenting styles, Gordon sets up oppositions between harsh punitiveness on the one hand and reasoned persuasion on the other; between "other-imposed discipline" and "self-imposed discipline"; between autocratic relations with children and participatory ones; between authoritarianism and permissiveness. These are all false oppositions, as I have argued throughout this book. Authoritative parenting, guided participation, and respectful engagement are all balanced methods of socialization whose effectiveness results from avoiding every such polarization. Gordon's one-sided solutions, in contrast, cannot provide the sustained and consistent guidance that all children need.

Gordon writes about parenting: ". . . most adults fall into a trap: rather than use only influence methods, they impose limits, give orders, send commands, punish, or threaten to punish. These control-type methods don't actually influence youngsters: they only coerce them or compel them."[24] Gordon's assumption is that external coercion must always be incompatible with the kinds of long-term, positive influence that enable children to acquire internal standards. As I shall show below, this is an assumption that runs contrary to the best psychological evidence. Concerning those adults who would try to control children, Gordon writes: "Most controllers, I'm certain, feel that they know what's best, because they're older,—whatever."[25] The tone suggests skepticism over the very legitimacy of adult authority over children. Yet parents *are* wiser, more experienced, better trained, and do usually know best when it comes to their children. And children need the guidance that this greater wisdom affords, even when it may not suit their wishes of the moment.

Gordon writes that "discipline is hazardous to children's health and well-being" and that "we must urgently adopt the goal of finding and teaching the alternatives to authority and power."[26] No doubt he is reacting against the kinds of authoritarian, highly punitive, and sometimes abusive practices that I described in my Chapter 5 discussion of adult-centered imbalances. Gordon's revulsion against such practices is understandable. But his child-centered alternatives are just as imbalanced in their own way. Gordon's own one-sided position leads him to some astonishing conclusions. Gordon claims that "children don't really misbehave" and suggests that, if adults *perceive* misbehavior on the part of a child, they might "find out what a child needs" and then "modify the environment" to better suit the child's interests.[27] In one truly remarkable passage, Gordon dismisses the "myth" that children can ever be spoiled by overgratification of their wishes.[28] All of this sounds like a recipe for producing willful, disobedient, and self-absorbed children; but this is not a danger that appears on Gordon's radar screen. Perhaps not surprisingly, Gordon expresses more of a concern about children's self-esteem and what discipline may do to wound it.[29]

Gordon and others in his movement are certainly correct in their arguments against harsh and arbitrary punishment. As I have noted, *authoritarian* (as opposed to authoritative) parenting is no more effective in fostering good values and habits than permissiveness. But it is a mistake to reject all forms of external control on children's behavior. There are times in the socialization process when children require more direction than their own self-discipline is capable of producing. At such times, the parent's choice is not limited to either harsh punitiveness on the one hand or simply appealing to the child's reason on the other. It is possible, and wise, to raise children with *both* firm discipline and reason, to *combine* control *and* communication in family edicts. This is the way of authoritative parenting, respectful engagement, guided participation, and the other socialization approaches that I have described in this and the previous chapter.

Children's spontaneous, voluntary interests are fundamental for energizing their growth, but these interests are not sufficient in themselves to mold their competence and character. All throughout development, children benefit from, and indeed require, external guidance that is supported by judicious amounts of discipline and control. This has been confirmed in a large body of studies from experimental child psychology.[30] In particular, studies that have compared and contrasted three parental disciplinary strategies—power assertion, love withdrawal, and "induction"—have provided us with valuable evidence about the importance of combining communication and control in childrearing.

The classic authoritarian strategy for discipline is *power assertion*. This method consists of coercion and threats of punishment when children refuse to conform to parental wishes. Often parents attempt to force children to adopt new attitudes and behavior through unmitigated assertions of their power, backed up by severe sanctions for disobedience. This can be highly effective in the short term, particularly when the adult is there to enforce the sanctions. But experimental evidence has shown that power assertion does not lead to long-lasting, dependable formation of habits or beliefs. For one thing, its effectiveness fades when parents are absent. Moreover, too much power assertion may have unintended side effects, and even countereffects, on the child's behavior. The clearest demonstration of this has come from a "forbidden toy" experiment that several researchers have used to examine children's responses to adult directives.[31]

In the forbidden toy experiment, some children are told that they will receive a mild punishment if they play with a desirable (but forbidden) toy and other children are told that they will receive a severe punishment for doing so. Neither group ever chooses to play with the toy in the immediate situation, because of course the adult experimenter is right there. But when the children return to the laboratory on a later occasion when the adult is not present, the children who were severely threatened prove to be very likely to play with the toy; whereas the children who were only mildly warned usually devalue the toy and refuse on their own to play with it. In a similar vein, it has been observed that the severity with which parents assert their power to punish does not determine the extent to which a child will follow their directives. If anything, it seems that too-strenuous power assertions may interfere with an adult's long-term influence over a child's attitudes and behavior.

A more subtle and indirect disciplinary strategy is *love withdrawal*. Parents implicitly threaten to withdraw their love from a child through direct expressions of disapproval ("I don't like you when you act like that!"), through emotional coldness, or through expressions of disappointment and disinterest, such as ignoring the child for a long period of time after a disobedient act. Observations of contemporary parenting have shown that many parents use love withdrawal in response to all types of child misdeeds, including harm to persons, harm to property, and loss of self-control.[32] Indeed, love withdrawal is a more effective strategy of gaining immediate compliance from children than power assertion.[33] But despite its immediate effectiveness, love withdrawal cannot accomplish the main goal of socialization: influencing children to adopt improved attitudes and behavior that children will consider to be their own. There is no evidence that love withdrawal leads to the internalization of habit or beliefs. Rather, love withdrawal only leads to limited changes in children's overt behavior. It may increase the likelihood that children will "put on a good show" and inhibit any tendencies they might have to be discourteous or disobedient. But it does not lead to the adoption of permanent new standards that children will maintain on their own, apart from any consequences having to do with their parents' approval.

A third disciplinary strategy has been identified in the work of developmental psychologist Martin Hoffman as *"informational internalization,"* or, more plainly, *induction*.[34] According to Hoffman's observations, disciplinary techniques that induce children to internalize key information about the parent's directives are the ones that are most successful at permanently changing children's attitudes and behavior. Such techniques succeed because they lead children to understand, and accept, the *standards* that their parents are trying to communicate rather than focusing only on the *sanctions* through which parents enforce these standards. An effective parental influence encounter, Hoffman writes, will ensure that the aspect of the encounter most salient to the child will be the attitude or behavior that the parent is trying to instill rather than the child's punishment for refusing to comply. In the most productive of such encounters, the child may forget the sanction entirely. In fact, the child even may eventually forget the parent's role in promoting the standard: the child will come to endorse the standard so wholeheartedly that its origin becomes irrelevant. This does not mean, however, that the origin of the standard is immaterial in a developmental sense. Without the parent's introduction and inducement of the standard, the child may never have come to it.

In contrast to power assertion or love withdrawal, induction fosters the permanent internalization of moral habits and standards. The way in which this works can be seen most clearly in the context of a typical disciplinary encounter between parent and child. Right before such an encounter, the child has acted in an improper way. The parent then may stop the child's actions; or the parent may punish the child after the fact. In either case, the child will not be likely to repeat the unwelcome act in the parent's immediate presence. But will the child continue to refrain from this behavior when the parent is not around? This depends upon the type of discipline that the parent administers. If a discipline method is to foster moral internalization, it must use reason and explanation to induce the child to anticipate the effect of behavior on others.

Such inductions can take many forms, depending upon the situation and upon the age of the child. For example, an induction to a very young child will emphasize the direct effects of the child's actions: "If you keep pushing him, he'll fall down and cry." With an older child, the parent may focus upon the fairness of the child's actions in terms of the others' actions and intentions: "Don't yell at him, he was only trying to help." Or the parent may point to the psychological, rather than the physical effect of the child's actions: "He feels bad because he was proud of his tower and you knocked it down." Inductions nourish the child's concern for others, and they offer the child information about how his behavior can adversely affect others. Such information helps a child better understand interpersonal causality (that is, the relation between the child's own act and the physical and psychological well-being of another); although, as I noted above, the child's maturity places some limits on the type of inductive information that the child is able to process.

Even messages presented through inductions cannot by themselves socialize the child. This is because, for socialization to occur, it is essential that the child pay attention to the message, and the induction alone will not suffice to motivate sustained attention. Hoffman believes that the child must be placed in an "optimum state of arousal" if the induced message is to effectively influence the child. This can be done by combining the induction with a mild amount of power assertion or love withdrawal. In other words, an inductive disciplinary technique places a message concerning welfare of others in the context of the parent's mild warnings, disapproval, disappointment, or other moderately arousing parental sanctions. Without the sanction, the child will not be aroused enough to take the induced message seriously. On the other hand, if the punishment or love withdrawal is too severe, the child's arousal will be so great that it will interfere with the child's attention to the induced message.

Inducing children to adopt improved habits and standards is an enterprise that psychologists traditionally have called "attitude change." The psychological literature has distinguished two main processes of attitude change: compliance and internalization.[35] Compliance means changing one's behavior in the present in order to conform to externally mandated standards. Internalization means adopting these standards as one's own, both for the present and the future.

Some social psychologists have claimed that compliance and internalization are fostered under different conditions. Tangible rewards and punishments, they assert, promote compliance; whereas persuasion, argument, and reasoning promote internalization. Many of today's popular experts who give parents advice about childrearing have accepted these theoretical claims, setting compliance in opposition to internalization and advising parents to aim only for the latter. Much like Thomas Gordon and his PET movement, many of these experts argue that internalization is more likely than compliance to cause children to improve their behavior.

But empirical research with children has shown that long-term improvement in a child's behavior is a more complex process than this. The main problem with the internalization/compliance opposition is that internalization itself generally cannot occur without an initial act of compliance.

An experimental demonstration of this was offered in a well-designed series of studies conducted by social-psychologist Mark Lepper and his colleagues.[36] Lepper and his colleagues arranged two types of situations to investigate the conditions under which children internalize standards. The first situation was a variation on the forbidden toy experiment mentioned above. In this first situation, Lepper followed the usual procedure prohibiting children from playing with an attractive toy, using mild threats for some children and severe threats for others. He replicated earlier findings that children in the mild-threat condition were less attracted to the toy in a subsequent session. He also found that these children were more likely than those severely threatened to resist temptation in an entirely new situation. Lepper concluded that "prior compliance in the face of . . . relatively minimal extrinsic pressures, in general terms, seemed to increase subsequent internalization or private acceptance of the standards implicit in the adult's initial request; previous compliance in the face of more salient external pressures seemed to decrease later internalization."[37]

Threats and prohibitions aside, a similar relation was found between the positive *rewards* offered to children and children's likelihood of continuing a pattern of activity. In their second type of experimental situation, Lepper and his colleagues asked children to play with Magic Markers for a period of time. Lepper knew that the children in his study found Magic Markers interesting, because the children were selected for the study by surreptitious observations that identified a group of children who clearly enjoyed this type of activity. Once in the experimental situation, the children were exposed to one of three reward conditions. One group of children was told that they could win an attractive "Good Player" certificate by working with the Magic Markers, and in fact, they were awarded the certificate at the end of the session. Another group of children was told nothing, but these children were awarded the certificate unexpectedly at the end of the session. A third group of children was simply asked to use the Magic Markers without any reward, expected or unexpected. Several weeks later, all three groups of children were again given a chance to play with the Magic Markers, but this time they were not explicitly urged to do so. The children who had obtained no previous reward for such play—the third experimental group—showed by far the greatest interest in using the Magic Markers again. Lepper concluded that "the use of unnecessarily salient extrinsic incentives . . . undermined children's intrinsic interest in the activity per se."[38]

In order to explain the combined results of his studies, Lepper proposed what he called a "minimal sufficiency" principle of socialization. The principle states that the most effective methods of permanently improving a child's behavior are those that are applied with just enough coercion or reward to engage the child in the new behavior but not so much coercion or reward that the child finds this to be the most memorable part of the experience. In other words, the external incentives that the adult provides must be *minimally sufficient* to change the child's behavior without being more salient in themselves than the standards that the adult is trying to promote. Under these conditions, the child's attitudes and behavior will be permanently transformed, because the child will internalize the new standards. Lepper uses his minimal sufficiency principle to explain the findings from previous socialization research by Diana Baumrind, Martin Hoffman, and others. For example, Lepper reconceptualizes Diana Baumrind's distinction between authoritarian and authoritative parents as a distinction between parents who use overly sufficient coercive techniques and parents who combine minimally sufficient techniques with reasoning and argument. Parents in the latter group—the authoritative parents—establish the optimal conditions for their children to internalize socially appropriate standards. This is why children with parents who use authoritative methods soon come to exhibit socially responsible behavior on their own initiative. In contrast, authoritarian parents foster compliance rather than permanent attitude change in their children. Permissive parents fail to provide their children even with the minimal coercions or rewards necessary to change their behavior in the first place.

The minimal sufficiency principle accounts for the long-term effectiveness of subtle social influence techniques, especially when compared with more heavy-handed techniques like power assertion and love withdrawal. The principle implies that children must be encouraged to attend to the behavioral standards that parents must communicate if children are to internalize these standards. Parental actions, such as too-severe punishment, that draw the child's attention away from the standards themselves inevitably will work against the internalization process. The key to success, according to this principle, is to guide a child toward acting out the desired standards, relying on disciplinary tactics that are not themselves particularly noticeable to the child. The child will then focus on the standards themselves, and on the reasons behind them, and will ultimately incorporate the standards into his or her own attitudinal repertoire.

Informational internalization through induction, the minimal sufficiency principle, and authoritative parenting in general, all share an interactional approach to socialization. In each of these strategies, long-lasting influence upon a child's behavior is achieved through consistent and reasonable family controls along with clear parental communications to the child about the moral significance of the controls. The controls must be convincing, but they should only be mildly arousing in an emotional sense. The communications must be adapted to the child's developing cognitive abilities, so that the parent's message of moral significance may be understood by the child.

Parents exert discipline in the home not only by punishing unwelcome behavior but also by honoring good behavior. Parents always have a number of material rewards at their disposal, but the most potent and ubiquitous reward of all is praise. A parent's use of praise is as fundamental to the parent's disciplinary strategy as the parent's use of sanctions. Praise can be a means both of controlling children's behavior and of communicating standards and other moral messages. Like all other forms of discipline, praise is most effective when used judiciously. It can be counterproductive when used in an excessive, inconsistent, or arbitrary manner.

Many of the same principles apply to praise as to punishment, including the minimal sufficiency principle. Recall that the forbidden toy experiment has been used to test children's reactions to praise (a "Good Player" certificate) as well as to punishment. In both cases, the experiment's conclusion was the same. Praise can play a role in encouraging children's good behavior, just as punishment can play a role in controlling their unwelcome behavior; but neither praise nor punishment is effective in the long run if they become so obtrusive that they mask the message that they are intended to convey. Like punishment, praise should be carefully modulated to the child's actions. Whenever possible, it should be joined to clear parental communication about the reason for the praise.

This may run counter to some popular slogans that are currently in vogue. (Two bumper stickers that I frequently see on cars read "Praise your child every day," and "Children thrive on constant praise.") Indeed, children *do* thrive on praise, and it may seem curmudgeonly to advocate any manner of allocating it—or, at times, withholding it. Yet it is important to realize that constant praise is by no means a universal value in parenting. Indeed, parents in many traditional cultures around the world are far less prone to praise their children than are parents in modern Western culture. Anthropologists have observed that children in such cultures are expected to act well, help their parents, and try their best to acquire useful skills.[39] Since such efforts on the child's part are assumed, parents do not go out of their way to praise them. (Parents from such cultures do punish, however, when their expectations are disappointed.) According to the anthropological reports, children living under these conditions do not wilt from lack of praise. There are some contrasts between these children's early social behavior and that of Western children, but these contrasts do not necessarily favor the Western way. For example, children in cultures where parents refrain from praising good behavior are less likely to "show off" or to engage in blatant attention-seeking behavior. They demonstrate less egocentrism and a stronger sense of responsibility for making contributions to the family's common good.[40]

The dangers of excessive praise in fact have been noticed by some of the experts who offer childrearing advice to parents. Thomas Gordon, for example, writes that "getting rewards, especially praise, can become addictive and can undermine a child's motivation."[41] He goes on to say:

> I have come to believe that praise as a method for controlling children is grossly overrated, because it is usually ineffective and is often damaging to the adult-child relationship. In addition, praise may bring out a number of undesirable and unsociable characteristics in children.[42]

Here Gordon correctly observes that children who are routinely and heavily praised come to see the primary purpose of their good behavior as earning praise. Such children expend their efforts in order to be awarded praise rather than in order to learn something, help someone, and so on. Apart from this being an ignoble intention to cultivate, it distorts the nature of children's efforts. Aiming first and foremost at praise, children become attuned to the public relations value of their behavior instead of to its benefits for others or for their own improvement. As a consequence, their efforts become hollow, performed without conviction, and ultimately devoid of meaning. Children cannot be expected to sustain such efforts for long. In this manner, excessive praise and severe punishment share the same shortcomings as parental influence strategies.

But this does not mean that praise and other forms of extrinsic reward are always harmful, nor even that they are wholly expendable in parental communications. Gordon and other experts of similar persuasion swing too far in rejecting extrinsic reward on principle. Once again, false oppositions are at work: extrinsic *versus* intrinsic motivation, parental control *versus* parental influence, praise *versus* self-reward.[43] Similar to mild sanctions, moderate rewards can persuade children to engage in the types of effort that only later the children will find valuable. Without the initial sanction or reward, children may not have come to the activity on their own; or they might not have stuck with it long enough to reap its extrinsic benefits. This is why parents are well advised to encourage their children with praise when the children take on daunting or arduous tasks. Even though at some point a child may thrill to the sounds of the music that she is performing, the parent's inducements may have been needed in order to encourage the child to bear with the inevitable drudgery of the early lessons.

To be of value, the parental inducements cannot have been so powerful as to define the entire purpose of the child's efforts. The purpose comes from elsewhere—learning, service, the beauty of art, and so on. The inducements do not create the purpose but support and sustain the child's efforts in essential ways. To do so, the inducements must be used in moderation and accompanied by communication about the higher purpose of the efforts.

Parental influence—whether by means of discipline or inducement, and whether bolstered by sanction or reward—is not an end in itself. The influence must lead the child in the direction of intellectual and moral growth. It must impart to the child an improved standard of conduct, skill, or belief. This is the same communicational bridge that must be built in all socialization encounters, including those initiated by discipline and control. The communications that accompany parental control are not at all arbitrary: in one form or another, they must relay to the child a vision of character and competence. It is this vision, compiled in bits and pieces over years of interaction between parent and child, that provides the child with a framework of guidance for development.

Because any framework of guidance relies on a particular vision of character and competence, parents must make choices about which purposes and directions to lead their children toward. In their communications with their children, parents will stress certain standards: What should those standards be?

In *The Moral Child*, I argued that there is a core set of standards that steers children's moral development in our society.[44] While parents vary in many of the incidental attitudes and beliefs that they hold, there is a broad consensus in our culture (and probably universally) about the moral standards that parents want children to attain. Most parents want to raise children who are honest, kind, dependable, socially responsible, fair-minded, and respectful of others. It is the rare parent who does not value moral virtues such as decency, self-control, modesty, empathy, and truthfulness. Many of these are the same virtues that children are prepared to develop by their native endowments, as I discussed in Chapter 6. In order to bring these virtues to fruition, an abiding framework of parental guidance is crucial. This is the bridge that draws the child's early moral tendencies into the mature world of parental and societal standards.

Parents communicate such standards to their children in many ways. In this chapter, I have shown how the right socialization practices, along with congruous forms of discipline, enable parents to communicate standards clearly and effectively to their children—as well as encouraging children to be open and receptive to the standards that their parents introduce. Beyond socialization practices, the very nature of the parent/child relationship itself provides a communicational vehicle for the parent's standards. An honest relationship imparts the standard of truth more clearly than any disciplinary encounter. An empathic relationship demonstrates the value of empathy more powerfully than any lesson or induction. Children's relations with their parents are among the closest and longest-lasting interpersonal relations that they will ever have. Participating in a parent/child relationship that is caring, responsible, truthful, and fair offers the child a magnificent moral education in and of itself.

The moral quality of the parent/child relationship overrides all other communications that the parent might attempt.[45] This is one place in which the medium really is the message: Aesop got it right in his fable about the youngster ignoring what his mother said in lieu of how she acted. When the quality of the relationship is in line with the parent's message, the message becomes convincing to the child. When a parent's socialization practices are also sound, a positive, enduring, and powerful influence on the child's character is established.

9
Schooling

Practically every institution that once enjoyed a secure societal mandate to provide guidance for the young has come under pressure in recent years. It was not long ago that families, churches, workplaces, union halls, local volunteer associations, and even city neighborhoods were regarded as safe and reliable places to raise young people. Economic and cultural forces have changed all that. Even the strongest institutions that have provided care for the young have found their capacities as well as their credibility severely weakened. To add to the pressure, many critics have blamed the institutions themselves (or the people who currently manage them) for the causes of their own present incapacities.[1]

Of all the besieged institutions that serve the young, it is the public school that has borne the most withering attacks. The pressure has come from both within and without. From within, students have dropped out, acted out, or sat impassively through teachers' vain attempts at instruction. From without, critics have hurled contemptuous invectives at teachers; at those who train teachers; at the "bloated" education bureaucracy; at the "obstinate" teachers' unions; and generally at any professional who comes in regular contact with the public schools.

Some have suggested, with their actions or their arguments, that our society should abandon the enterprise of public schooling entirely. To the ringing approval of those who consider public schools to be waste-

189

lands of bad values, over a million parents in the United States now school their children at home.[2] Other parents have turned to independent schools that have a mission to educate no more than a small spectrum of the student population. During the past decade, the percentage of families who send their children to independent schools has risen steadily year by year, with the exception only of 1992, when it declined by a mere half a percentage point.[3]

Critics of the public schools have found many serious shortcomings within the classroom walls to decry—shortcomings that contribute to, or at least fail to address, the mediocre and disengaged nature of students' academic performances. Some critics have pointed to the low standards of school officials; the disjointed, "bits-and-pieces" nature of instruction; and the passive, dispirited student participation required by the traditional classroom discourse.[4] Others have denounced the curriculum's emphasis on pointless facts rather than real skills and understanding—and the resulting tilt towards rote memory over thinking.[5] Still others have condemned the invalid, arbitrary assessment procedures through which students' potentials are evaluated—and according to which educators make key decisions about students' future lives.[6] Indeed, the shortfalls in our predominant ways of schooling have been so broadly exposed that the very institution of the public school seems on the verge of being discredited.

The burgeoning inclination to give up on public schools has lured entrepreneurs into a new type of American business: schools-for-profit. As long as adults have tried to educate children in groups, there have been nonprofit independent and parochial schools, many of them highly distinguished. Trying to turn a profit on educating children is a recent twist. It speaks volumes about the extent to which our society is prepared to abandon public schooling. A business chartered to create money-making private schools was formed with great fanfare in 1992.[7] Apparently this appeared to be a sufficiently promising opportunity that the president of Yale quit his university post and joined in. The interest with which this venture was reported in the press and readily endorsed by some civic leaders provides an indication of how far the public school has declined in the nation's esteem. It is a turn of events that would have shocked the Horace Manns, James Conants, and Admiral Rickovers of more idealistic eras. It may be yet another sign of how much our willingness to provide a wholesome childrearing climate for all our children has deteriorated in recent years. The once-revered public school, instrumental in creating an affluent, unified nation from a melting pot of immigrants, now stands in competition with profit-seeking franchises.[8]

Is there any other period in American history when such a combination of events would have failed to provoke at least some sense of public indignation? This is but one more sign of how benumbed our instincts concerning children's welfare have become.

The Importance of Good Schooling for Every Child

For at least a century, public schools have played a central role in the flourishing of democratic societies throughout the world. They have enabled millions of children to rise from backgrounds of poverty and limited expectations to lead lives of success and fulfillment. In America, public schools have enabled generations of "teeming masses" to see their children enjoy the full opportunity to succeed in a thriving society.

What institution, other than the public school, has access to all children in a society? What other institution is in the position to offer *every* child nurturance, support, guidance, and a chance for a successful future? What other institution is in a position to ensure the kinds of widespread dissemination of basic knowledge and skill that can bind a democratic society together and secure its stable governance? Only public schools have this kind of universal reach. This is why the schools are what Amitai Etzioni has called our essential "second line of defense" against the cultural disintegration that threatens both our young and our society. Etzioni writes that "if the moral infrastructure of our communities is to be restored, schools will have to step in where the family, neighborhoods, and religious institutions have been failing."[9]

Our schools must be improved and reformed, but this does not mean that we can afford to abandon them. Because schools, when they are working well, have instructional capacities that go far beyond those of any other institution, we must extend, rather than weaken, the universal reach of schooling. Whatever their present-day shortfalls, public schools are still the last, best hope for millions of young people. Family ties have loosened to the point of disintegration in many households. Whatever we may do to reverse this trend (and of course we must try), there is no realistic hope that we will be able entirely to eradicate the problem in the foreseeable future. The contributing causes are too stubborn, and the trends are still all in the wrong direction. No matter how many new social programs we put in place, there will still be large numbers of children growing up in dysfunctional families, in negligent families, or with no families at all.

Although many of our public schools badly need reforming, the institution itself deserves defending, particularly at this time when so many are turning to alternatives such as home tutelage and for-pay instruction. Schools will always remain the best contexts for imparting the most advanced forms of thinking available in any society, and public schools grant every child the opportunity to acquire such thinking. Only the institution of public schooling can provide all of a society's children with systematic instruction in the academic disciplines, with a teaching staff trained in the craft of pedagogy, and with the presence of peer learners to collaborate and compete with.

The value of formal schooling for children is so great that simple fairness demands that we provide exemplary versions of it for every child. If we fail in this, our beliefs in sustaining democracy will ring hollow, and our prospects for future social stability will become dismal. Comparative studies of how children acquire literacy in and out of school reveal the unique importance of formal school instruction.[10]

Despite the trenchant critiques—many of them justifiable—that have been leveled at today's public schools, many children do come out of them with a reasonable assortment of advanced skills and knowledge. Even though far from perfect, our current system of schooling still offers children an irreplaceable opportunity for developing their intellectual powers. The potential of the institution is so great that an improved system realistically could aspire to fostering optimal growth in every child's competence.

Schooling also can play an invaluable role in the shaping of children's character. In today's world, for most children, it may be a central role. Of course this was not always so: until schools became widely available, children generally acquired strong habits and values when working with adults in the home, on the farm, or in the shop.[11] But the days of working families and childhood apprenticeships are largely gone. In their place have emerged the many years of extended schooling necessary for learning the advanced literacy and numeracy skills required by a technological society. These years of extended schooling provide a major share of the vital interpersonal relationships that will shape the child's habits and standards.

In schools, children observe the conduct of adults who represent, for the child, the norms and standards of society. Teachers communicate these standards verbally and through their behavior. While at school, students are subject to them in their own behavior. Students also are subject to explicit school codes of conduct, ranging in importance from dress to honesty. Even the implicit respectfulness and orderliness of the school atmosphere sends a message to students about what is deemed proper in the social world that schools represent. Peer relations in school give students a further chance to discuss and negotiate standards, to examine and confirm the rules, to communicate and to uphold shared values. Amidst this rich and highly structured environment of interpersonal relationships, children develop a sense of expectations for themselves. They also strive to meet these expectations. Out of such striving, character is fostered.

Most importantly, schools provide children with the tools that they need to find their purpose in life. In schools, children develop sustaining interests, discover what they are good at, and acquire a multitude of skills, dispositions, aspirations, and working knowledge. Not only are all these important in themselves, but, to put it bluntly, they also tend to keep children out of trouble. A child with a passion for music or math will be less likely to drift into trouble than a child with no interests, no skills, no hope. A child with a disposition towards open-mindedness will be less likely to harbor prejudices against others than a child whose unenlightened attitudes have never been challenged by exposure to new ideas.

When a group of teenagers is spending every afternoon playing for their school hockey team, it is obvious that the children in the group are not at the same time out on the neighborhood streets committing mayhem. They are, in fact, participating in a supervised activity with rules, rational standards, and a wholesome purpose. And the quality of the activities and relationships that the child participates in will determine the course of the child's intellectual and moral development.

Every gardener knows that healthy plants are less prone to disease and infestation than are poorly nourished ones. In a similar vein, children and adolescents who acquire positive interests, values, and skills are far less prone to antisocial engagements than are children who have not had a chance to develop such natural forms of resistance. In the course of human development, the acquisition of positive interests, standards, and skills will dispose a child towards harmonious social engagements while reducing the child's exposure to risky activities and experiences. Moreover, the child's positive interests, standards, and skills themselves provide psychological tools for averting dysfunctional behaviors such as violence. These tools include a belief in nonviolence and harmony; social skills that enable the child to resolve disputes peacefully; and the self-confidence to know that one can achieve one's desired goals without resorting to force.

Through such psychological tools, children acquire multiple means of blocking antisocial responses. In the case of violence, a great deal of redundancy becomes built into most children's internal systems of control. Several distinct types of cognitive, affective, and behavioral systems reinforce and substitute for one another—much like an airplane that, for safety's sake, has both automatic and manual means of accomplishing all basic functions.

For example, children have *empathic* reasons not to hurt someone (to avoid causing another pain); they have *rational* reasons (to avoid getting into trouble themselves); they have *normative* ones (to respect another's rights, the law, or the dictates of their own conscience); and they have *behavioral* ones (habits of good conduct formed over years of self-control and obedience). When children commit violent acts, it means that *all* of these control systems have failed at once—or that none of them has been adequately developed. Schooling is an antidote to both of these risks, because it provides a fertile ground for nurturing each of the operative control systems. In well-managed school environments, children learn codes of conduct, nonviolent habits and values, moral rules and virtues, and a sense of purpose that provides them with prosocial rather than antisocial motivation.

In any context where normal developmental processes have had a chance to take root, violence and other antisocial behaviors will remain highly unusual. Children who are deeply and truly engaged in schooling spend much of their lives in such a context. This is one fundamental reason why such children do not often appear in the courts as perpetrators of the grisly youth crimes now reported almost daily in our newspapers.[12]

What is true of violence and antisocial behavior is also true of the broad range of self-destructive and counterproductive activities that are damaging the futures of so many young people today. As I discussed in Part I of this book, these activities arise from the same source and are fed by the same cultural streams. A child who murders another child, a young teen who joins a criminal youth gang, a teenager who commits suicide, an adolescent who drifts into drugs or early pregnancy, all may be reacting to the same inner void: a lack of meaning and purpose in their lives, a sense of hopelessness, a cynicism about both the present and the future.[13] All of these problems have common roots in the widespread demoralization that has weakened the standards and sapped the natural energies and virtues of today's young.

Most problems of so-called "wayward" youth will yield to a common preventative treatment: good schooling. Like a broad-spectrum vaccine that can block the growth of many dangerous viruses at once, a child's wholehearted engagement in schooling can stop destructive and wasteful activities before they begin to consume the child's life. One of the great questions for our times is how we can create the kinds of school environments that will encourage *all* of our children to become wholeheartedly engaged in life-enhancing quests such as learning, aspiring, and achieving.

Where Today's Public Schools Fall Short

Despite the public school's importance, unique capacities, and noble tradition of service, it is now in serious trouble. Those who have sniffed a chance for profit by displacing the public schools indeed have found serious weaknesses to exploit. Opportunism, after all, needs a real opportunity to feed upon.

The great unresolved dilemma of today's schools is how to communicate with the vast populations of students who resist instruction. Schools cannot manage, let alone educate, students who arrive in their classrooms unprepared for learning and who remain disengaged from all that takes place there. Nor can they prevent such students from undermining the learning atmosphere of the entire school. Of course every school that ever has operated has had some such students among its ranks. But today their numbers are legion.

From my own work in the public schools, my guess is that more than half of today's students find little interest in the lessons that schools have to offer.[14] They do not see school as a resource created for their benefit. They do not see school as an opportunity to learn something that they will need to know. They certainly do not see school as a privilege that they are incredibly fortunate to have. (I recently tried out this notion of "privilege" on some high-school students and received the predictable groans, chuckles, and eye-rolling.) Instead, most of today's students see school as an imposition—or, at best, as a responsibility that they perform with stoic reluctance.

The frail academic motivation of many of today's students is matched by their shaky understanding of what goes on in school. For many students, coursework seems little more than an obscure set of rituals that they must labor to fake their way through. They are able to penetrate neither the instructional materials nor the methods that schools use to deliver these lessons. By the time they have reached high school, many of our students have long ago given up the goal of understanding their course material. Barely intelligible regurgitation at the teacher's demand is all they want or expect to achieve.

In many schools, neither the lessons nor the instructional methods have changed much since the turn of the century. What educational historians have called the "factory model" of schooling still prevails worldwide.[15] In fine nineteenth-century fashion, the schools try to "deliver" instruction in the most efficient manner possible. This means treating students as homogeneous products to be filled with identical information, sorted, and tested, all through a standardized procedure. At the end of the production line, the units are certified and ready for service. The pleasantries of graduation day, with its ceremonial rituals for those who have made it through, barely masks the mechanical nature of the process that gets diplomas into student hands.

The one thing that *has* changed has been the moral atmosphere of the school. This clearly has changed for the worse. It is worse partly because of the conduct of students, which is often violent and disorderly. But students' conduct is not the only problem—and, in any case, schools cannot be held wholly responsible for the behavioral habits of their students, however abysmal these habits may be. The moral atmosphere of the school has declined also because of changes in the ethos of teaching. In today's schools, it is rare to find teachers who hold high academic and moral standards for their students. Instead, too many of today's teachers work with an air of professional detachment from their students, allowing students to just get by with minimal contributions and efforts. As I noted in Chapter 2, this is the infamous "compromise" that Theodore Sizer has called the *modus operandi* of teaching in today's public schools. In effect, the teacher tells the student: If you show enough "learning" so as not to embarrass either of us, I will let you pass through this course with the credentials that you need to complete your requirements.[16] Mediocrity becomes the norm—even a dreary goal of sorts—for both teacher and student.

One thing that has fed the moral detachment of today's teachers is the increasingly impersonal and bureaucratic nature of our public schools. As sociologist Gerald Grant has noted, the period since World War II has seen the virtual disappearance of small, intimate public schools that infused with community spirit and local values.[17] In their place have developed larger, centrally administered institutions that—at best—stand for a distant and diffused set of values. Such institutions cannot provide children with the individualized instruction and personal relationships that children need for building competence and character. These institutions, in fact, have become inhospitable places for teachers as well as for students. There is no doubt that our schools must be reformed, as I shall discuss later in this chapter; although this is no way implies that they should be abandoned or further weakened by a lack of public support. It is the nature of the institution as it has evolved in recent years that must be questioned, not its very existence.

In most of today's public schools, teachers consider themselves to be both specialized professionals and unionized workers. This has proven to be an unholy combination when it comes to the estimable calling of educating young people. The problem is that this particular role mixture leaves little room for developing personalized relations with one's "clients"—that is, one's students. Together, the professional and union mentalities create a double layer of job-related attitudes that filter out the kinds of sentiments that once led teachers to take students under their wings. A professional will deliver a particular service in an expert manner but is not always inclined to take responsibility for the whole person.[18] A union member will work hard by the book, guided by well-defined obligations and prerogatives. When these two orientations are combined to structure the teacher's role, teaching becomes a narrow, rule-bound endeavor that focuses more on delivering a set curriculum than on bringing out the best human potential in every student. As a consequence, many teachers no longer consider it their role to advise students on their moral beliefs, conduct, or academic motivation. To advocate standards—whether moral or academic—is not a part of a teacher's job description in the current epoch.

In fact, the highly charged legalistic atmosphere of today's educational institutions threatens to turn the job description itself into a more powerful referent than the teacher's ancient responsibility as a mentor of youth. In my visits to schools in recent years, I have been struck by the clock-punching mentality that has arisen among many of the teaching staff. It is no longer common for teachers to remain after school in order to counsel, or to discipline, a student who is in trouble. Few teachers are willing to spend extra time (their "own time," they protest) with children who are creating problems for themselves or others. Instead, teachers these days are quick to remove errant children from their classrooms by trying to get them transferred, suspended, or expelled. Our society abounds with children whom teachers have given up on. Part of the reason is that these children indeed have acted badly and have performed poorly in their schools. But another part of the reason is that many teachers no longer see it as "part of their job" to devote extra attention to children who need it.

Nor do many of today's teachers readily join in efforts to make schooling more stimulating for children who are looking for an extra challenge. It has become practically impossible to recruit teachers for special assignments outside of normal school hours, even when such assignments open up new avenues for their students' learning. Any attempts at educational innovation must be squeezed into the regular school day, which is already crammed and rigidly programmed with mind-deadening exercises. In my observations, this is not because teachers are slackers: in fact, I believe they are among the most responsible and dedicated professionals in our society. Rather, their nine-to-five (or, more accurately, eight-to-three) orientation has been engendered by the stubborn bureaucratic atmosphere that has overtaken our educational institutions. Teachers have become demoralized; and so it is little wonder that many of their students have too.

The lackluster results have been plain for all to see. Each year brings new signs of further deterioration in students' social conduct, both in and out of school. Academic standards for the vast majority continue to crumble without respite. By virtually any measure, most students' academic achievement is uninspired at best. Their knowledge of the world is scanty, their thinking skills are uneven, and their motivation for serious learning is appallingly weak. As educational researchers have discovered, there are many high school students today who do not know where Antarctica is on a map. I would add that many of these students could not figure out how to use a map to find Antarctica if given one, could not find a map in a library if sent looking for one, and would not go near a library in the first place unless forced to do so.

At gravest risk are children whose backgrounds are far removed, in experience and awareness, from the kinds of learning that formal schooling demands. This is particularly true for young children who are new to the school context. Large-scale government programs, such as "Chapter 1," have tried to help such students when they are identified and targeted for special instruction.[19] Such efforts have proven insufficient for the magnitude and scope of the problem. Educational reformers are now recognizing that, in order to consistently bring out the intellectual potential of all children, we need to build better schools in general rather than rely on patchwork remediation programs.

In terms of the bridge metaphor that I introduced in Chapter 7, there is a missing link between many children's backgrounds—their abilities, interests, knowledge—and the demands of formal schooling. In many of our schools, there are severe gaps in the interpersonal and communicational bridges necessary for instruction. Too many children are falling through these gaps: a very large proportion of today's children are not fulfilling their academic potentials.[20] Some of these children come from disadvantaged backgrounds, others from affluent backgrounds. Students from every sector of the population have become disengaged and demoralized. Rather than placing the problem of disengagement *within* these children, as if there were something wrong with the multitudes of students who are not thriving in today's public schools, we must examine and correct the shortcomings in our school settings. The only feasible agenda for our public schools is to create programs that meet *all* our children's needs.

Reforming Our Schools

It is hardly possible to talk about education these days without bringing up the idea of reform. The air is full of revolutionary notions about virtually every aspect of schooling, from how it is financed to what is taught. The ways in which schools are managed and financed, the length and sequencing of class periods, the instructional practices, the curricular materials, the examination procedures, and the way in which teachers are trained are all being reexamined and reworked. Today in education, change has become a shared assumption—almost, paradoxically, a new orthodoxy in itself.

Many of today's reform ideas have been put forward by social policy makers who focus on the economic characteristics of institutions and the benefits of altering them. "School choice" has been the primary example of this kind of solution. The driving notion behind school choice is to unleash forces of the free market. By offering parents the freedom to send their children to any public school they choose, better schools will be rewarded with more students and higher levels of funding, and worse schools will be faced with withdrawal of public support. In this manner, incentives will be created for all schools to improve, since they will feel the need to compete.

Incentives and competition can play a positive role in improving schools, just as they can play a positive role in spurring children's development. In addition to spurring competition, there is a further benefit: school choice offers parents a greater sense of control over their children's education. This is important for at least two reasons. First, parents deserve the freedom to select the moral and intellectual environments that their children will be guided by; and second, parents will be more likely to understand and support a school that they have chosen for their children than schools that have been forced on them. School choice, therefore, is a necessary starting place for all serious efforts to reform our schools.

Still, school choice is no more than a starting place. Any choice is meaningless when there are no good options to choose from. And all the incentives and competition in the world will not automatically endow teachers with the tools they need to reach unmotivated students. In order to make school choice a real solution rather than just another empty political exercise, we must create public schools worthy of choosing.

The most promising routes to school reform aim directly at the pedagogical environment of our schools. Teaching is at the very heart of schooling. Because a child's learning requires a framework of guiding relationships, as I have shown in Chapter 7, the teacher is the most important resource of any school. Teachers can never be replaced, not by books, not by new buildings, not even by the advances in technology that seem to promise final answers every few years.[21] In the end, if children are to acquire competence and character, they need to have sustained relationships with people who care about their intellectual and moral growth. Any improvement in our schools must begin by making sure that these kinds of relationships are available to all students. It must also ensure that teachers have effective conceptual and instructional tools to help them guide their student's development in the right direction. The instructional relationship between teacher and student is always the place "where the rubber meets the road": that is, where academic knowledge is communicated, where student curiosity is piqued, where skills and work habits are nurtured, and where lifelong dispositions towards learning are shaped. For this reason, a focus on the quality of the instructional interactions in the classroom is necessary for identifying the key educational guidelines that cannot be derived from an institutional focus alone.

The only true avenue to educational reform lies through the instructional interactions between teacher and child. There are some structural changes in schools that could indirectly aid teachers' instructional capacities: for example, breaking down large schools into smaller units, increasing the classroom time dedicated to core subjects, reducing the numbers of students under a teacher's supervision, and so on.[22] Such structural changes would improve the conditions that many teachers work under, thereby indirectly facilitating their instructional capacities. But at best these are secondary improvements that make improvement possible: they do not themselves constitute improvement in the critical "bottom line" of schooling, which is the quality of instruction. The fact is that mediocre teaching can and does happen under the best of conditions. Conversely, inspired teaching can take place anywhere. In the long run, the most effective educational reforms will be the ones that target instruction.

I say "in the long run," because there are no immediate ways to change instructional habits that have grown up over generations of factory-style teaching. As in all things worth doing, there are no quick fixes or silver bullets that can transform our schools overnight into places where every child becomes deeply engaged in learning. Anyone who claims otherwise is offering the modern equivalent of snake oil.

Improving teaching throughout our public schools will require us to adopt an odd mix of sustained patience and creative adventure. We must be willing to try new methods, even shake things up a bit, without expecting immediate results from everything that we try. Above all, we must keep in mind the central purpose of making schooling useful to children of all backgrounds, talents, and interests. As Howard Gardner, one of the nation's most thoughtful and serious educational reformers, has written, schooling must become a *personalized* experience for every child.[23] Only in this way, Gardner maintains, can schools help children acquire the kinds of deep understanding that they will need to succeed in their working lives. Our factory-model schools have not encouraged teachers to personalize their instruction; nor have teachers been given the materials or training that it takes to teach for understanding. To accomplish this, our schools will need to adopt some radical new procedures. They must turn to the innovative sorts of methods that have come out of recent breakthroughs in educational research.

Over the past two decades, new integrations of research and practice in the field of education have opened the way for dynamic new approaches to the craft of teaching. Research in human development, closely interwoven with school-design experiments that try out new ideas in practice, have contributed some promising solutions to the present-day educational malaise. These are the sorts of solutions that focus on students—or, more precisely, on what transpires between students and teachers—rather than on institutional characteristics of the school.

School reformers who focus on instructional interactions emphasize that schooling must be set in relation to where students have been as well as to where they should be heading. They realize that educational programs must build upon children's natural abilities as well as on the spontaneous interests that children acquire out of their own experience. As Howard Gardner has written, educational programs must be designed so as to engage, nurture, and extend the child's "unschooled mind"—that is, the child's spontaneous interests and naive theories about the world.[24] Accordingly, reformers in the developmental tradition, including Gardner himself, are creating programs that focus on the crucial interactions between teacher and student. These programs build upon the skills and interests that children themselves bring to school while at the same time providing children with essential new skills, powerful new ideas, and the thirst for further knowledge. It is this kind of two-way bridge-building—extending backward from the child's prior abilities and forward to understanding within the academic disciplines—that is key to an effective approach for reforming schooling.

Developmental school reformers seek to transform schools into places that we can count on to foster competence and character in all children. In order to accomplish this, three goals must be achieved. First, schools must become places where all children can find personal relationships that guide them toward shared community standards while at the same time treating each child as an individual. This means that teachers must present high intellectual and moral standards to their students; they must be prepared to recognize each child's particular talents and interests; and they must personalize their instruction in a manner that brings out the best in every child. Second, schools must engage children in activities that foster disciplined understanding. This means that teachers must make their instruction both rigorous and meaningful for students; that teachers must steer a path between the common classroom pitfalls of rote exercises on the one hand and directionless diversions on the other. Third, schools must uphold clear standards that lead children to develop good habits and dispositions of character. This means both academic and moral standards. Schools must represent the highest values in society and must expect excellence in intellectual and social comportment from every student.

The remaining sections of this chapter will examine three elements of teacher-child interaction that must be reformed. The first is *assessment*, including both the standards that teachers use to evaluate students' performances and the tests that teachers use to evaluate students' knowledge and skills. Although assessment is very old enterprise, it is one that reformers are have reexamined from the ground up; and they have reached dramatic new conclusions about its best manner and uses.

The second element is another traditional concern for educators: the nature of the *curriculum*, or, more precisely, the systematic knowledge that schools are in business to impart to new generations. Together, the reforms in assessment and curriculum that have been driven by developmental theory and research are on the verge of becoming an integrated approach to instruction—and one tailored to the diverse talents, skills, and interests of individual learners.

The third element of teaching that I discuss is the intellectual and moral *manner* of teachers themselves. Considering the pressing need of today's young people for guidance from respected mentors, I believe this to be the most central of all our reform priorities.

Standards and Assessment

There has been so much noise and confusion surrounding academic standards in recent years that it has drowned out the most important point of all: Children do best—intellectually, personally, morally—when they are striving for excellence. Any activity that encourages children to strive for excellence will enhance their motivation to learn; and any instruction that shows them how to achieve excellence will advance their competence.

It seems obvious that schools should focus on the pursuit of excellence. Unfortunately, many schools have become distracted from this mission by misplaced concerns and oppositional thinking. In Part II of this book I documented some of the distractions: concerns about the "stress" caused by urging children to achieve, concerns about the "damage" to a child's self-esteem caused by communicating high expectations, concerns about whether schools and teachers should advocate fixed standards at all.

In recent years, I have visited many classrooms where teachers refrain from introducing advanced material to students out of the fear that it is not "stage-appropriate" for their students. This is what I referred to in Part II as a distorted Piagetianism. I have spoken with many teachers who believe that "pushing" children to do things that they cannot yet do will create "pressures" that may harm a child's sense of self (the words in quotations are phrases that I often hear in today's elementary school circles). How then, I sometimes ask, can a child ever learn anything new? "Self-discovery," is the usual answer that I get from teachers in the early grades. In the later grades, teachers are more willing to demand effort from their students; but by then, they find the students unprepared in skill and motivation for the learning of disciplined knowledge.

A former student of mine, now a public school teacher, told me of an experience that bewildered her—and shocked me too when she described it to me. Shortly after receiving her certificate, this young teacher was assigned to a New York City elementary school in a thoroughly multicultural district. Soon after she started, the teacher started receiving what seemed to be an orchestrated series of complaints from a group of parents. They told her that she was spending far too much time on math instruction. Their children, they said, were suffering. The teacher tried to make the instruction more accessible to these children, but the complaints continued. Finally she spoke with the principal. Yes, he told her, a large and organized group of parents from this school district had become convinced that children from their minority group were not adept at, or inclined towards, mathematics. Therefore, these parents had concluded, math instruction—and the math testing that inevitably followed—was discriminatory. In order to create an even playing field, these parents wanted the school to teach less math. To his credit, the principal did nothing more than reassure my former student that she was doing her job properly. Yet it is disturbing that such misplaced fears could so capture a group of concerned parents. One wonders whether another principal, in another setting, might bend more with the prevailing winds.

To repeat what I said earlier in this book: (1) Children are inspired, not stressed, when faced with challenging tasks. They crave the chance to achieve something meaningful. (2) It is always "developmentally appropriate" to introduce new ideas to children and to encourage them to acquire new skills. Good teaching requires linking the new ideas and skills to the child's present interests and capacities, not discouraging them from taking on challenges. (3) Children's self-regard is stunted far more by the message that nothing is expected than by the message that they must try harder to meet high expectations. (4) Schools and teachers are shirking their responsibilities as guardians of the young if they do *not* advocate core standards such as honesty, respect, integrity, and the pursuit of excellence.

As for concerns surrounding the value of particular intellectual pursuits for different children, the proper cut here is at the individual level. It is true that individual children have particular patterns of talents and interest. One child may be fascinated by literature, another by math, and schools should work with rather than discourage these individual leanings. But to claim that entire ethnic groups (or, for that matter, genders) have such leanings does nothing more than stereotype children and constrain their future choices.[25] Boys and girls from every background have the potential to excel in any endeavor that inspires them. Public schools are in business to provide *all* children with precisely such an opportunity.

Schools and teachers communicate standards to children most clearly when they evaluate student progress through assessment procedures of one kind or another. Assessment has traditionally been considered to be the final step in the educational process: in factory model language, first you produce the goods, then you check their quality through some sort of control device. This model of assessment has it exactly backwards. Because assessment always reflects standards, and because standards are central to the very mission of schooling, it is essential that the practice of assessment be considered at the outset as an integral, defining component of the school's instructional program.

In too many of our schools, assessment is seen primarily as a means of "testing" children. Such schools give their students exams for two reasons: to find out how smart they are or to find out how much they have learned from their current teachers. In the first case, the information is used to "sort out" students: to determine, that is, who are the bright students and who are the slow ones. When used in this manner, test results can severely constrain a student's future choices in life. In the second case, the information is used to evaluate the teacher. How much has she been able to teach this class of students? When used in this manner, test scores can have a great impact on a teacher's career.

Both uses of assessment severely distort the teacher's instructional mission. Sorting out students through school tests should not be a teacher's task, especially in the early years of schooling when children have had little chance to explore or express their talents. It is both unfair and a waste of human potential to "sort out" young children on the basis of early test scores. Yet it is done all the time in today's schools. As for evaluating teachers according to their students' test scores, this is a practice that discourages teachers from doing their best by using high-quality, innovative instructional methods. As many educational critics have shown, assessment practices strongly shape teacher and student behavior. If teachers use assessment primarily as a means of evaluating their students or themselves, they will inevitably "teach to the test"— trying, that is, to raise children's test scores rather than teach them deeper competencies that will serve the students better in the future.

Fortunately, some school reformers at last are recognizing assessment as more than merely a way of evaluating students and teachers. Rather, if approached in the right way, assessment serves essential pedagogical functions. It can play a key role: (1) in helping teachers define the kinds of learning that they wish students to achieve; (2) in providing teachers with multiple means of recognizing students' talents in all their diversity; (3) in enabling teachers to provide students with immediate and useful feedback on their academic performances; and (4) in helping students become able to learn from feedback, monitor their own work, and surpass their own past efforts.

Single-minded uses of assessment for grading (and sorting) students have been challenged before, particularly in some "progressive" education movements that threw out testing altogether. Utopian school communities, such as the British private school Summerhill, have spurned the practice of grading students out of a distaste for extrinsic rewards and the competitive atmosphere that they promote.[26] Educators in the progressive tradition have articulated the fear that standardized grades lead to invidious comparisons between students. Such comparisons, these educators believe, are invalid, because they do not recognize unusual talents that individual students may have. Not only can such comparisons result in detrimental misdiagnoses of students' talents; they also can discourage students from pursuing special interests that schools do not normally test for.

While such concerns are legitimate, the progressive solution of dispensing with grades altogether is untenable. It weakens the school's assessment function irreparably, and it removes some essential communication instruments from the educator's tool kit. Many students need the spur of extrinsic rewards to get them going, or to keep them going in the face of learning challenges that they find too daunting, too frustrating, or too unfamiliar to tackle on their own initiative. Many students, for example, never discover the intrinsic joys of reading until given an extrinsic push that enables the student to overcome the anxiety of cracking a formidable-looking book. As I noted in Part II, the notion that intrinsic and extrinsic motivation are incompatible, and that educators must choose between them in formulating their strategies for working with students, is just another myth based upon a false dichotomy.

In addition to bolstering students' motivation, grades and other assessment devices serve to communicate standards and expectations to students. They do so by providing unambiguous feedback to students about the merits of their performances. Feedback is certainly the most important educational function of assessment. Students need feedback about their work if they are to improve; grades and other assessments offer schools a systematic means of providing such feedback to all students on a regular basis. Without such a means, the teacher's feedback will seem inconsistent and directionless to many students. Probably the greatest single reason behind the failure of the progressive school movement was its loss of the ability to motivate and communicate with students through systematic assessments based upon clear, unequivocal standards.[27]

Developmental Approaches to Curriculum

Developmental researchers working on educational reform are rediscovering an old idea: inducing children to acquire basic skills and knowledge by engaging them in long-term "projects" with highly motivating missions. Educational projects are authentic tasks that accomplish important goals at the same time as teaching academic skills. Examples might be designing and building a play area by using advanced mathematical calculations; or producing a community newsletter with advanced literacy strategies; or creating an original science exhibition. Project-based instruction is just one of several promising ideas in curricular reform today. I shall focus on it here because it exemplifies virtually all of the developmental principles imbedded in such reform efforts.

Project methods of instruction originally were introduced into American education by early twentieth-century innovators who were influenced by the same progressive movement that questioned traditional assessment practices.[28] In both early and contemporary versions, educational projects include creating works of art, drawing maps, writing and staging dramatic plays, conducting science experiments, and running small commercial enterprises. The unifying notion is to engage children in authentic tasks that spontaneously motivate them while at the same time fostering core academic skills. While working on a project, children pursue a specific goal over an extended period of time. Ultimately, project activity should yield a product, performance, or event. By nature, projects tend to be multidisciplinary and mission-driven. They offer students chances to acquire and practice diverse literacies. Reading, writing, numerical calculation, scientific expertise, and aesthetic knowledge all can be built into well-designed educational projects.

Despite its promise as an educational tool, and despite some genuine success in classroom settings, in its early incarnation the project method quickly became relegated to the status of an educational frill. This was largely because the method was never organized by a systematic pedagogy that could fully exploit its potential for comprehensive instruction.[29] Nor were the consequences of projects ever adequately assessed, with respect to their motivational effects, their developmental outcomes, or their value vis-à-vis other pedagogical techniques. Consequently, the project approach came to be seen by educators as marginal and even flawed. While some classroom use of projects continued, for many years the educational research literature presented little discussion of projects as a serious part of curriculum and instruction.

Recent breakthroughs in educational research and developmental psychology have made it possible to transform the use of projects from an occasional diversion into a systematic pedagogy. These research breakthroughs have suggested new insights about the context in which projects may be encountered; about the educational goals that they can serve; about the ways in which students may work productively on such projects; and about the means by which the effectiveness of project work can be demonstrated. Developmental researchers working on problems in cognitive science, social learning, and student assessment have been carrying out work that addresses each of these issues. In particular, recent work on cognitive apprenticeship, epistemic forms, peer collaboration, and alternative assessment suggests specific strategies for teaching that help teachers establish contexts, goals, learning arrangements, and assessment procedures that take full advantage of the educational opportunities that projects offer.

Cognitive apprenticeship suggests that projects can be more than just a meaningful and motivating context in which students develop literacy skills. Projects provide a chance for students and teachers to work together in an apprenticeship relationship. In such a relationship, students are engaged in joint activity with a teacher.[30] The teacher models the use of skills and thinking processes and provides scaffolding to help the students carry out the activities. Gradually, the teacher "fades" by slowly reducing her support until the students can accomplish the task independently. Throughout, the teacher serves as a coach who oversees the students' learning by selecting appropriate tasks, diagnosing problems, providing challenges, and offering feedback.

Projects also give students a chance to go beyond the use of basic skills and develop "higher-order" literacies including the use of epistemic forms. Epistemic forms are basic conceptual structures like comparison and contrast and form-fits-function analysis that provide organized ways of encoding and understanding knowledge. Epistemic forms serve thinking and learning in many different fields.[31] These powerful forms of thinking may be used by people of all ages—scientists, historians, and of course students—to understand any academic discipline. They also have great applicability to daily life. For example, form-fits-function analysis provides a powerful way of seeing the "logic" of many things. Engineering can be viewed from a perspective in which vehicles have purposes (to fly; to hover) as well as characteristics and features adapted to the achievement of those goals. Engaging in this form of analysis or using other epistemic forms can help students to explore and come to a deeper understanding of a wide variety of concepts and topics; students who develop generative use of these forms should emerge as better thinkers in school and out.

Also enhancing the value of projects are opportunities for peer learning. Many researchers and practitioners in recent years have discovered the great educational potential of peer interaction. Experimental formats such as peer tutoring, cooperative learning, peer collaboration, and "groupwork" have proven effective in a wide variety of settings.[32] Peer collaboration and "groupwork," both of which foster equal-status teamwork relationships between students, have special value for helping students understand the conceptual intricacies of challenging subjects such as math and physics.[33] Peer collaboration is particularly appropriate to a project-based method of instruction because it encourages task sharing and communication among children who have similar levels of ability. Moreover, there are theoretical reasons for believing that peer collaboration is an especially powerful learning experience when it is combined with other compatible instructional methods such as cognitive apprenticeship and performance assessments.[34] Projects offer a unique opportunity to combine these diverse instructional methods in one continuous setting.

Long-term, mission-driven projects embed essential literacy and numeracy skills as well as powerful epistemic forms of thought. They are highly motivating, since they are built around missions that are immediately apparent to students. They encourage group work among students and apprentice-type relations between student and teacher. Engagement in long-term projects fosters curiosity, an ability to plan, responsibility, perseverance, understanding, and the disposition to learn among all kind of students—even, it is important to note, among students who have not previously found convincing reasons of their own to learn academic skills.

Project-based learning advances not only students' cognitive capacities but their dispositions, motivations, and habits as well.[35] Essentially, dispositions for thinking and learning are psychological elements with two basic components: inclination and sensitivity. Inclination refers to a student's tendency toward a behavior, such as fairness or carefulness. Sensitivity, in contrast, refers to a student's alertness to occasions when that behavior is appropriate. In brief, to say that a student has a disposition for good thinking and learning is to say that he or she has the sensitivity to detect occasions for the use of a particular behavior and the inclination to follow through.

The recent work on assessment that I discussed above provides the tools necessary both to facilitate student learning during projects and to evaluate the effectiveness of projects. Over the past several years, increasing attention has been paid to developing ways to look directly at skills, understandings, and performances of importance in the course of meaningful activities.[36] These assessments provide both students and teachers with occasions to reflect upon the learning process. This active consideration produces feedback that facilitates revision and the further development of valued skills. Simultaneously, these assessments can serve as a record of students' levels of understanding and skill in a wide range of areas and can document any changes in the students' performances over time.

Such methods, of course, rely upon teachers wholeheartedly to endorse and adopt innovative change in their own instructional practice. Many promising innovations have not been fully utilized due to inadequate teacher support or understanding. The more successful new programs have worked with teachers and parents in a fully collaborative manner from the outset.[37] Teachers and researchers share the program agenda, frequently discuss instructional strategies, and together refine the methods that are finally used with students. In this manner, teachers take ownership of the innovations and understand them from the inside. The successful experimental programs have provided us with a model for working with teachers in developing instructional projects that make strategic use of the educational methods noted above.[38]

I have singled out project methods in this section because, in their current uses, they combine all the major insights that have arisen out of developmental work on educational reform. For one thing, project methods encourage an apprenticeship relationship between teacher and student: as the teacher provides challenges and tools, opportunities arise for the teacher to model and support literate approaches to complex endeavors. Projects also encourage rich interchanges among the students themselves. They provide students with a chance to explore rich conceptual problems over significant lengths of time, developing the capacity to use powerful epistemic forms of thinking in diverse domains of knowledge. In the process, enduring dispositions towards learning and exploration may be established.

In the area of assessment, projects offer an assessment environment in which students' products, performances, and understandings may be documented in the course of motivating and meaningful activities.

Such constructive assessments enable the educator to enhance academic skills through strategic interventions geared to the individual student's strengths and weaknesses.

Teaching

All instruction flows from relationships; in turn, all relationships have distinguishable features that shape the quality of instruction that they impart. Relationships have both intrinsic features (a peer relationship will always have some sense of equality) as well as features particular to its participants (some peers are friendly, others rivalrous or contentious, others distant, and so on). By its very nature, the teacher/student relationship has certain intrinsic features that affect its quality. Most importantly the teacher in any teacher/student relation occupies a position of authority over the student. But different teachers exercise their authority in different ways: this constitutes the particularistic element of the instructional relationship.

The intellectual quality of a particular teacher-student relationship derives from (1) the standards and expectations that the teacher holds for the student, (2) the teacher's understanding of the student, (3) the teacher's ability to communicate with the student, (4) the teacher's willingness to innovate and to individualize instruction, and (5) the teacher's own grasp of the subject matter. The moral nature of the teacher/student relationship derives from the legitimacy of the teacher's authority and the manner in which the teacher wields it.

In many ways, the moral nature of the teacher/student relationship is prior to its intellectual nature. As a practical matter, a student will lose respect for the teacher and come to distrust the relationship if the teacher violates the legitimacy of her authority. As a moral matter, teachers have a responsibility to embody good values in their interactions with their students. If teachers shirk this responsibility, they harm their students by leading them in the wrong directions. A teacher exemplifies and communicates good values to students by exercising authority in a legitimate manner. Legitimate authority in teaching has three benchmarks: *fairness, specificity*, and *truthfulness*. Of these three important benchmarks, the last is both the most difficult and the most critical.

Fairness is a moral imperative of all relationships. In a teaching situation, it usually arises in issues of evenhandedness while dealing with different students and in concerns of judiciousness in doling out rewards or punishments. A common example is a teacher's response to uncompleted homework. There are many reasons why a teacher may be more patient with some students than with others, ranging from the teacher's history with particular students to the forcefulness of a student's excuses. Some of these reasons may be good ones, and even necessary. But students are highly sensitive to such variations in response, and unless they perceive the variations as benignly motivated and justly administered, the teacher places her moral authority at risk.

Specificity is one of the benchmarks determining the legitimacy of authority in asymmetrical relationships. It means that an authority's directives to those under its command must be restricted to specific areas in which the holder of authority has a legitimate claim to leadership. A legitimate claim can derive from a number of socially recognized attributes, such as competence, experience, status, and so on. All such claims hold only for properly designated spheres of authority. They do not constitute a license for the unconstrained exercise of power. Authority figures must not overstep the boundaries of their specific area of command. It is fine for a teacher to tell a student what classroom to be in on Tuesday morning but not what church to be in on Sunday morning or whom to vote for in the next election.

Like fairness, the third benchmark—*truthfulness*—is also a general moral criterion of human relationships. Yet truthfulness raises a particular set of problems in instructional relations. These problems revolve around the most difficult and important moral challenge that teachers face: pursuing moral ends with moral means. Teachers—and other adults as well—often shade the truth when talking to children, out of the common conviction that the whole truth can lead young minds astray. No matter how well-intentioned, this is a mistaken and dangerous conviction. It inevitably imparts a harmful moral message and can jeopardize student's trust in their teachers.

Truth shading can take many forms in the classroom. A science teacher working with a health curriculum may exaggerate the risks of unsafe behavior (smoking, drinking, eating high-fat foods) for the benign purpose of getting the warning across in a dramatic way. A history teacher may skip over facts that could cast revered figures in the wrong light. The acute sensitivity of many groups in a pluralistic society creates constant pressure on social studies teachers to tread lightly, if at all, in presenting possibly derogatory facts about historical figures that the groups hold up as heroes.

My purpose here is not to sermonize against the common but morally questionable practice of "shading the truth." More to the point, I wish to focus on the *instructional* risks that doing so can create. The teacher/student relationship is based upon trust. In this regard, it is like any other relationship. But since the purpose of the teacher/student relationship is to communicate knowledge, it is essential to the viability of the relationship that the accuracy of the imparted knowledge be trusted. A student's crucial sense of trust can be undermined by an awareness that the teacher is more committed to a certain message—however noble—than to the truth.

Beyond its serious threat to instructional credibility, truth shading undermines a large part of the moral meaning of the teacher/student relationship. As I have discussed throughout this book, the developmental effects that relationships have upon children derive directly from the interactional qualities of the relationship. In this sense, the medium is very much the moral message in any relationship. Piaget understood this when he wrote that relations that are characterized by constraint can only engender unilateral respect, moral realism, and a host of other "heteronomous" leanings; whereas relationships that are characterized by cooperation lead directly to mutual respect and an autonomous moral orientation.[39] The forms of interaction within the relationship themselves have a moral meaning *and in the course of development become internalized by the relationship's participants.*

The greatest educational pitfall of a dishonest communication is that it will embody, and therefore transmit, a value of untruthfulness. This is a powerful form of moral education in the wrong direction. The demoralizing legacy of a dishonest communication far outweighs any verbal exhortation towards honesty that a teacher could convey. Yet, in my observations, this is the single most common miseducative experience that students encounter during their education. It also is the single most difficult misstep for teachers to avoid in their practice. It is common and difficult to avoid for the same reason: in human affairs, there always are compelling reasons why certain momentous ends seem to justify any means.

In the world at large, absolute consistency between means and ends may not always be within reach. Certainly there are times, for example, when deceit has served an essential moral purpose—as when a lie saves an innocent person from the hands of an evil dictator.[40] But here I emphasize the *particular* moral risks of dishonesty between teacher and student—risks that derive from the purpose and nature of the instructional enterprise. The purpose of the instructional enterprise, most educators agree, is to foster the student's intellectual and moral development; and the nature of the enterprise, as I have noted, is a communicational relationship in which the teacher takes on an authoritative role. Dishonest communications weaken and corrupt every aspect of the enterprise, because they impart a message that truth is not valued; they create a miseducative encounter between teacher and student; and they undermine the teacher's legitimate authority in the classroom. It is difficult for me to imagine any shading or distortion of the truth that could be justified in an instructional relation where the teacher has assumed responsibility for the student's development. The means and ends of instruction are so intertwined that their congruence is essential—for effective teaching as much as for the usual moral considerations.

Although it is by now commonly accepted that teaching has a moral dimension, there is still a curious ambivalence in the profession concerning a teacher's proper stance on moral issues. I have seen this most clearly in moral education seminars that I have taught for student teachers. I often begin such courses by asking whether it is appropriate for teachers to bring their values into the classroom at all. When phrased in this general manner, the question provokes a wide range of opinion and disagreement. It is normal for student teachers to express great reservations about any assertion of moral or personal values in the classroom. This is commonly considered unprofessional and unfair to pupils who would not share the teacher's values.

But when the seminar moves on to consider the general goals of teaching, it quickly becomes clear that there is widespread support for the universal assertion of at least two values. In every discussion of teaching goals that I have had with teachers or student teachers, I have found strong consensus that teaching should foster, if nothing else, tolerance and critical thinking. Within our educational culture, these two goals are so widely accepted, and so little questioned, that I often have trouble getting teachers to see that they are values at all. It always astonishes me that many teachers, for example, see a commitment to absolute tolerance in the classroom as perfectly consistent with the belief that teachers should not allow their values to affect their classroom judgments and behavior. Similarly, teachers often show a tendency to place the goal of critical thinking in a kind of natural "metacategory" outside the realm of values, as if there were no rational choice to be made in the matter. Since critical thinking is seen as an objective procedure for subjecting choices to the tests of reason and truth, it is not usually seen as itself being subject to evaluation.

The anecdote that I relate in my seminars on this point is an incident that I witnessed at a conference in Toronto, Canada, about ten years ago. It is one of those rare stories that is more timely now than when it first occurred. The occasion was a presentation by a researcher from The Ontario Institute for Studies in Education about new methods for fostering "critical thinking" in adolescents. Her ideas seemed noncontroversial enough to me, but they were met with indignation and even some outrage from a pair of local school board members. Didn't these new techniques, they asked, inculcate what at the time was called "divergent thinking?" And didn't Canada, that loose affiliation of diverse cultures, need to encourage more *con*vergent thinking in its young people? Who was this researcher to interject her own antinationalistic values into curriculum materials designed for public schooling?

No doubt many of us non-Canadians in the audience were oblivious to the shifting fault lines that even then were threatening to tear that sprawling nation apart. But even some of the Canadians there that day also dismissed this objection as nationalistic hyperanxiety. I suspect that, if the same incident were to take place at the present time, many more might be more persuaded.

My point here, though, is not to argue for these particular nationalistic concerns. Personally, I am an employer of critical thinking! Rather, my point is that even the most widely accepted values can come under attack in situations where the values do not function in ways that are perceived to be adaptive (and therefore valued). Who is to say that nationalism should not be an educational priority in a certain time and place? And who is to say that critical thinking may not undermine nationalistic sentiment? All educational choices—from direct moral instruction to curricular priorities—reflect values; and no matter how unassailable such values may appear at a particular time and place, they may be questioned at a different time and place.

This can be a jarring experience when one has assumed that certain choices are beyond question. Teachers cannot make such an assumption; and yet they must be prepared to take stands on core matters of values and to defend their deeply held views on such matters. The first challenge of teaching is to acquire a coherent framework of values for making educational choices. Fortunately, like any members of society, teachers need not (and should not) construct their frameworks independently. There is a solid legacy of basic values available to them in the communities where they teach.

Of all the complex issues that arise in classrooms, ethical questions are the ones that teachers say they are least prepared to deal with. Yet such problems offer unparalleled opportunities to communicate moral values to students. The rule of thumb is similar to that concerning the teacher's general manner when engaging with students: teachers do best by modeling the values that they are trying to impart. As long as they respond to classroom problems with principles of fairness, respect, and honesty, they may feel confident that their responses are serving the purpose of moral guidance.

The enterprise of teaching children values in schools is more often than not an indirect one. Where core values are concerned, teachers communicate more by their manners than through explicit messages. A habit of being scrupulously honest with one's students is far more powerful for teaching the value of truthfulness than a thousand lectures on the subject. Students are acutely aware of times when teachers are shading the truth, when they are favoring some students over others, and when they are turning a cold shoulder to students in need. Students are acutely aware of their teachers' efforts to be honest, fair, and caring. Such efforts are the school's surest and most lasting means of communicating good values to children.

No matter how well they function, schools can be only a limited part of the solution to today's youth crisis. The problem is too large for any one institution alone; and, in any case, many central areas of guidance are better left to a young person's family, friends, and spiritual leaders. As pioneer educator James Comer has written, schooling will contribute little to a child's life unless it is supported by high-quality interpersonal relationships.[41] Comer reminds us that we must focus first and foremost on children's *development*—social, moral, and intellectual—and adapt our schools to that end, rather than (as so often happens) subjugating children's developmental needs to the institutional requirements of an unresponsive bureaucracy. Comer and others who make children's development their highest priority understand that school is but one of the multiple influences that must play a role in the building of a child's competence and character. *All* the people and institutions that come in contact with young people must play a constructive role in their growth. Schools cannot shoulder the entire responsibility themselves. We should neither expect this of them nor blame them for every ill consequence that follows from our inaction.

But neither can schools shirk the responsibility that legitimately falls on their turf. Until and unless schools dedicate themselves to creating within their own walls a climate of positive guidance for their students, it will be difficult if not impossible to stop the downward drift.

10
Community and the Spirit of Youth

In this book, I have emphasized the importance of ideas and practices when it comes to raising children. After describing signs of demoralization among many of today's youth, I discussed in Part II some misdirected ideas and practices that have dominated our present-day society. Part III has been devoted to ideas and practices that I believe to be more promising than those which have come to represent modern approaches to childrearing. Naturally, like any author, I hope that my message will suggest a constructive new approach to readers of this book.

But improving the quality of childrearing throughout our society will take more than simply convincing individual people to adopt better ideas and practices. No parent or teacher, however dedicated, can long withstand the overpowering forces of an unwholesome and oppositional culture. In order to be sustained, good ideas and practices must become widely shared among families, schools, and other institutions that provide services to children. In fact, childrearing must become a *collective* effort extending across neighborhoods. What is more, a culture of childrearing based upon a shared set of lofty standards and expectations must replace the unfocused and dispirited sensibilities of our present epoch. All of this requires building communities that support the

219

essential but risky enterprise of parenting. Without community support, even parents with the best of ideas and intentions will rarely be able to find the resources they need to properly guide their children.

Chapter 8 advocated a parenting style that builds bridges between the child's own inclinations and the civilized world. In a "bridging" style, parents connect their children with wholesome activities, events, and people in the neighborhood. In contrast, many parents today isolate their children in a misguided attempt to protect them from danger. As sociologist Frank Furstenberg puts it, parents living in highly dangerous neighborhoods often retreat to a kind of "lock up" strategy, keeping their children inside the home or with the parent whenever possible.[1] This strategy is counterproductive because it deprives children of a chance to develop the personal competence that in the long run will provide their best protection. Nor is this even the safest way to go in the long run. As Furstenberg writes, "The tactic is costly for it helps sustain the social paranoia that prevents many parents from banding together. . . ." Although bridge-building may feel risky at times, active engagement in neighborhood life is a surer route to safety than withdrawal.

Yet to many parents, lockup is less a "style" or "strategy" than it is a forced choice. Some parents live in so bleak a state of social isolation themselves that they see no way to bridge their child to anything constructive. Their neighborhoods are fearsome places with few social networks to rely upon. Still, until the parents sense some hope of community support, they will see this tactic as their only realistic response to the dangers that their children face daily.

The Primacy—and Elusiveness—of Community

There is an ancient old-world proverb that has gained widespread currency among people concerned about the uncertain prospects of children today: "It takes a village to raise a child." There is indeed much wisdom in the saying. A growing child's need for an extended network of community support is primary. Yet community remains an elusive notion, because it is located in the *transactions* among societal institutions rather than in the institutions or people themselves. For example, institutions like school and family establish a community for raising children only when they collaborate effectively with one another. The nature and quality of the collaboration—its harmony, its openness to communication, its capacity to handle sudden misfortune—is the key determinant of sustained community.

For exposition's sake, I have organized this last section of the book around separate chapters on parents, schools, and communities. But in reality this is like separating air, yeast, and dough in a loaf of baking bread. It is only the combination that brings the mixture to life. In cultures that thrive, families and schools work together cooperatively to communicate standards, skills, and knowledge to each new generation of children. Through all the daily transactions of family, school, and neighborhood, young people living in such communities encounter a unified consensus of core values—what Frances Ianni has referred to in his book as a "youth charter."[2] This is the one and only way that cultures can preserve themselves over the ages. It is also the principal way in which young people refine their moral senses and acquire higher purposes in life. As Common Cause founder John Gardner has written:

> Families and communities are the ground-level generators and preservers of values and ethical systems. No society can remain vital or even survive without a reasonable base of shared values. . . . They are generated chiefly in the family, schools, church, and other intimate settings in which people deal with one another face to face.[3]

We have drifted very far from this ideal in modern times. Many of our neighborhoods now are more like unconnected aggregates of people than like true communities. Rather than presenting children with a shared consensus of values, they present discordant, fragmented messages that demoralize rather than inspire. Elements of the social system have become so disconnected from one another that, where children's developmental needs are concerned, they constantly work at cross-purposes.

A 1994 *Boston Globe* story on welfare benefits to parents of disabled children serves as a dismal example of how *not* to build community through social action.[4] The story begins with the case of an eight-year-old boy who had some tantrums in school. The school placed the child in a special needs class for "disabled" children. The mother disliked the idea, believing that the outbursts were just "something he would outgrow." Then she was told that the boy's "disability" would bring her almost $500 in additional monthly welfare payments. She agreed to the boy's disability classification, although her doubts remained. She said,

"He wants things his way. He isn't really disabled. . . . I just think he needs help in terms of his attitude . . . and we need the money." One of the teachers agreed, saying that the boy was an intelligent child who simply engaged in some disruptive behavior. (As the reporter notes, such behavior "is the kind that in another generation would have been handled by the parents.") The teacher went on to say that she has seen this governmental procedure mislabel at least four other students of hers, and that she believes "this is bad for the kids."[5]

Such incidents, repeated countless times daily in our society, are creating a subculture of children who have been classified as "disabled" for no good reason beyond financial advantage. Misdiagnoses of this kind not only stigmatize the children but also obstruct the efforts of parents and teachers to help such children improve their attitudes and behavior. For rather than receiving the rousing message that they should be working towards higher standards of conduct, the children are hearing the demoralizing message that there is something wrong with them. The system's rigidity and irrationality obstructs the very mission of child welfare that it was designed to advance. By standing in contradiction to parents' valid perceptions and values, the system undercuts the possibility of a community that could promote youth development.

Irrationality is one thing, intentional discord another. It is especially hard to get community when civic leaders polarize rather than unite by playing on fears and controversies among the citizenry. A wildly disproportionate share of public debate concerning education focuses on hot but marginal issues such as condom use and multicultural awareness programs. Why are we not joining forces to tackle the more central problems, such as the conduct and competence of our schoolchildren? In their harsh comments and critiques, political leaders teach young people to distrust the very institutions, such as schools, that are needed to provide them with guidance outside of the home.

Our society's orientation towards legal advocacy may serve the cause of social justice, but it has not played a constructive role in the contexts of family and community. By fueling discord, it undermines the goals of arriving at a community consensus of values for youth and delivering clear messages about positive directions for children's development Legal rights groups have urged young people to contest the authority of their teachers and, in some cases, even that of their parents. Legal oppositions also have contaminated family dynamics: In many families that are breaking apart, as they win Pyrrhic victories in contentious divorce proceedings, parents are induced by oppositional court proceedings to damage one another's credibility with their own children. This destructive enterprise is aided and abetted by a family court system that still operates on an advocacy principle, despite the reams of evidence showing that parental divisiveness in any setting inevitably harms children.[6]

Children everywhere seek a coherent framework of guidance. Without a strong community, there can be no such coherence. A parent may offer a sterling example for the child, a teacher may provide a moving insight or admonition, but in the long run the child will experience confusion unless the child finds synchronous notes elsewhere in the community. This confusion sows the seeds of demoralization. In turn, demoralization inevitably will lead to either apathy or rebellion, depending upon the child's inclinations and circumstances.

It is not too late for us to build communities that are capable of raising confident and inspired children. Modernity may have endangered community, but it has by no means killed it. Rather, modernity has altered the conditions under which communities may be established. It also has taught us some lessons about children, about society, and about human nature. These lessons should make it possible for us to build communities that we may rely on to promote intellectual, moral, and spiritual growth in young people. By learning from the mistakes and discoveries of our recent past, we shall be able to reconstitute, in the world of today and tomorrow, virtual villages for raising our children.

Building Communities for the Coming Generations

In a time of megalopolises and social isolation, where may we find the communal "villages" for raising our children? In a time of societal conflict and disintegrating families, how may we create the extended networks that provide young people with coherent guidance? In a society divided among people with vastly different economic advantages, how may we build communities that will support the development of *all* the children in our society?

In searching for answers to these questions, we may look to examples of people who are rebuilding communities in places that have been devastated by economic decline and social disintegration. Sometimes principles useful to all may be found while working in extreme and difficult circumstances. Earlier in this book, I have mentioned the courageous efforts of urban youth organizations that provide safe havens for young people in some of our most ravaged neighborhoods.[7] At the present time, boys' clubs and girls' clubs, YMCAs, athletic associations such as community basketball leagues, and small storefront church groups are engaging young people in wholesome activities and offering them the guidance of mentoring adults. Many of these organizations operate on a shoestring, their work usually unheralded: "This is the greatest untold story in America," says Milbrey McLaughlin, a chronicler of these groups. By all signs, these grassroots organizations are saving the lives and futures of thousands of children who have fallen through all other societal cracks.

These organizations are successful for two key reasons. First, they are authentic. They are a product of the same environment where the young people whom they serve are growing up. The most effective organizations have been on site for a long time and have demonstrated their commitment to stay through thick and thin. Often the organizations employ as workers some older members of the neighborhood who have made it though similar circumstances in their own youth. Often these "survivors" have been in trouble themselves and have learned from their mistakes. Their voices speak with special force and clarity to the next generation in line.

Second, the organizations place strict demands on all who participate. There are rules and expectations that must be heeded. Their young members know that they will be out if they do not meet the well-defined standards. It is instructive that the young people do not chafe under such regulation. Rather, reports McLaughlin, "The youths *welcome* the rules and limits that these groups set for them." As I noted above, we may all learn from the principles revealed by this work.

Still, despite their proven effectiveness, these organizations receive little civic support. They scrape by from year to year with few funds, and they often must turn away many young people who desperately need their services. Sometimes, for want of sufficient resources, they wither away, unnoticed by anyone other than the inarticulate youth population whom they have served. In order to ensure their effectiveness and their survival, such organizations need to be linked to businesses, schools, public agencies, and other institutions that could support their essential work. In other words, they must become part of a coordinated set of efforts that nurture the development of young people. Creating a coordinated set of efforts around the developmental needs of children requires building a sense of community: in fact, assuming collective responsibility for all children in a society is the essence of community. In all too many parts of today's society, this is not happening. Community has become an elusive hope.

This may be our new frontier, an especially hard one to reach because it seems to recede further in the distance with each passing year. But even on this most challenging front, there are pioneers who are making headway, their trials and their progress setting useful examples for the whole society. One such is Ernesto Cortes, Jr., a community builder in south Texas. Cortes learned his organizing skills from veteran activist Saul Alinsky, and he has brought Alinsky's social action vehicle, the Industrial Areas Foundation, to new life around the missions of education and public service. Cortes pulls together all the functioning institutions in a metropolitan area to combat social problems such as crime, drug use, economic decline, and school failure. He teaches people in local neighborhoods how to identify and pursue their common goals. The goals may be as earthy as obtaining a new sewer system or as ethereal as engineering progressive school reform. Whatever the project, Cortes begins with the people's own goals for themselves and their families. Cortes insists that the locus of action remain with the citizenry: a classic organizing rule that he learned from Alinsky is never to do for others what they can do for themselves. By reminding citizens of the common interests that they share, by pressing them to make commitments to one another, and by forging connections among people and institutions which too often operate in isolation from one another, Cortes builds community in the most literal sense.

As may be predicted in these fractious times, Cortes draws criticism from both ends of the political spectrum. For some conservatives, he is too closely associated with the radical Alinsky to be worthy of trust. For some radicals, he is too committed to improving our society rather than tearing it down in order to start anew. The reason that Cortes draws fire from all political extremes is that he tries to bridge oppositions rather than further polarize them. He understands that creating a nurturing community for raising young people requires consensus rather than divisiveness among those to whom the young look for guidance. Cortes *makes use of* the institutions that survive in our society rather than attacking them. Although he advocates revolutionary reforms in schools and local governments, he works constructively with these institutions rather than trying to tear them down. The following interchange between Cortes and television host Bill Moyers is instructive:

MOYERS: Some of your critics say that you are actually too conservative. They say that you're bringing more people into a system of existing institutions that are ossified and out of date, when you should be changing that system.

CORTES: Well, I've seldom been privileged to be called too conservative, but I guess in some ways we are advocating a culturally conservative strategy. It's important for people to be connected to institutions. We have to make a distinction between tradition, which is the living ideas of the dead, and traditionalism, which is the dead ideas of the living. If you say I'm conservative because I think the family's important, I plead guilty. If you say I'm conservative because I think the church is important, I plead guilty. If you say I'm conservative because I think the public schools could be made to work, then I plead guilty. And if you say I'm conservative because I believe America can work, then I plead guilty as well.[8]

Through a number of local partnerships that are linked through a support network called the Texas Interfaith Education Network, Cortes and his colleagues have used their community-building approach to revitalize public schools all across south Texas. With names such as COPS (Communities Organized for Public Service), ACT (Allied Communities of Tarrant), and EPISO (El Paso Interreligious Sponsoring Organization), the partnerships are working to replace factory-style schools with "communities of learners." In a statement of its vision for future public schools, the Interfaith Network describes this idea in the following manner:

Successful schools will act more as "communities of learners" than as the lowest rung on a bureaucratic ladder. They will be characterized by the creation of a variety of learning environments and strategies that are adapted to the particular and varied needs of their children. Students are seen not as passive learners but as members of collaborative learning communities. Teachers and administrators share a commitment to continuously improve their teaching, learning from experience, from each other, and from the school's children. Successful schools will be characterized by energized and collaborative relationships among all stakeholders, including parents, teachers, administrators, and community leaders. . . . Successful schools will recognize and support the important role of families in the education of their children.[9]

Local partnerships such as COPS hold community-wide meetings to promote the cause of school improvement. The meetings are large and personal at the same time. Some would say that they have a "revival-style" atmosphere. Speakers share their own experience with education and request support from the parents, civic leaders, business men and women, and other citizens who are in attendance. Often students are there as well, and they too share their experiences and their hopes. By the end of the meeting, all members of the community are asked to make public statements of commitment to the school reform enterprise.

As undertaken by Cortes and his followers, the community-based school reform movement is a powerful blend of the timeless and the contemporary. It is timeless in that it preserves the village-like intimacy and shared responsibility that have marked communities throughout the ages. It is contemporary in that it makes use of the most up-to-date educational methods that have come out of recent research and practice.

Cortes's organizing work captures the essence of community by building bridges between citizens and their institutions. Through such efforts, citizens gain the sense that schools, churches, and other public agencies are indeed *their* institutions. By making the goal of school improvement a public matter belonging to everyone, new channels of communication are created among parents and teachers, civic leaders and schools, church and lay people, and ultimately between children and an extended network of mentoring adults. The energized community conversation about education that results gives children a new sense of purpose in their academic pursuits as well as a new sense of connection with their elders. The common goals and values demonstrated though such efforts presents a clear consensus of expectation for the young. The school improvements that result from such efforts offer young people new opportunities to develop the kinds of skills and understanding that will serve them well in their current and future lives.

The particular school reform vision of the Texas Interfaith Education Network includes many of the elements of the program that I outlined in Chapter 9: the focus on students' active learning and understanding; the focus on each student's individual talents and interests; the reconfiguration of social relationships in the classroom so as to emphasize collaboration and mentoring; the use of peer learning methods such as group work and tutoring; and the use of performance-based assessments to provide students with constructive feedback about what they know and do not know. In addition, though, there is a strong commitment to teaching basic skills that children will need for jobs and for citizenship. In this approach, there is no senseless polarization between thinking and knowledge, between problem-solving and facts, or between children's spontaneous interest and high standards of achievement. It is understood that a good school promotes *all* of the above.

Nor is there polarization between the secular and spiritual needs of children in the Texas school reform efforts. The movement is unabashedly open to religious sentiment as it is expressed in the places where Cortes and his colleagues organize communities. People of many faiths join together in a common cause, but this does not imply a need to subdue any particular expression of faith. There is little sense that one person's beliefs will have an oppressive effect on someone else unless they are kept hidden. In fact, churches and other religious institutions are needed for the constructive roles that they can play in rebuilding the communities. What they have in common, of course, is their dedication to a transcendent propose; and it is this orientation to transcendence that they impart to children through their joint community presence.

The Texas community renewal movement is reformist in nature. It works closely with traditional institutions such as schools; but it presses these institutions to update their methods in order to improve their capacities to help today's young people. Accordingly, the movement endorses nontraditional educational reform methods such as collaborative learning and performance assessment in an effort to revitalize these institutions. The focus of the effort is on the skills and values that children will need now and in the future. There is no attempt to harken back to a nostalgically remembered past or to preserve practices that freeze younger generations in time.

There are indeed communities in today's society that have tried to do this. Some have met with at least partial success. Through the loyalty of people determined to raise their families in same circumstances that they and their own parents once enjoyed, such communities have fought hard to preserve their safety and their solidarity in the face of deteriorating societal circumstances. In many regards, one must admire what they have been able to accomplish.

Sociologist Frank Furstenberg describes one such community in

Philadelphia. It is "one of a handful of urban villages . . . that has survived successive waves of urban deterioration and gentrification."[10] The community is marked by a "rich supply of resources and dense network of adults who come in contact with children [and] serve as an effective system of sponsorship as well as a source of social control." Yet it is by no means a wealthy neighborhood: it comprises mostly working-class people whose families have lived there for generations. Rather than material, the communities main resources are interpersonal. People feel an obligation to one another's children. They watch out for them: "the streets have eyes," as one parent comments. Schools, athletic leagues, and local businesses all show a strong interest in the neighborhood's children. They communicate frequently with parents. "Parenting is a shared activity" in this neighborhood, writes Furstenberg. On matters of core standards, the community speaks to the young with one voice: parents "can reasonably expect that adults would act as they would if an adolescent gets out of line." The children of the community enjoy the protection and guidance that only a caring network of people and institutions can provide. In this regard, these children are far more fortunate than many of their peers.

Still, one cannot be sanguine about this particular community's future. It is fighting the rising forces of social anomie with archaic weapons. Some of the community's values are obsolete as well as mean-spirited. Furstenberg comments on the "fierce racism" that helps contain discord among neighborhood residents. Exclusionary sentiments such as racism are no way to provide an uplifting community charter for youth. Communities cannot be preserved through attempts to seal themselves off from outsiders. This is a losing effort. Eventually the walls will break down. Those who are unprepared for interacting constructively with the full range of people in our diverse society will be unable to adapt.

Nor does a community do well by forever fighting every manifestation of social change. Schools and other institutions must be constantly renewed so that they have the capacities to serve the present and future generations. If they are to serve the young, the institutions must respond to the times. This does not mean that institutions should lose sight of their traditional missions or abandon their traditional values. But it does mean that they must speak to the interests of contemporary youth in a language that young people can hear. If young people come to perceive their community's schools and churches as dusty old museums with nothing useful to offer, the young will not participate whole-heartedly in them. They will develop no loyalty to the institutions—nor, very likely, to the community itself. Much of the value that young people find in their communities is provided by the contributions of institutions such as school, church, and youth organizations. When the institutions become obsolete, the young will soon leave, in body or in spirit.

Communities develop just as young people do: in fact, the developmental trajectories of communities and the young are intertwined. Each new generation brings with it new interests and new needs that provide opportunities for changes to communities and their institutions. One compelling example is school reform that takes account of the skills that children will need in today's world—and that uses the most effective, up-to-date methods to foster such skills. Another example is the restructuring of youth organizations and local business to provide engaging activities for young people in need of guidance. When communities and their institutions keep in touch with the spirit of today's youth, they will be able to make such changes; and, by making such changes, they will themselves keep growing and thriving. They will keep finding new ways to serve their ancient purpose of nurturing the younger generations.

I do not wish to belittle the valiant efforts of communities that are fighting to preserve the safety of their streets by fending off what they see as dangerous encroachments from the outside world. Although I believe that such a strategy cannot long prevail without progressive reforms, such efforts have provided some children with the fundamental protections that they need to grow up in a risk-laden environment. There is much that we should learn from such efforts, no matter how limited their ultimate prospects. The first priority for any community must be to protect *all* its children from violence, abuse, neglect, and exploitation. In order to achieve this, communities must once again make themselves into save havens for the young. Communities must provide these havens in every corner of every neighborhood, outside of the home as well as within it. Why should this be seen as beyond our reach? If private profit centers such as theme parks can create large fantasy worlds where children can roam without undue danger, why is this no longer possible in the public domain?

I ask this out of vexation and concern rather than out of naiveté. I know full well the relentless cultural forces that have led to our widespread present predicament of unsafe neighborhoods: indeed, I have devoted Parts I and II of this book to unveiling these forces. But despite the incontestable realities of our modern society, young people still need a certain degree of freedom to explore the world. It is through spontaneous exploration that young people acquire much of their skill, self-confidence, and insights into life's possibilities. This is one of the key avenues to competence. As they freely explore the world, young people exercise their powers and discover their interests. They learn about people, places, and themselves in profound ways that are unavailable to them in schools and other less "contextualized" settings.[11]

Continually curbing a child's thirst for exploration inevitably will cause a child to become dejected and apathetic. It is a sure way to turn a high-spirited youth into a demoralized one. Young people from all sectors of society benefit from living in communities where they can safely wander at will. We must give them no less. In a society where responsible parents feel that they can no longer give their children the freedom that they need to explore the world, children are growing up with a serious developmental handicap.[12]

It is certainly within our reach to make our communities safe and child-friendly. Above I have noted the importance of supporting indigenous community organizations that, on their own, have been providing havens for youth even while the neighborhoods around them have crumbled. This alone would be a useful and cost-effective measure. There are a large number of groups that accomplish miracles for many children with practically no outside support. Some are formal organizations that have been in the neighborhood "forever" and by now seem almost institutionalized: boys' and girls' clubs, storefront churches, and the like. Others have sprung up spontaneously in response to the specter of children in desperate need. They go by names such as "Gideon's Army" and "the Network of Marginality," and they scrape by from day to day with whatever help they can get.[13] If linked to our public agencies and offered a small portion of the resources that we routinely dole out to these agencies, they could do wonders. They deserve our support precisely because they go where children are in greatest need.

Urbanologists such as Jane Jacobs and sociologists such as Amitai Etzioni have offered a number of other solutions that are both workable and economically feasible. We should encourage, through a variety of incentives, the return of small-scale housing and storefront enterprises to our cities. We should win back our city streets through community patrolling. And we should rebuild rather than abandon our older neighborhoods, knowing full well that even the most decrepit of neighborhoods always will be populated by some families with children.

A decent society will take responsibility for all its children. We cannot turn our backs on children who are consigned to unsafe neighborhoods and pretend that they are living outside the boundaries of our own society. We must do everything in our power to see that *all* our children have communities where they can live and grow with well-founded feelings of security. This is not pure altruism: a society that provides advantageous developmental conditions for all its young members ultimately ensures its own security as well.

Recapturing the Moral Voices of Communities

In the end, we must help our communities recapture what sociologist Amitai Etzioni refers to as their "moral voices." Etzioni writes: "*Communities speak to us in moral voices. They lay claims on their members.*"[14] Etzioni shows how our modern-day disinclination to "lay moral claims" has eroded the routine moral reactions of our communities and their members. He offers a compelling example of a psychiatrist who argues that doctors should not ask someone to make a risk-free bone marrow donations in order to save a sibling, because refusing to do so might produce guilt in a person who was asked and refused. Etzioni's reply: "If they refuse, they *should* feel guilty."[15]

The present-day disinclination to lay moral claims has been at the heart of our failure to maintain communities that could provide protection and guidance for today's young people. We hesitate to take responsibility for other people's children, and we harbor few expectations that others should watch out for ours. Moreover, we rarely show children that we expect them to assume responsibility for the welfare of others in their community. Our points of reference concerning children's well-being have become increasingly internal. We ask whether children are comfortable, whether they are overburdened and overstressed, whether they are feeling good about themselves. We are becoming unaccustomed to asking whether they are being responsible, whether they are contributing something to the world, whether they are being *diligent*, to use an old-fashioned word.[16] We are hesitant to foist "guilt trips" on them. If we were truly concerned for their well-being, we instead should be hesitant to withhold our moral sensibilities from them.

Articulating a community's moral voice helps children find the guidance that they need to form their own perspectives. A community's moral voice communicates expectations to all its members. In the course of development, children orient towards these expectations. They direct their energies towards them, work to acquire the skills needed to meet them, and choose friends, interests, and engagements accordingly. Nothing is more stultifying for a child's development than a vacuum of expectations from those around him. Nothing is more inspiring than high expectations communicated with encouragement and support. This is the essence of a "youth charter." Clear expectations are the main conduit for imparting standards to children.

Communities that expect nothing of their children will see them grow with stunted standards, poor self-control, and little personal or social responsibility. Communities that consistently hold strong expectations for *all* their children will see them grow with high standards, worthy aspirations, social awareness, and a readiness to take responsibility for their behavior.

The disinclination to "lay moral claims" that has robbed communities of their moral voices is closely linked to the cultural relativity of modern times. Because people have lost confidence in the universality of their standards, they hesitate to foist those standards upon others. This hesitation provides a formidable point of resistance against the building of a youth charter. How can we urge children to adopt a belief that may reflect only our own biases? How can we insist that all children follow a code of conduct that may reflect only one set of choices among many? A youth charter cannot be built without a firm conviction that its guiding principles will lead young people in the right direction. Such convictions have been worn down by an incessant posing of one nagging question: Whose moral voice should the community express?

The question, of course, assumes diversity of opinion—as well as some degree of conflict arising from this diversity. Neither the diversity nor the conflict can be denied. Modern society is by nature pluralistic. Few communities will ever again be homogeneous in any meaningful sense. In many ways, this is a good thing. The history of nations, including that of the United States, shows how important cultural diversity is for a society's growth. For democratic societies, pluralistic debate and contention is crucial for social progress. *But this does not mean that a diverse democratic society cannot arrive at fundamental areas of consensus.* A community's youth charter is one area that demands such consensus, no matter how pluralistic the community many be.

When I have complained throughout this book about the divisiveness and polarization of political discourse in our society, I have been referring to one particular misdirection: the unnecessary politicization of matters related to childrearing, education, and youth. Political argumentation is valuable in many areas of social life, and as a citizen I welcome it. But it is counterproductive to argue over core assumptions that constitute the very basis of a civilized life. Among the most important set of core assumptions that any society has concerns its goals and expectations for young people. As a society we *do* share a set of common goals and expectations for our young. We hope that they are kind, decent, respectful, honest, fair, and responsible. We hope that they are competent and self-controlled. We must believe that it is our duty as elders to help them become this way.

There is not in actuality much controversy surrounding these core assumptions, but there is a great deal of confusion concerning how we ought to act regarding them. Should we advocate them or should we simply hold them quietly? Should we expect all parents and children to promote them, or should we withhold our judgments where others are concerned? Should we act as if these assumptions indeed are "givens," or should we keep them open for debate? The confusion, I believe, stems from our respect for the democratic process and for diversity of opinion. This respect is understandable and commendable, but it is misplaced. Just because even the most divisive forms of debate are generally legitimate in a democratic society does not mean that everything is always up for grabs. The standards that encourage young people to acquire character and competence, to achieve their full intellectual and moral potentials, are not up for grabs. There may be variations around the edges, and certainly we should discuss these. But we should not act as if our adult society is torn over the basics. We should not act as if we cannot agree that it is better for a child to resolve disputes nonviolently rather than violently; that it is better for the child to tell the truth than to lie and cheat; that it is better for the child to work hard in school rather than to goof off; that it is better for a child to treat parents and peers with respect rather than with contempt. I could provide many more such examples, but so could any reader of this book. That is precisely my point.

Communities must recapture their moral voices and express them in ways that will foster the younger generation's character development. In order to promote moral growth in the young, expressions of a community's moral voice should adhere to three general principles:

1. The expressions must come from a variety of sources. Whenever possible, parental messages should be bolstered by extended family, teachers, peers, neighborhood mentors, sports coaches, churches, and so on. The multiple expressions will have a cumulative influence that is far more powerful than that from any single source. Not only will the multiple expressions enhance one another's credibility, but they also will help the youngster understand the various ways that moral aims may be pursued in different relationships and circumstances.

2. The various expressions must be reasonably consistent with one another. Parents, teachers, peers, and others should advocate roughly similar goals and expectations for young people. (As noted above, I refer to *core* goals and expectations and not to the large assortment of political and cultural matters about which civilized adults differ—and about which young people should be urged to make up their own minds.) Core consistency in a community's basic goals and expectations for its young is the essence of a constructive youth charter.

3. A community must express its moral voice in ways that build bridges to the interests and abilities of its young people. Only in this way can effective socialization of the young be accomplished. Building bridges means communicating standards in a manner that young people can understand, engaging young people in compelling activities and experiences that reflect these standards, and conducting relationships with young people in a manner that embodies these standards.

Combined, these three principles create a powerful condition of influence on young people's personal development. The principles provide coherent yet diverse guidance for the formation of a moral perspective. The three principles also offer young people extended opportunities to strengthen their moral motives and habits, because the principles are played out in active experience as well as in verbal messages.

As I have discussed previously in this book and elsewhere, it is the combination of action and reflection that ensures the development of sustained moral commitment.[17] Children who are encouraged to take real responsibility and to perform service to others, who grow up within relationships that are honest, caring, and fair, and who have been instructed in the moral meaning of the choices that they and others make, will stand by far the greatest chance to develop lifelong commitments to moral goals. Communities that raise young people to such standards will do well by themselves, in the present and in the future.

Community and the Spirit of Youth

The surest antidote to youthful demoralization is a sense of purpose: acquiring, that is, a belief in (and dedication to) something larger than oneself. In the individual child, this transcendent sense of purpose takes the form of what is commonly called a spiritual belief. But a sense of purpose is not a matter of individual belief alone: rather, it is intricately linked to a community of persons that has inspired the child's commitment to others beyond the self.[18] This is why, as I shall argue in this chapter, community and spirituality go hand in hand. Together they make possible the child's development of competence and character; together they enable children to reach their full intellectual and moral potential; together they ensure the preservation and improvement of the culture.

In Chapter 5, I wrote of how modern culture has elevated the self and derogated the spiritual, to the detriment of its younger generations. The defeat of the spirit has not been total, of course. Robert Coles and others have documented the rich spiritual life that many young people continue to carve out in the midst of modern society. The question for us is not how to turn the clocks back and undo the social advances of recent history but rather how to make modern culture more "spirit-friendly" (to put it in a modern way) for the developing child.

The concern that led me to write this book was a gnawing fear that contemporary society has become an unwholesome environment for young people to grow up in. And each year the conditions for young people get worse, not better. I have not found my worry to be especially idiosyncratic or controversial: friends, colleagues, and many parents with whom I speak share my concerns. Most people in our society are aware of the rising tide of youthful crime and violence. Most people have witnessed for themselves multiple indications of the youthful demoralization that I have discussed in this book.

Many people look to the images of corruption and degradation that fill our media and wonder whether these unsavory messages are not the culprit. Are such influences the source of our cultural decline? My skin crawls too at the depraved content of today's mass media programming, but I do not believe that this has much to do with the troubles that beset today's youth. The reprehensible events that children encounter in the public media are more a reflection than a cause of the problem. Rather, the root of the problem is the culture's failure to provide children with what they need for their spiritual growth. The culture is failing children not so much for what it is giving children but for what it is not giving them. It is not the influences that children are receiving from the culture that lead them astray but rather the influences that they are *not* receiving.

The same can be said for the various instruments and artifacts of modern culture. Television is not so much a problem because of its vile contents but rather because it is an enormous waste of precious time. While children are spending their typical four hours per day gazing into the tube, they could be reading, exploring, exercising, honing their skills, learning about people, places, and things. They could be developing character and competence in the generative arena of real life experience. Instead, they place their energies and their spirits in a state of suspended animation for huge chunks of their formative years. This tragic loss of opportunity far outweighs the damage that any televised gunfight or steamy romance could deal to their psyches. This is why the most constructive solution for children's incessant TV watching is to curb it rather than to censor it. Censorship accomplishes little. In fact, it removes a fruitful opportunity for adult guidance. When a responsible adult offers the child a moral interpretation of a repugnant event, the adult gives the child a framework of guidance that can help the child deal with such events whenever they occur (as they inevitably will in the course of any life).

But adult guidance is one of those priceless commodities that has become rarer with each passing year. The reasons for the scarcity are stubborn, varied, and deep. Some families have disintegrated, leaving (at best) one overburdened and undersupported parent to fill the entire parental role. Other families are still intact but, with both parents working, the children spend most of their time in unstructured, poorly supervised settings where little is expected of them. And beyond the reduced family circumstances of today's children, a cultural vacuum of expectation greets them everywhere they turn. The culture has come to view children as fragile and incompetent creatures with little capacity for active engagement in challenging endeavors. It also has come to see children as playful and amoral creatures who cannot be trusted either with real responsibility or with honest discussion. Standards for children's achievement have declined to far as to have practically vanished. At the same time, communities are fast on their way to forgetting their own standards of conduct; and they have lost the voices to urge high standards on the young. Sound means for transmitting standards to the young are also becoming a lost art. To the extent that anyone discusses socialization, discipline, or moral education in a public forum these days, it is usually with accusatory, divisive language and with political intent. Out of such polarized discussion arise false oppositions rather than the constructive solutions we need for bringing adult guidance back into all children's lives.

In order to achieve a spirit-friendly society for youth, we need a radical reordering of our family priorities; and we need to revise our thinking about children and what is best for them. Children's developmental needs must become more central to our families, no matter how beleaguered with stresses and outside occupations they may be. But this does not mean that families should revolve around children's every whim. It is the long-term development of their children that families must pay more attention to. For many families, this may mean paying *less* attention to their children's short-term desires and demands. Children need the kind of parental guidance that is effected through the hard, time-consuming effort of working with children on challenging tasks and responsibilities. Busy or otherwise distracted parents too frequently buy their way out of this hard job by letting their children off the hook: coddling their children, releasing them from any obligations, giving them easy praise, allowing them to drift about in idle (or even harmful) pastimes, as long as they stay out of their parents' hair. Parents must ask both more of themselves and more of their children than this. Parents must take the time to provide sustained guidance for their children, and they must see that their children take the time to experience the rewards of providing meaningful service to others.

To be effective, parental guidance must build bridges to the child's interests and lead towards clear goals and high standards, as I discussed in Chapters 7 and 8. Moreover, if parental guidance is to truly support the child's development of character and competence, it must lead the child in the direction of service to others. Service and spirituality are intimately connected in a child's development. Children learn to dedicate themselves to matters beyond themselves by performing service to others. In the course of the selfless act, children first discover the joys of preoccupations that transcend their own immediate desires. For many children, this experience leads directly to a spiritual sense of transcendence: that is, a faith in, and devotion to, something over and above the self. A readiness to be of service to others, a sense of transcendence, and a faith in life's deeper meaning all foster the child's spiritual growth. In turn, spirituality sustains the child's intellectual and moral pursuits through good times and bad.

Even in an affluent society, adults must become accustomed once again to offer children opportunities to serve others—not for the benefit of those whom they serve, but for the child's own benefit. Opportunities for service begin in the home, and a habit of orienting towards the needs of others is best formed early. This is why parents are in a unique position to guide a child towards service activities that will nourish the child's spiritual growth. But the child's development does not stop in the home. Schools and communities also must offer children opportunities to contribute to the welfare of others. Every adult who acts as a mentor to the young is in a position to do so in one way or another. When adults expect children to help out, even in small ways, they teach children to assume responsibility for others and for themselves.

There is an alternative to communicating high standards of achievement, service, and responsibility to children. It is the alternative that increasingly is being played out in millions of homes today: raising children to be self-centered, irresponsible, and ultimately demoralized. Our culture cannot endure a drift in this direction for many more generations. Either we reconstitute our families and our communities so that they once again can provide spirit-friendly conditions for all children's development or we shall forever lose the qualities that we cherish most in human civilization.

Epilogue—Another Fable for Our Times

I began this book with a nightmare of sorts—a bleak view of what the future could hold if we are unable to revise the misdirected ideas and practices that have permeated our way of raising children. That bleak future is not entirely here yet, although our cultural life at present should be giving us enough intimations of it that we should be taking pause. In fact, we are now starting to reap what generations of misguided views and practices have sown. The demoralized attitudes and antisocial directions that many of today's young have taken pose a threat to the very survival of our society. If our society is once again to become a wholesome climate for young people to grown up in, it must reorient itself and provide young people with a more uplifting set of directions for their lives. And it must do so soon. Each generation raised with insufficient guidance, low standards, and uncertain expectations will speed the pace of the decline and bring us further away from the possibility of a correction.

There is another, more hopeful fable that fits our times, a story drawn from a literature of the past and recently revived in movies and a popular musical. It is *The Secret Garden*, the story of an overprotected and frightened young boy who discovers his strength only after some people close to him stop treating him like an invalid. When I first read the novel, years ago during my own childhood, the story left little lasting impression. But last year I took one of my own children to a movie version, and this time around the Victorian-era tale struck me as eerily prophetic. The young boy's predicament looked like a symbolic representation, albeit extreme, of the fate faced by too many young people growing up today. Their powers and potentials have been unrecognized by those in charge of them. Their zest for exploration has been curtailed by a stultifying bubble of overprotectiveness. Their self-centered attitudes and habits have been left uncorrected. Their natural desires to gain strength and competence have been discouraged. Their spontaneous interest in the world has been diminished by too much empty experience and too many fearful warnings. They have grown up in a setting devoid of expectation, standards, or guidance, and they have been deprived of a chance to take on real responsibility and to be of real service to others. In all these ways, many children today see little choice but to turn inwards and shut down.

Like the boy in the book, today's young people may look to their friends for stimulation and support; but unlike the boy, they may not be lucky enough to have peers who keep their best interests in mind. In a child's life, friends can be as much a source of trouble as a source of hope. For children who have benefited from strong family and school guidance and who are able to make sound judgments about choosing and listening to friends, peers are an invaluable developmental resource. For children without other moral guidance or support, peer influence can be a risky business.

It must be noted that the boy in the book was the scion of a wealthy family. This did little to solve his problem: in fact it compounded it. Yet it would be disingenuous to ignore the advantages that affluence brings to some children and not to others. Even though many children of the middle classes are growing up demoralized, at least they are well-fed, living in safe housing, and attending well-maintained schools. These things count. The demoralization of youth in our poorer communities tends to be a far more lethal affair.

Still, in the end, I see more commonality than differences among the children of the rich and poor these days. All of our children are growing up in a culture that has lost touch with what children need in order to forge character and competence. They are all growing up in a society where the essential practices of guiding, instructing, and disciplining children are fast becoming lost arts. They all are growing up in communities that are losing their moral voices. The poor indeed may be in greater danger at present. But unless we raise standards and expectations for all children in our society, our affluent communities will turn into places that are just as deadly as the downtrodden ones are today. This is why I take standards, and not material resources, to be the heart of the matter.

The novel about the overprotected boy has a happy ending. At the initiative of the boy's plucky cousin, his windows to the world were thrown open, literally and figuratively. As the fresh air came flooding in, the boy came to life. Like children everywhere, the boy's natural energies and vitality were too resilient to be extinguished, even during years of neglect. Unbeknownst to his family—and perhaps even to himself— the boy had been long lying in wait for a chance to discover his potential and realize his unarticulated dreams. When he finally received that chance, his spirits rose to the occasion, his strength waxed, and his many talents shone through.

It is within our reach to provide a such a chance for every child in our society. What could be a more worthy, or more pressing, mission for our times? But to do so will require some new thinking and new action among those charged with raising the young. It will require us to assume a collective sense of responsibility for all of our children. It will require us to build communities—modern villages—that reflect this collective sense of responsibility by providing all the guidance and educational opportunities that every child deserves. It also will require us, individually as well as in community, to present children with high standards and expectations that can inspire them throughout their life-long development. In all of these ways, the mission will require us to bring some very old ideas to life again: the reinvention of ancient wisdom in a modern world.

Notes

Preface

1. For a recent account of one group of such children living in a New York housing project, see T. Williams and W. Kornblum (1994), *The Uptown Kids: Struggle and Hope in the Projects* (New York: G. P. Putnam's Sons).

Chapter 1. Introduction

1. J. Fox and G. Pierce (1994), "American Killers Are Getting Younger," *USA Today Magazine*, January, pp. 24–26.
2. Report of the National Commission on Children, U.S. Government Printing Office, 1991.
3. *International Herald Tribune*, January 19, 1994, p. 3.
4. "Children Rob Tennessee Teacher at Gunpoint," *Boston Globe*, May 3, 1994.
5. Fox and Pierce, "American Killers Are Getting Younger."
6. "Children Wounded by Gunfire Plead with Congress for an End to Violence," *New York Times*, February 8, 1994.
7. The Winter 1994 *Carnegie Quarterly*, published by the Carnegie Corporation of New York, reports: "An alarming new phenomenon is the rise of violence among girls, often in complicity with violent boys. . . . Girls increasingly join previously all-male gangs. All-girl gangs tend to be as violent as all-boy gangs" (p. 3).
8. Fox and Pierce, "American Killers Are Getting Younger."

9. "Children Wounded by Gunfire Plead with Congress for an End to Violence."

10. National Commission on Children report (1991) Washington, DC: U.S. Government Printing Office.

11. "Answers Leave a Confounding Picture in Poll of Mass. High School Students," *Boston Globe*, May 20, 1994.

12. National Center for Health Statistics (1992), "Advance Natality Statistics"; see also Charles Murray, "The Coming White Underclass," *Wall Street Journal*, October 29, 1993, p. A14.

13. F. F. Furstenberg Jr., J. Brooks-Gunn, and S. P. Morgan (1987), *Adolescent Mothers in Later Life* (New York: Cambridge University Press).

14. Murray, "The Coming White Underclass."

15. A typical example is a story that appeared in the *Belmont Citizen-Herald* on June 16, 1994 ("Educators see changes in kids' behavior"). The story reports that, over the past five years, local teachers have observed among their students: increased aggressiveness, more disrepect for classroom property, more obscene and rude language, more difficulty paying attention, more depression, more psychosomatic illness, and more "material indulgence" centered around expensive toys and clothes (p. 9A).

16. U.S. Department of Justice, F.B.I. report (1990), *Crime in the United States: The United States Crime Report for 1989* (Washington, DC: U.S. Government Printing Office).

17. U.S. Department of Education report (1988); "College Board Verbal Scores Decline to an All-time Low," *New York Times*, August 27, 1991.

18. J. Condry (1993), "Thief of Time, Unfaithful Servant: Television and the American Child," *Daedalus, 122*: 259–278.

19. Ibid.

20. National Board of Physicians report (April 1993), Washington, DC.

21. T. Achenbach and C. Howell (1993), "Are American Children's Problems Getting Worse? A 13-Year Comparison," *Journal of the American Academy of Child and Adolescent Psychiatry, 32*: 1145–1154.

22. Helen Haste, in conversation, quoted in *The Guardian*, November 1992.

23. See J. M. Baldwin (1902), *Social and Ethical Interpretations in Mental Development*, 3d ed. (New York: Macmillan); and G. S. Hall (1904), *Adolescence: Its Psychology and Its Relations to Physiology, Anthropology, Sociology, Sex, Crime, Religion, and Education*, 2 vols. (East Norfolk, CT: Appleton-Century Crofts).

24. I borrow the "grotesque" descriptor of unbalanced truths from Sherwood Anderson's *Winesburg, Ohio*.

25. A. Etzioni (1993), *The Spirit of Community: Rights, Responsibilities and the Communitarian Agenda* (New York: Crown); and J. Q. Wilson (1993), *The Moral Sense*. (New York: Free Press).

Chapter 2. Growing Up the Easy Way

1. I. Sigel, A. McGillicuddy-DeLisi, and J. Goodnow (Eds.) (1992), *Parental Belief Systems: The Psychological Consequences for Children* (Hillsdale, NJ: Erlbaum).
2. U.S. Joint Economic Committee (1992), *Economic Indicators* (Washington, DC: U.S. Government Printing Office).
3. I have gleaned the material for this "quick look" from informal discussions with parents whom I have met while giving talks across the U.S. and Western Europe. I have also drawn upon observations of family life in communities that I have visited. As a middle-class person myself, my relation to the material in the present chapter is quite different from my relation to the material in Chapter 3. Here I am intimately familiar with the conditions and have shared many of the illusions that I discuss. There, as an outsider, I have needed to draw heavily on fieldwork by ethnographers, journalists, and other writers who have experienced those troubled conditions in depth and over sufficient stretches of time to gain insight.
4. Here I focus on children during the school years. I shall discuss infancy and the preschool years in Chapter 4.
5. For the harsher ones see T. Sizer (1992), *Horace's School; Redesigning the American High School* (New York: Houghton Mifflin); J. Kozol (1991), *Savage Inequalities; Children in America's Schools* (New York: Crown); and C. Finn (1992), *We Must Take Charge: Our Schools and Our Future* (New York: Free Press). For more sympathetic takes see S. Lightfoot (1983), *The Good High School: Portraits of Character and Culture* (New York: Basic Books); D. Perkins (1993), *Smart Schools: From Training Memories to Educating Minds* (New York: Free Press); T. Kidder (1989), *Among Schoolchildren* (Boston: Houghton Mifflin); and H. Gardner (1991), *The Unschooled Mind* (New York: Basic Books).
6. T. Sizer (1984), *Horace's Compromise; The Dilemma of the American High School* (Boston: Houghton Mifflin); Kozol, *Savage Inequalities*; and Finn, *We Must Take Charge*.
7. Lightfoot, *The Good High School*; Perkins, *Smart Schools*; Kidder, *Among Schoolchildren*; and Gardner, *The Unschooled Mind*.
8. W. Damon (1983), *Social and Personality Development* (New York: Norton).

9. Sizer, *Horace's School*; Sizer, *Horace's Compromise*; and Gardner, *The Unschooled Mind*.

10. I draw this conclusion from my own conversations with parents after talks that I have given on the topic.

11. L. Cheney, "Hard Work, Once as American as Apple Pie," *Wall Street Journal*, December 5, 1993.

12. Ibid.

13. *Boston Globe*, April 26, 1989.

14. Ibid.

15. B. Baldwin (1990), *Beyond the Cornucopia Kids: How to Raise Healthy Achieving Children* (Wilmington, NC: Direction Dynamics).

16. F. Gosman (1992), *Spoiled Rotten: Today's Children and How to Change Them* (New York: Villard Books), p. 3.

17. *New York Times*, July 24, 1993.

18. Ibid.

19. Ibid.

20. J. D. Vigil (1993), "Gangs, Social Control, and Ethnicity: Ways to Redirect," in S. B. Heath and M. W. McLaughlin (Eds.), *Identity and Inner-City Youth: Beyond Ethnicity and Gender* (New York: Teachers College Press); and J. D. Vigil (1988), *Barrio Gangs: Street Life and Identity in Southern California* (Austin: University of Texas Press).

21. *Boston Globe*, April 10, 1994.

22. *Wall Street Journal*, June 29, 1992.

23. Ibid., p. 1.

24. S. Davis, K. Grover, and A. Becker (1992), "Academic Dishonesty: Prevalence, Determinants, Techniques, and Punishments," *Teaching of Psychology, 19* (1): 16.

25. I use the term "warped" advisedly, in the sense introduced by Harry Stack Sullivan in his classic *Interpersonal Theory of Psychiatry* (New York: Norton, 1953). In Sullivan's theory, a personality "warp" was a character distortion engendered by maladaptive interpersonal experience during the childhood and early adolescent years. Such warps can create severe fault lines in the cornerstones of one's mental health, and they predict the possibility of continued sociopathologies throughout life. Warps are prevented by early, intense experience with intimacy in mutually caring relationships—and especially, Sullivan emphasized, by close relations with peers.

26. American Association of University Women (1993), *Hostile Hallways* (Washington DC: A AUW), June.

27. *New York Times*, July 14, 1993.

28. *Issues Quarterly, 1* (1994) (New York: National Council for Research on Women).

29. I draw here on an excellent account of the Spur Posse by Joan Didion, from *The New Yorker*, July 26, 1993, and also from the *New York Times* coverage of March 19, 1993.

30. R. T. Ammerman (1991), "The Role of the Child in Physical Abuse: A Reappraisal," *Violence and Victims, 6* (2): 87–101.

31. J. Didion, "Trouble in Lakewood," p. 50.

32. *Redbook*, April 1989; *Newsweek*, August 2, 1993.

33. Didion, "Trouble in Lakewood," p. 54.

Chapter 3. Growing Up the Hard Way

1. National Academy of Sciences (1993), *Losing Generations: Adolescents in High-risk Settings* (Washington, DC: National Academy Press).

2. Ibid., p. 2.

3. M. L. Sullivan (1989), *Getting Paid: Youth Crime and Work in the Inner City* (Ithaca, NY: Cornell University Press), p. 38.

4. W. Damon (1988), *The Moral Child* (New York: Free Press).

5. C. West (1993), *Race Matters* (Boston: Beacon Press).

6. Sullivan, *Getting Paid*, p. 2.

7. See West, *Race Matters*, for an excellent, balanced critique of two polarized positions, both of which he considers oversimplified: on the one hand, economic conservatives who look to values and behavior rather than poverty as the roots of inner-city youth problems; and, on the other hand, the "liberal structuralists" who blame poverty for most every problem, including poor behavior. West asserts, and I wholly agree, that cultural values and poverty are inseparable, both in their intricate causal relation to one another and in their multiple adverse effects on young people growing up.

8. For a vivid account, see Jonathan Kozol (1991), *Savage Inequalities: Children in America's Schools* (New York: Crown).

9. M. Czikszentmihalyi (1993), "Contexts of Optimal Growth in Childhood," *Daedalus, 119*: 42.

10. E. Anderson (1990), *Streetwise: Race, Class and Change in an Urban Community* (Chicago: University of Chicago Press).

11. Ibid., p. 69.

12. Ibid., p. 71.

13. Ibid., p.72.

14. M. McLaughlin (1993), "Embedded Identities: Enabling Balance in Urban Contexts," in S. B. Heath and M. W. McLaughlin (Eds.), *Identity and Inner-City Youth: Beyond Ethnicity and Gender* (New York: Teachers College Press), p. 54.

15. Ibid.

16. The work of Watts community organizer "Sweet Alice" Harris, a recent Templeton Award winner.

17. D. Hart (1993), "Altruism and Caring in Adolescence: Relations to Moral Judgment and Self-understanding," in M. Killen and D. Hart (Eds.), *Morality in Everyday Life* (New York: Plenum).

18. F. Villarruel (Ed.) (in press), "Learning Out of School: New Contexts for Youth Development," in *New Directions for Child Development* (San Francisco: Jossey-Bass).

19. Heath and McLaughlin, *Identity and Inner-City Youth*.

20. Ibid., p. 57.

21. Ibid., p. 47.

22. National Academy of Science, *Losing Generations*, p. 14.

23. J. Sander (1991), *Before Their Time: Four Generations of Teenage Mothers* (New York: Harcourt Brace Jovanovich).

24. Ibid., p. 178.

25. M. Konner (1991), *Childhood* (Boston: Little, Brown); R. LeVine (1979), "Adulthood among the Gusii," in N. Smelser and E. Erikson (Eds.), *Themes of Work and Love* (Cambridge, MA: Harvard University Press).

26. Sander, *Before Their Time*.

27. Csikszentmihalyi, "Contexts of Optimal Growth."

Chapter 4. Misconceptions of Modern Times, I: The Elevation of Self and Derogation of the Spirit

1. E. Campos et al. (1994), "Social Networks and Daily Activities of Street Youth in Belo Horizonte, Brazil," *Child Development, 65*: 319–331.

2. For an excellent discussion of modernity's implicit assumptions, see D. Bell (1976), *The Cultural Contradictions of Capitalism* (New York: Basic Books). For his core definition of modernity, Bell quotes Irving Howe: "Modernity, [Howe] writes, 'consists in a revolt against the prevailing style, *an unyielding rage against* the official order'" (Bell, p. 46).

3. A. Etzioni (1993), *The Spirit of Community: Rights, Responsibilities and the Communitarian Agenda* (New York: Crown), p. 116.

4. Ibid., p. 259.

5. F. Nietzsche (1967), *The Will to Power*, trans. by W. Kaufmann and R. J. Hollingdale (New York: Random House).

6. Bell, *Cultural Contradictions*.

7. See, for example, C. Lasch (1992), *The Once and Future Heaven* (New York: Random House).

8. I. Sigel, A McGillicuddy-DeLisi, and J. Goodnow (Eds.) (1992), *Parental Belief Systems: The Consequences for Children* (Hillsdale, NJ: Erlbaum).

9. Bell, *Cultural Contradictions*, p. 49.

10. Ibid., p. 28.

11. W. Kaminer (1992), *I'm Dysfunctional, You're Dysfunctional: The Recovery Movement and Other Self-Help Fashions* (Reading, MA: Addison-Wesley).

12. M. Levine and J. Seligmann (1973), *The Parent's Encyclopedia of Infancy, Childhood, and Adolescence* (New York: Thomas Y. Crowell), p. 423.

13. T. Rubin (1990), *Child Potential: Fulfilling Your Child's Intellectual, Emotional, and Creative Promise* (New York: Continuum), p. 39.

14. M. McKay and P. Fanning (1988), *Self-Esteem* (New York: St. Martin's Press), p. 309.

15. T. Gordon (1989), *Teaching Children Self-Discipline at Home and at School: New Ways Parents and Teachers Can Build Self-Control, Self-Esteem, and Self-Reliance* (New York: Random House), p. 135.

16. In the McKay and Fanning book, cited above, parents are urged to "Find occasion to frequently praise your child. . . . Display your child's work, trophies, stories, or Play-Doh sculptures. . . . Recount how patient, inventive, determined, or creative he or she was" (pp. 314–315). As I have discussed in *The Moral Child*, such on emphasis on praise would seem odd to parents in more traditional parts of the world, where cultural norms require no more than silent acknowledgment when children do something right (and firm sanctions when they do something wrong). Anthropologists have suggested that the effort to praise children extensively for every small deed may be linked to a behavioral pattern that is also largely absent in traditional societies: the attention-seeking "showing-off" that many modern-day children exhibit often and without embarrassment. See R. A. LeVine, P. M. Miller, and M. Maxwell (Eds.) (1988), "Parental Behavior in Diverse Societies," *New Directions for Child Development, 11*: 40.

17. W. Damon and D. Hart (1988), *Self-Understanding in Childhood and Adolescence* (New York: Cambridge University Press).

18. R. Wylie (1979), *The Self-Concept: Theory and Research on Selected Topics* (Lincoln: University of Nebraska Press).

19. Ibid., p. 690.

20. For one critical perspective on this "finding," see C. Sommers (1993), *Who Stole Feminism?* (New York: Scribners).

21. Damon and Hart, *Self-Understanding*.

22. Asking this question systematically assumes a longitudinal design: that is, a study of *the same girl* at different times. Comparisons between statements of *different* girls from separate age cohorts would provide even weaker evidence for such a "loss," since we would not be able to determine whether variation among the statements were due to an age change or to some other cohort difference. Since I have not seen formal journal articles with methodology sections on this matter, I do not know the nature of the data that supports the publicized claims; but I have yet to see any reports that would suggest that longitudinal data has been collected.

23. W. Damon (1988), *The Moral Child* (New York: Free Press); interview originally reported in the *New York Times Magazine*, May 24, 1975.

24. *Diagnostic and Statistical Manual of Mental Disorders, DSM-III-R*, 3rd ed. rev. (Washington, DC: American Psychiatric Association, 1987).

25. For an excellent philosophical treatment of this point, see J. Feinberg (1992), "Psychological Egoism," in *Freedom and Fulfillment: Philosophical Essays* (Princeton, NJ: Princeton University Press). As Feinberg notes: "An exclusive desire for happiness is the surest way to prevent happiness from coming into being. Happiness has a way of 'sneaking up' on persons when they are preoccupied with other things, but when persons deliberately and single-mindedly set off in pursuit of happiness, it vanishes utterly from sight and cannot be captured" (p. 11). It is my contention here that every word of Feingold's statement is true also of self-esteem.

26. N. Noddings (1993), *Education for Intelligent Belief or Unbelief* (New York: Teachers College Press).

27. N. Garmezy (1983), "Stressors of Childhood," in N. Garmezy and M. Rutter (Eds.), *Stress, Coping, and Development in Children* (New York: McGraw-Hill), pp. 43–84.

28. B. Spock (1988), *Dr. Spock on Parenting* (New York: Simon & Schuster).

29. Ibid., p. 270.

30. B. B. Whiting and J. W. M. Whiting (1975), *Children of Six Cultures: A Psychocultural Analysis* (Cambridge, MA: Harvard University Press); and B. B. Whiting and C. P. Edwards (1988), *Children of Different Worlds* (Cambridge, MA: Harvard University Press).

31. D. Elkind (1981), *The Hurried Child: Growing Up Too Fast Too Soon* (Reading, MA: Addison-Wesley). The Fall 1994 catalogue of Harvard University Press announces a new David Elkind book entitled *Ties That Bind*. The cat-

alogue describes the book as claiming that "childhood innocence has been superseded by the illusion of childhood competence." According to the blurb, this is one of the factors that has "undermined the well-being of children and adolescents." Among the other factors is that "the needs of hurried children have been sacrificed to the needs of their harried parents" (p.3).

32. L. J. Stone, H. T. Smith, and L. B. Murphy (1973), *The Competent Infant: Research and Commentary* (New York: Basic Books).

33. R. W. White (1960), "Competence and the Psychosexual Stages of Development," in M. R. Jones (Ed.), *Nebraska Symposium on Motivation* (Lincoln: University of Nebraska Press), pp. 97–141.

34. E. J. Susman (1991), "Stress and the Adolescent," in R. M. Lerner, A. C. Petersen, and J. Brooks-Gunn (Eds.), *Encyclopedia of Adolescence* (New York: Garland); and A. G. Gray (1987), *The Psychology of Fear and Stress* (Cambridge: Cambridge University Press).

35. G. Elder (1972), *Children of the Great Depression* (Chicago: University of Chicago Press).

36. For a description of this effort, see R. M. Lerner and F. A. Villarruel (Eds.) (1994), *Promoting Community-based Programs for Learning* (San Francisco: Jossey-Bass).

37. I note for the record that the project later was funded by other agencies with the foresight to ignore such conventional wisdom. By now we have shelves of videos and other records documenting the deep reserves of energy that children can display when they are given tasks that challenge their abilities. Of course, if children are to unleash their formidable energies in the right directions, they must be given the message that they can rise to the challenge—that they *can* contribute, they *can* learn, they *can* accomplish.

38. "Even the word spiritual may make [some people] a bit suspicious," he writes, "as if it might be a disguise for religion." (Spock, *On Parenting*, p. 269). Spock then goes on to give his broader definition that I have quoted above.

39. See R. Coles (1990), *The Spiritual Life of Children* (Boston: Houghton Mifflin), for a moving account of this struggle within the psychiatric profession.

40. S. Freud (1964/1927), *The Future of an Illusion* (Garden City, NY: Anchor Books).

41. J. Piaget (1929), *The Child's Conception of the World* (London: Routledge and Kegan Paul).

42. A. M. Rizzuto (1991), "Religious Development: A Psychoanalytic Point of View," in F. K. Oser and G.W. Scarlett (Eds.), *Religious Development in Childhood and Adolescence* (*New Directions for Child Development No. 52*) (San Francisco: Jossey-Bass).

43. J. W. Fowler (1989), "Strength for the Journey: Early Childhood and the Development of Selfhood and Faith," in D. Blazer (Ed.) *Faith Development and Early Childhood* (Kansas City, MO: Sheed and Ward).

44. J. Fowler (1991), "Stages of Faith Consciousness," in F. K. Oser and G. W. Scarlett (Eds.), *Religious Development in Childhood and Adolescence* (*New Directions for Child Development No. 52*) (San Francisco: Jossey-Bass).

45. Ibid., p. 35.

46. Coles, *The Spiritual Life of Children*.

47. Ibid., p. 100.

48. Ibid., p. 127.

49. Ibid., p. 109.

50. *The Moral Child*, pp. 9–10.

Chapter 5. Misconceptions of Modern Times, II: The False Oppositions

1. Phi Delta Kappa/Gallup Poll, 1993.

2. "Efforts to Promote Teaching of Values in Schools Are Sparking Heated Debate Among Lawmakers," *Wall Street Journal*, May 10, 1994.

3. Ibid.

4. D. Tannen, "A Destructive Culture of Critique," *International Herald Tribune*, January 18, 1994, p. 7.

5. G. H. Elder Jr., J. Modell, and R. D. Parke (1993), *Children in Time and Place: Developmental and Historical Insights* (New York: Cambridge University Press).

6. F. Ianni (1989), *The Structure of Experience* (New York: Free Press).

7. See W. Damon (1993), *Social and Personality Development* (New York: Norton).

8. P. Aries (1965), *Centuries of Childhood* (New York: Vintage).

9. J. J. Rousseau (1798/1979), *Emile* (New York: Basic Books).

10. For the most comprehensive and accessible statement, see J. Piaget (1983), "Piaget's Theory," in P. Mussen (Ed.), *Handbook of Child Psychology: Volume I, Theory and History* (New York: Wiley).

11. J. Flavell (1986), *Cognitive Development*. (Englewood Cliffs, NJ: Prentice-Hall).

12. B. F. Skinner (1965), *Science and Human Behavior* (New York: Free Press).

13. J. Piaget (1966), *Etudes Sociologiques* (Paris: Presses Universitaires). See also M. Chapman (1988), "Contextuality and Directionality of Cognitive Development," in *Human Development, 31* (2): 92–106. Unfortunately, most of Piaget's essays on social interaction have never been translated into English. For this reason, many social scientists are unaware of the social components in Piaget's theory and have criticized it on that basis. Yet even if its social components are removed (a thought that would have horrified Piaget), the theory remains fundamentally interactionist due to its vision of how people learn through feedback from the real world. Of course Piaget knew full well that people are a part of the real world, that they communicate with one another all the time, and that their learning is constantly affected by such communication. It is therefore absurd to ignore the contributions of social interaction to learning—and a prominent form of social interaction in a young learner's life is *instruction*, or "teaching," as we call it in our schools. Piaget's theory, therefore, does not support an unguided, laissez-faire approach to children's acquisition of skills and knowledge.

14. Especially work with the Vygotskian tradition—see J. V. Wertsch (1985), *Vygotsky and the Social Formation of the Mind* (Cambridge, MA: Harvard University Press).

15. C. T. Fosnot (in press), *Constructivism: Foundations, Perspectives, and Practice* (New York: Teachers College Press); and C. T. Fosnot (1989), *Enquiring Teachers, Enquiring Learners* (New York: Teachers College Press).

16. See H. Gardner (1992), *The Unschooled Mind* (New York: Basic Books), for an excellent statement about young children's preparedness for serious learning. Gardner argues that it is essential for early childhood education to prepare children for knowledge of academic disciplines such as math, science, history, and the humanities. Without sound early preparation, we cannot expect children to master these disciplines in the later school years: instead, we are doing nothing more than setting them up for eventual school failure.

17. I refer, of course, to frequently quoted musings of Socrates and Plato on the matter. The quotes are used to support the concept of education as letting the student's inner ideas unfold—a concept that indeed was built into the ancient root of the term education: *educe*. Though charming and evocative, such musings do not constitute either an adequate philosophy or science of learning. The interactive process, as I have noted, is more complex and dynamic than the ancients imagined.

18. D. K. Cohen (1990), "Revolution in One Classroom (or Then Again, Was It?)," *American Educator*, Fall.

19. Ibid., pp. 21–22.

20. M. Nissan (1992), "Beyond Intrinsic Motivation: Cultivating a 'Sense of the Desirable,'" in F. Oser, A. Dick, and J. L. Party, *Effective and Responsible Teaching: The New Synthesis* (San Francisco: Jossey-Bass), pp. 126–139.

21. By no means, though, are modern classroom practices the main source of this problem. Television programming, from *Sesame Street* down to the more commercial children's shows, appears almost consciously intent to create in young people short, impatient, and scattered attentional capacities.

22. E. D. Hirsch, Jr. (1988), *Cultural Literacy* (New York: Vintage). For a more complete discussion of Hirsch's treatise, see W. Damon (1990), "Reconciling the Literacies of Generations," *Daedalus, 119*: 33–55.

23. C. Lightfoot and J. Valisiner (1992), "Parental Belief Systems Under the Influence: Social Guidance of the Construction of Personal Cultures," in I. Sigel, A. McGillicuddy-DeLisi, and J. Goodnow (Eds.), *Parental Belief Systems: The Consequences for Children* (Hillsdale, NJ: Erlbaum).

24. M. Wolfenstein (1955), "The Fun Morality," in M. Mead and M. Wolfenstein (Eds.), *Childhood in Contemporary Cultures* (Chicago: University of Chicago Press).

25. Ibid.

26. Lightfoot and Valisiner, "Parental Belief Systems Under the Influence," p. 404.

27. Ibid., p. 407.

28. D. Eyer (1992), *Mother-Infant Bonding: Scientific Fiction* (New Haven: Yale University Press).

29. Ibid., p. 2.

30. M. Klause and J. Kennell (1976), *Maternal-Infant Bonding: The Impact of Early Separation or Loss on Family Development* (St. Louis: Mosby).

31. Quoted in Eyer, *Mother-Infant Bonding*, p. 4.

32. See M. Lamb (1982), "The Bonding Phenomenon: Misinterpretations and Their Implications," *J. Pediatrics, 101*: 555–557, in which he writes: "findings provide very little support for the beneficial effects of early contact." See also M. Lamb and C. Hwang (1982), "Maternal Attachment and Mother-Neonate Bonding: A Critical Review," in M. E. Lamb and A. L. Brown (Eds.), *Advances in Developmental Psychology*, Volume 2 (Hillsdale, NJ: Erlbaum).

33. In a popular book intended for parents, researcher Burton White wrote:

"Even I, a non-expert on infant research, could see through the spurious statements early on" (*A Parent's Guide to the First Three Years of Life* [Englewood Cliffs, NJ: Prentice-Hall, 1980], p. 14). In a 1983 textbook (W. Damon, *Social and Personality Development*, New York: Norton), I wrote that careful research "found virtually no signs of a biologically based bonding process arising out of mothers' initial contacts with their infants" (p. 29). I include my own writings here not to claim prescience but to do exactly the opposite. The word on bonding was out over a decade ago, so much so that many of us well outside the inner circles of work in this area knew enough to dismiss the notion. Yet the medical profession still continues to exploit the idea.

34. I am convinced that a main reason for the bonding notion's broad and quick acceptance within the medical community is the rhetorical similarity between the terms "attachment" and "bonding." If this is so, bonding is the cowbird of the behavioral sciences. It has fed off a grand tradition of theory and research going back to Freud, Bowbly, and Mary Ainsworth, and that continues to produce sound new insights about normal and abnormal personality development. Just as the idea of bonding stole attachment's glory when it was introduced, it may shed unfavorable light on attachment as its errors are revealed. I have, in fact, seen signs of this already, to my distress. One differences that I have with Eyer, Michael Lamb, and others who have helped us see through bonding's delusions is that their skepticism appears to generalize beyond bonding to attachment, which in my mind is an unfortunate and unnecessary conclusion that throws the baby out with the bathwater.

35. The most well-documented instance of this was documented by Anna Freud after World War II. Six young war orphans were brought from a Nazi concentration camp to an orphanage in England. These children had been one another's primary source of consistent human interaction since early in their infancies. Even in England, they continued for quite some time to rely on one another and to reject the overtures of adults. Nevertheless, they were diagnosed as well-functioning in most essential linguistic, cognitive, and social-emotional ways and eventually adapted successfully to their new lives. Their own peer support system seemed to suffice for establishing the rudiments of psychological health. See Damon, *Social and Personality Development*, pp. 52–54, for an extended account of this case.

36. T. B. Brazelton (1985), *Working and Caring* (Reading, MA: Addison-Wesley).

37. S. Fraiburg (1979), *Every Child's Birthright* (New York: Basic Books).

38. For excellent summaries, see J. Kagan (1979), "Family Experience and the Child's Development," *American Psychologist, 34*: 886–891; and K. McCartney (1990), *Child and Maternal Employment: A Social Ecology Approach.* (San Francisco: Jossey-Bass).

39. Brazelton, *Working and Caring*, p. 55; also quoted in Eyer, *Mother-Infant Bonding*, p. 193.

40. "Miss Manners" column, quoted from the *Boston Globe*, October 19, 1989.

41. Historian Philip Greven has reviewed many of these books in his own impassioned treatise, *Spare the Child: The Religious Roots of Punishment and the Psychological Impact of Physical Abuse* (New York: Knopf, 1991). As I discuss below, however, Greven's revulsion against corporal punishment leads him into some imbalances of a different sort.

42. See J. Stormer (1984), *Growing Up God's Way* (Florissant, MO: Liberty Bell Press), especially pp. 70–71.

43. My intention here is not to endorse spanking as a disciplinary practice but to avoid caricaturing and demonizing all those who occasionally do it. To do so would be to commit precisely the same mistake that I am arguing against in this part of the book: oversimplifying and exaggerating the differences between childrearing strategies. In fact, as I mention elsewhere in this chapter, a vast majority of parents throughout the history of the world have practiced corporal punishment in some form or another. Some have done so abusively, but many have done in a manner that is very far from any reasonable definition of abuse. Although I believe that there are far more effective and less risky forms of discipline available to parents, I cannot accept the view that all parents who ever have spanked a child have caused grave or lasting harm.

44. Greven, *Spare the Child*.

45. Ibid., p. 37.

46. Greven's point, and that of many others who are justifiably concerned about the high incidence of child abuse, is that such distinctions are too slippery to be sustained. He writes: "All levels of violence against children, including the various forms of physical punishments, are hurtful and harmful." (Ibid., p. 9) By this standard, Greven would consider practically all living adults (including, he writes, himself) to have been harmed by physical punishment when children. I find this claim a bit exaggerated.

47. J. Durant, "Adult Beliefs about the Use of Physical Punishment with Children," paper presented to the Society for Research in Child Development, New Orleans, April 1993.

Chapter 6. The Native Virtues

1. Other behaviorist metaphors for the supposedly passive child included a camera recording observed events and lower-species organisms (rats, pigeons, and so on) responding to reward contingencies.

2. V. Zeligser (1984), *Pricing the Priceless Child* (New York: Basic Books).

3. L. H. William, H. S. Berman, L. Rose (1987), *The Too Precious Child: The Perils of Being a Super-Parent and How to Avoid Them* (New York: Atheneum).

4. M. H. Bornstein and M. E. Lamb (Eds.) (1992), *Developmental Psychology: An Advanced Textbook*, 3d ed. (Hillsdale, NJ: Erlbaum).

5. Yet when things go wrong in a young person's life, people increasingly turn first to superficial influences such as the media for the blame. The daily papers are an excellent indication of this sort of misattribution. Practically every time a juvenile crime story is reported, someone cites TV, music, or movies as the cause. As I write, today's paper (*Boston Globe*, October 21, 1993) has the following quote about a student convicted of gang rape: "He [the student's father] said the young man had watched 'negative' sex and violence on television. . . . 'how can we stop all this sex on television and violence?' he asked." I chose this quote not for its pithiness but because it is from the paper that sits on my desk today. If I looked yesterday, or tomorrow, or the next day, I could have found a similar quote about a similar incident.

6. And not just adult laypersons: for a psychologist's romantic fantasies about the nature of childhood, see S. Fraiburg (1968), *The Magic Years* (New York: Basic Books). Fraiburg's charming but fanciful book has influenced a generation of concerned parents to guard their children from engaging "prematurely" in the more serious realities of life.

7. For a classic paper on this point, see R. W. White (1960), "Competence and the Psychosexual Stages of Development," in M. R. Jones, *Nebraska Symposium on Motivation* (Lincoln: University of Nebraska Press), pp. 97–141. White's essay, which had an enormous impact on the field of psychology when it was first written, unfortunately ran counter to the mainstream of modern thinking and has not left its mark on popular views of children's development. The essay is as fresh and pertinent today as it was a generation ago.

8. Ann Brown, president of the American Educational Research Association and herself an eminent developmental researcher, recently complained of this in a talk at Harvard. She said that too many professionals were filled with notions that she described as "bad Piaget." Especially onerous in this

respect, she commented, was the notion that one can harm a child's intellectual growth by introducing an idea or a skill too early.

9. Nor was it at all what Piaget meant. Like many great creative figures, Piaget wrote voluminously, and some of his early writings did appear to reify the notion of "stage" in ways that may have led to the constructive imbalances that I have discussed. But in most places where he discussed the process of change, Piaget showed himself to be an interactionist who appreciated the importance of new ideas and social feedback in the child's development. Nowhere did Piaget suggest that new stages grow by themselves, which is the impression that has been left by constructivism's worst excesses.

10. L. Kohlberg and R. Mayer (1972), "Development as the Aim of Education," *Harvard Educational Review, 42*: 449–496.

11. My favorite statement of the former position, precisely because it is so baldly cynical, was made by the charmingly crotchety philosopher George Santayana: "In human nature, generous impulses are occasional or reversible. . . . They form amiable interludes like tearful sentiments in a ruffian, or they are pleasant self-deceptive hypocrisies acted out, like civility to strangers, because such in society is the path of least resistance. Strain the situation, however, dig a little beneath the surface, and you will find a ferocious, persistent, profoundly selfish man."

12. J. Q. Wilson (1993), *The Moral Sense* (New York: Free Press).

13. A. Etzioni (1988), *The Moral Dimension: Toward a New Economics* (New York: Free Press).

14. Some would say that the formative interaction between culture and nature occurs even earlier than birth, through mechanisms such as reproductive selection and prenatal stimulation. See M. Cole (in press), "Culture and Cognitive Development: Interacting Minds in a Life-Span Perspective," in P. Baltes and U. Staudinger (Eds.), *Interactive Minds: Life-span Perspectives on the Social Formation of Cognition* (Chicago: University of Chicago Press).

15. Wilson, *The Moral Sense*.

16. J. Kagan (1984), *The Nature of the Child* (New York: Basic Books).

17. E. Turiel, M. Killen, and C. C. Helwig (1987), "Morality: Its Structure, Functions, and Vagaries," in J. Kagan and S. Lamb (Eds.), *The Emergence of Moral Concepts in Young Children* (Chicago: University of Chicago Press), pp. 155–244.

18. W. Damon (1977), *The Social World of the Child* (San Francisco: Jossey-Bass); W. Damon (1983), *Social and Personality Development* (New York: Norton); and C. Shantz (1983), "Social Cognition," in P. H. Mussen, J. H.

Flavell, and E. M. Markamn (Eds.), *Handbook of Child Psychology: Vol. 3. Cognitive Development* (New York: Wiley), pp. 495–555.

19. W. Damon and D. Hart (1988), *Self-Understanding in Childhood and Adolescence* (New York: Cambridge University Press).

20. N. Eisenberg and J. Strayer (1987), *Empathy and Its Development* (New York: Cambridge University Press); and J. Strayer (1980), "A Naturalistic Study of Empathetic Behaviors and Their Relation to Affective States and Perspective-taking Skills in Preschool Children," *Child Development, 51*: 815–822.

21. N. Eisenberg (1989), "Empathy and Sympathy," in W. Damon (Ed.), *Child Development Today and Tomorrow* (San Francisco: Jossey-Bass).

22. J. Campos, R. Campos, and K. Barrett (1989), "Emergent Themes in the Study of Emotional Development," *Developmental Psychology, 25*: 8–32.

23. J. Piaget (1951), *Play, Dreams, and Imitation in Childhood* (New York: Norton).

24. A. Sagi and M. L. Hoffman (1976), "Empathetic Distress in Newborns," *Developmental Psychology, 12*: 175–176.

25. J. Kagan (1984), *The Nature of the Child* (New York: Basic Books).

26. E. H. Erikson (1950), *Childhood and Society* (New York: Norton).

27. D. Miller and G. Swanson (1960), *Inner Conflict and Defense* (New York: Holt).

28. Damon, *The Social World of the Child*; W. Damon (1988), *The Moral Child* (New York: Free Press); P. Ekman (1972), "Universals and Cultural Differences in Facial Expressions of Emotions," in *Nebraska Symposium on Motivation, 19*: 513–537; P. Ekman (1984), "Expression and the Nature of Emotion," in K. R. Scherer and P. Ekman (Eds.), *Approaches to Emotion* (Hillsdale, NJ: Erlbaum); and C. Izard (1977), *Human Emotions* (New York: Plenum).

29. M. L. Hoffman (1984), "Interaction of Affect and Cognition on Empathy," in C. Izard, J. Kagan, and R. B. Zajonc (Eds.), *Emotions, Cognition and Behavior* (Cambridge, England: Cambridge University Press).

30. R. Selman (1980), *The Growth of Interpersonal Understanding* (New York: Academic Press).

31. See Damon, *The Moral Child*.

32. E. Tronick (1989), "Emotions and Emotional Communication," *American Psychologist, 44*: 112–119.

33. C. Trevarthen (1992), "The Self Born in Intersubjectivity: An Infant Communicating," in V. Neisser (Ed.), *Ecological and Interpersonal Knowledge of the Self* (New York: Cambridge University Press).

34. L. Murray and C. Trevarthen (1985), "Emotional Regulation of Interactions Between Two-month-olds and Their Mothers," in T. Field and N. Fox (Eds.), *Social Perception in Infants* (Norwood, NJ: Ablex).

35. Damon, *Social and Personality Development*.

36. P. Guillaume (1926/1971), *Imitation in Children* (Chicago: University of Chicago Press).

37. Damon, *Social and Personality Development*.

38. Damon, *The Moral Child*.

39. Piaget, *Play, Dreams, and Imitation in Childhood*.

40. Damon, *The Social World of the Child*.

41. N. Mueller (1989), "Toddler's Peer Relations," in W. Damon (Ed.), *Child Development Today and Tomorrow* (San Francisco: Jossey-Bass).

42. W. Damon (1980), "Patterns of Change in Children's Social Reasoning: A Two-year Longitudinal Study," *Child Development, 53*: 831–857.

43. L. A. Sroufe (1988), "The Role of the Infant Caregiver: Attachment in Development," in J. Belsky and R. Nezworski (Eds.), *Clinical Implications of Attachment* (Hillsdale, NJ: Erlbaum), pp. 18–40.

44. M. Lewis and J. Brooks-Gunn (1979), *Social Cognition and the Acquisition of Self* (New York: Plenum).

45. Campos et al., "Emergent Themes in the Study of Emotional Development."

46. W. Damon and D. Hart (1982), "The Development of Self-Understanding from Infancy Through Adolescence," *Child Development, 52*, 841–864; and Damon and Hart, *Self-Understanding in Childhood and Adolescence*.

47. G. Nunner-Winkler and B. Sodian (1988), "Children's Understanding of Moral Emotions," *Child Development, 59*: 1323–38.

48. W. Damon (1984), "Self-Understanding and Moral Development from Childhood to Adolescence," in W. Kurtines and J. Gewirtz (Eds.), *Morality, Moral Behavior, and Moral Development* (New York: Wiley); and Damon and Hart, *Self-Understanding in Childhood and Adolescence*.

49. S. Oliner and P. Oliner (1988), *The Altruistic Personality* (New York: Free Press); and A. Colby and W. Damon (1992), *Some Do Care: Contemporary Lives of Moral Commitment* (New York: Free Press).

50. A. Blasi (1984), "Moral Identity: Its Role in Moral Functioning," in Kurtines and Gewirtz, *Morality, Moral Behavior, and Moral Development*.

51. A. Blasi (1983), "Moral Cognition and Moral Action: A Theoretical Perspective," *Developmental Review, 3*: 178–210; and A. Blasi and R. Oresick (1986), "Emotions and Cognitions in Self-Inconsistency," in D. Bearison

and H. Zimiles (Eds.), *Thought and Emotion: Developmental Perspectives* (Hillsdale, NJ: Erlbaum).

52. Damon, "Self-Understanding and Moral Development"; and Damon and Hart, *Self-Understanding in Childhood and Adolescence*.

53. Blasi, "Moral Identity"; Blasi and Oresick, "Emotions and Cognitions in Self-inconsistency"; P. Davidson and J. Youniss (1991), "Which Comes First: Morality or Identity?" in W. Kurtines and J. Gewirtz (eds.), *Handbook of Moral Behavior and Development* (Hillsdale, NJ: Erlbaum); and A. Colby and W. Damon (1992), *Some Do Care: Contemporary Lives of Moral Commitment* (New York: Free Press).

54. A. Caspi, G. Elder, and D. Bem (1989), "Continuities and Consequences of Interactional Styles Across the Life Course," *Journal of Personality, 57(2)*: 376–406.

55. Colby and Damon, *Some Do Care*.

Chapter 7. A Framework of Guidance for Children's Intellectual and Moral Growth

1. I am grateful to Michael Cole for the "second nature" metaphor.

2. Probably the most famous examples of such polemics approach in recent years have been E. D. Hirsch's widely circulated books on "cultural literacy"—E. D. Hirsch, Jr. (1988), *Cultural Literacy* (New York: Vintage); and E. D. Hirsch, Jr. (1992), *The Dictionary of Cultural Literacy* (New York: Vintage). In his writings, Hirsch deplores the "natural development" theories that liken the child to an "acorn" growing into a "tree"—theories which he claims have spawned the "new kind of teaching"—and sets himself on the environmental/acculturation side. Whatever rhetorical fruits there are to be gathered from such an opposition, it certainly does not represent the current state of thinking in developmental psychology. Virtually all contemporary developmental theorists are interactionists. No serious scholar in child development today could disavow the dynamic interplay between culture and individual growth. No scientific position holds that children develop like acorns. The controversies in the field revolve not around the question of whether interaction occurs, nor even on whether it is critical to development; but rather on the form and direction of the interaction. Here we do find differences between those who would emphasize biological processes, those who would emphasize social processes, those who would emphasize linguistic processes, and so on. One would think that a scholar who pre-

sumes to set an agenda for educational reform—and particularly a scholar who claims to be committed to the accumulated knowledge of cultures—would attempt to understand and use the best knowledge available about such matters. But the intricacies of human development elude Mr. Hirsch, just as I am sure the intricacies of history or geography would elude any student whose education consisted of learning Mr. Hirsch's lists. A passing acquaintance with facts does not define the depths of functional literacy, "cultural" or otherwise.

3. For a review of how these terms have been used in the child development literature, see W. Damon (1983), *Social and Personality Development* (New York: Norton); and W. Damon (1988), *The Moral Child* (New York: Free Press). See also Barbara Rogoff's magnificently detailed analysis of "guided participation" in her recent book by that title—B. Rogoff, J. Mistry, A. Goncu, and C. Mosier (1993), *Guided Participation in Cultural Activity by Toddlers and Caregivers*, Monographs of the Society for Research on Child Development, Vol. 58, no. 8.

4. In many recent developmental writings, the process has been called "scaffolding" because of the supportive guidance that it requires. The idea is that, as the child assumes more and more of the adult's perspective, the adult instinctively removes the "scaffold" of support bit by bit. Many developmentalists are generally favorable toward this theoretical approach, but some have worried that it may miss some of the child's own creative contributions to the adoption of another's goals. As Peg Griffin and Michael Cole have written: "The scaffold metaphor leaves open questions of the child's creativity. If the adult support bears an inverse relation to the child's competence, then there is a strong sense of teleology—children's development is circumscribed by the adults' achieved wisdom." The same authors are also concerned with the model's seeming implication that the adult's guidance occurs mechanically, programmed to match the sequence in which the behavior is modeled. They argue that social influence is a more irregular, almost organic, process. It takes place on many psychological levels at once, and remains closely in tune with the child's own agenda: ". . . scaffolding—bolted together tiers of boards upon which humans stand to construct a building—admits far more easily of variation in amount than in kind. Yet the changes in adult support ordinarily reported in scaffolding research point to qualitatively distinct kinds of support. Sometimes the adult directs attention. At other times, the adult holds important information in memory. At still other times, the adult offers simple encourage-

ment." P. Griffin and M. Cole, "Current Activity for the Future: The Zoped," in B. Rogoff and V. Wertsch, *New Directions for Child Development, 23*: 47.

5. J. S. Brown, A. Collins, and P. Deguid (1989), "Situated Cognition and the Culture of Learning," *Educational Researcher, 18* (1): 32–42.

6. J. Lave and E. Wenger (1991), *Situated Learning: Legitimate Peripheral Participation* (Cambridge: Cambridge University Press).

7. Damon, *The Moral Child.*

8. D. Baumrind (1989), "Rearing Competent Children," in W. Damon (Ed.), *Child Development Today and Tomorrow* (San Francisco: Jossey-Bass).

9. W. Damon (1983), *Social and Personality Development* (New York: Norton); and W. Damon and D. Hart (1992), "Self-Understanding and Its Role in Social and Moral Development," in M. H. Bornstein and M. E. Lamb, *Developmental Psychology: An Advanced Textbook, 3d ed.* (Hillsdale, NJ: Erlbaum), pp. 421–464.

10. E. Turiel, M. Killen, and P. Davidson (1987), "Morality: Its Structure, Function, and Vagaries," in J. Kagan and S. Lamb (Eds.), *The Emergence of Morality in Young Children* (Chicago: University of Chicago Press).

11. W. J. Bennet and E. J. Delattre (1979), "A Moral Education: Some Thoughts on How to Best Achieve It," *American Education, 3*: 3–6; and Damon, *The Moral Child.*

12. When children regularly misuse their skills, they may drift toward delinquency and, eventually, the kinds of character disorders that may lead to intransigent psychopathologies. When they find no sustaining purpose for their skills, the skills will atrophy. I believe that this is why so many child prodigies lose interest in their early talents by the time that they reach adolescence. See D. Feldman and L. Goldsmith (1980), *Nature's Gambit: Child Prodigies and the Development of Human Potential* (New York: Basic Books).

13. In earlier times, this was considered no more than common sense. See, for example, the childrearing advice expressed in Anne Bradstreet's poetry, in J. R. McElrath and A. P. Robb (Eds.) (1981), *The Complete Work of Anne Bradstreet* (Boston: Twayne).

14. Hirsch, *Cultural Literacy*; and Hirsch, *Dictionary of Cultural Literacy.*

15. H. Gardner (1980), *Artful Scribbles; The Significance of Children's Drawings* (New York: Basic Books).

16. D. Perkins (1993), *Smart Schools* (New York: Free Press).

17. See A. Colby and W. Damon (1992), *Some Do Care: Contemporary Lives of Moral Commitment* (New York: Free Press).

18. Ibid.
19. Ibid.
20. Ibid.

Chapter 8. Parenting

1. In Massachusetts recently a bill was introduced before the state legislature that would hold parents civilly and criminally liable for misdeeds of their children. Many states now have laws that hold the parent at fault if their minor children provide alcohol or illegal substances to others on the premises of the family home or automobile, the parent's ignorance of the transaction notwithstanding.

2. P. Leach (1989), *Your Baby and Child from Birth to Age Five* (New York: Knopf).

3. Ibid., p. 316.

4. Ibid., pp. 316–317.

5. Ibid., pp. 460–461.

6. Ibid., p. 461.

7. Ibid., p. 463.

8. One learns in social science not to make too much of anecdotal evidence; but I cite these three examples as accounts that I have heard from friends and family and read in the newspapers just this past week. I consider this significant simply because it is so unexceptional. No week passes without similar stories. I wonder whether we shall become so inured to these types of things that they will cease being noteworthy altogether. At that point, I suppose (and fear), the stories will stop being told. Of course, a more hopeful prospect would be an improvement in our means of parental communication and control.

9. This observation was reported to me by Anne Colby.

10. A. Etzioni (1993), *The Spirit of Community* (New York: Crown).

11. "Reinventing 'the Good Mother' by Necessity," *Boston Globe*, May 8, 1994.

12. G. Elder (1975), *Children of the Great Depression* (Chicago: University of Chicago Press).

13. S. B. Heath and M. W. McLaughlin (Eds.) (1993), *Identity and Inner-City Youth: Beyond Ethnicity and Gender* (New York: Teachers College Press).

14. I say "today's society" because I wish to emphasize my belief that, despite the timeless nature of socialization principles, each new generation of children is different (as is each individual child); and successful parenting recognizes the difference. This is implicit in the communication component

of socialization: open, two-way communication will keep a parent in touch with the particular interests of contemporary children, as it must if the socializing connection is to be maintained throughout the child's entire youth.

15. D. Baumrind (1989), "Rearing Competent Children," in W. Damon (Ed.), *Child Development Today and Tomorrow* (San Francisco: Jossey-Bass), pp. 349–379.

16. T. Dix (1992), "Parenting on Behalf of the Child: Empathic Goals in the Regulation of Responsive Parenting," in I. Sigel, A.V. McGillicuddy-DeLisi, and J. J. Goodnow (Eds), *Parental Belief Systems: The Psychological Consequences for Children* (Hillsdale, NJ: Erlbaum), pp. 319–347.

17. Dix, "Parenting," p. 323.

18. Ibid.

19. I have found Dix's analysis valuable because of this taxonomy. The use that I make of his three classes of parental goals, however, is somewhat different from the use that Dix makes of them. Dix stresses the importance of empathic parenting. I agree with this point but make a somewhat different argument—namely that if parents are to succeed in socializing their children, they must achieve a balance between these different types of goals.

20. W. Damon (1983), *Social and Personality Development* (New York: Norton); W. Hartup (1989), "Social Relationships and Their Developmental Significance," *American Psychologist, 44*: 120–126; and J. Youniss (1980), *Parents and Peers in Social Development: A Sullivan-Piaget Perspective* (Chicago: University of Chicago Press).

21. Dix, "Parenting," p. 341.

22. To my dismay, I have heard this concern repeatedly when I give talks to parent groups about child development.

23. Thomas Gordon (1989), *Teaching Children Self-Discipline at Home and at School: New Ways Parents and Teachers Can Build Self-Control, Self-Esteem, and Self-Reliance* (New York: Random House).

24. Ibid., p. 6.

25. Ibid., p. 22.

26. Ibid., pp. 90, 98.

27. Ibid., pp. 106–111.

28. Ibid., pp. 205–206.

29. Ibid.; on page 135, Gordon writes "Self-esteem—or the lack of it—is critical in people's lives." He then goes on to recount a number of empirical associations between self-esteem and motivation, achievement, IQ, athletic ability, social skill, and personal attractiveness. As I have discussed at length

in Chapter 6, most of such associations are spurious. Even the correlational studies with some validity have the direction of causality wrong: self-esteem may result from achievement and hard work, but it does not produce it.

30. For a summary, see Damon, *Social and Personality Development*.

31. Ibid.

32. M. L. Hoffman (1984), "Interaction of Affect and Cognition on Empathy," in C. Izard, J. Kagan, and R. B. Zajonc (Eds.), *Emotions, Cognition and Behavior* (Cambridge, England: Cambridge University Press); and E. E. Maccoby and J. A. Martin (1983), "Socialization in the Context of the Family: Parent-Child Interaction," in P. H. Mussen (Ed.), *Handbook of Child Psychology*, Vol. 4 (New York: Wiley).

33. Maccoby and Martin, "Socialization."

34. Hoffman, "Interaction."

35. M. R. Lepper (1983), "Social Control Processes, Attributions of Motivation, and the Internalization of Social Values," in E. T. Higgins, D. N. Ruble, and W. W. Hartup (Eds.), *Social Cognition and Social Behavior: Developmental Perspectives* (New York: Cambridge University Press).

36. Ibid.

37. Ibid.

38. Ibid.

39. R. A. LeVine (1980), "Anthropolgy and Child Development," *New Directions for Child Development, 8*: 71–86.

40. Ibid.

41. Gordon, *Teaching Children*, p.43.

42. Ibid., p.45

43. Ibid., pp.44–58. Gordon's real objection, with praise as with punishment, is to the notion of parental control, whether implemented through sanction or through reward. Here is the crux of my disagreement with Gordon and his PET movement, as well as with the vast majority of childrearing experts writing today. Gordon argues against imposing external controls on children because it is more important to foster the child's internal controls; he assumes that the two types of control stand in opposition one another. Although I agree that imposing *overbearing* external controls on children is counterproductive, I do not believe that children can develop internal controls without participating in relationships that guide, inform, and, yes, at times control their behavior. Internal control certainly should be our goal for our children's development. But internal control only arises out of rela-

tionships that provide some external control; it cannot bypass the experience of external control entirely.

44. W. Damon (1988), *The Moral Child* (New York: Free Press).

45. In *The Moral Child* I recounted the story of a man who deceived his children about his own misdeeds because he felt that he needed to remain a hero figure in their eyes. When they found out the truth, they developed a strong mistrust of both him and the relationship. The children also conducted some misdeeds that their father found reprehensible; but he no longer was able to admonish them in a way that could reach them. In a vain pursuit of untenable "hero" status, the father had given away the moral credibility of his parental relationship. In my speaking tour following publication of *The Moral Child*, this was the single incident that garnered the strongest response. Many parents told me that they had experienced a shock of recognition when they read my account of the incident. I believe that this is the type of mistake that many well-intentioned people make, in smaller or larger ways.

Chapter 9. Schooling

1. For the harsher ones see T. Sizer (1992), *Horace's School; Redesigning the American High School* (New York: Houghton Mifflin); J. Kozol (1991), *Savage Inequalities; Children in America's Schools* (New York: Crown); and C. Finn (1992), *We Must Take Charge: Our Schools and Our Future* (New York: Free Press). For more sympathetic takes see S. Lightfoot (1983), *The Good High School: Portraits of Character and Culture* (New York: Basic Books); D. Perkins (1993), *Smart Schools: From Training Memories to Educating Minds* (New York: Free Press); T. Kidder (1989), *Among Schoolchildren* (Boston: Houghton Mifflin); and H. Gardner (1991), *The Unschooled Mind* (New York: Basic Books).

2. "Fed Up with Schools, More Parents Turn to Teaching at Home," *Wall Street Journal*, May 10, 1994. Not only are many parents removing their children from our schools; others are expressing their dissatisfaction by taking the schools to court. A lawyer for the National School Boards Association recently was quoted as saying: "It used to be if a student was accused of doing something wrong, the parent said: 'If the teacher said you did something wrong, they're right.' Now they say, 'We'll sue'" ("More Students and Parents Take Their Schools to Court," *Wall Street Journal*, July 6, 1994, p. B1).

3. P. Leach (1994), *Children First: What Our Society Must Do—and Is Not Doing—for Our Children Today* (New York: Knopf).

4. T. Sizer (1984), *Horace's Compromise; The Dilemma of the American High School* (Boston: Houghton Mifflin); and H. Gardner (1991), *The Unschooled Mind; How Children Think and How Schools Should Teach* (New York: Basic Books).

5. A. Collins (in preparation), *Epistemic Forms: Generative Structures for Inquiry and Understanding.*

6. L. B. Resnick (1987), "Learning in School and Out," *Educational Researcher, 16* (10): 13–20

7. J. Solomon (1993), "Mr. Vision, Meet Mr. Reality; Chris Whittle's Empire Is Shaken," *Newsweek*, August 16, pp. 62–65.

8. As of this writing, it appears that the "Edison Project" will have a more limited scope than originally intended, in part because of difficulty raising sufficient capital. From what I have read about the more limited work that this company is planning, my impressions are that the company has put together a highly qualified team of experts who have created a good educational plan for the small number of schools that they will create. My reservations do not concern the plans of this particular company but rather the whole notion of schools for profit, which eventually could lead to a further draining of talent and resources from the public schools. What will happen to the great majority of children who are left behind?

9. A. Etzioni (1993), *The Spirit of Community* (New York: Crown).

10. M. Cole and S. Cole (1989), *The Development of Children* (New York: Scientific American Books); S. Scribner and M. Cole, "Cognitive Consequences of Formal and Informal Education," *Science, 182*: 553–559; and L. B. Resnick, "Learning in School and Out."

11. P. Aries (1962), *Centuries of Childhood: A Social History of Family Life*, trans. by R. Baldick (New York: Vintage).

12. For example, according to news reports, the two ten-year-olds who recently murdered a toddler they had taken from a British shopping mall were hardly ever seen in school.

13. Neither the traditional field of clinical psychology nor the newer subdiscipline of developmental psychopathology has been able to distinguish between the etiologies of these various youth problems. This either means that they have the same general root or that the analytic tools of the profession are not yet fine enough to detect separate roots. In lieu of convincing evidence otherwise, I believe that the greater wisdom resides with the former hypothesis.

14. My modest estimate, based on my own observations and reading of the reports and data, probably understates the degree of apathy among students in most of today's schools. I challenge anyone to come up with indications otherwise.

15. T. James and D. Tyack (1993), "Learning from Past Efforts to Reform High School," *Phi Delta Kappan*, February.

16. Sizer, *Horace's Compromise*.

17. G. Grant (1988), *The World We Created at Hamilton High* (Cambridge: Harvard University Press).

18. It has been frequently commented that the medical profession has strayed down the same wrong path, to the detriment of the people it serves.

19. Such as "Chapter 1."

20. National Education Goals Panel (1991), *The National Education Goals Report: Building a Nation of Learners* (Washington, DC: Government Printing Office).

21. The past thirty years have seen the introduction of teaching machines, audiovisual equipment, computers, and teleconferencing into the educational world. Each in turn has been heralded as "the answer" to schooling; and each has prompted the more zealous advocates of the new technology to suggest that here, at last, may be a way to replace (or at least diminish the centrality of) the teacher. None has succeeded. To do so would be to repeal the natural laws of children's learning.

22. See Sizer, *Horace's School*, for a discussion of the structural changes that could improve the conditions for teaching in our public schools.

23. See Gardner, *The Unschooled Mind*.

24. Gardner, *The Unschooled Mind*.

25. There are two such claims that I have heard in recent years, both of them absurd as well as harmful to young students. One is that math instruction should be deemphasized among minority populations of students who have tested poorly in math because it does not mesh well with their culture and, as a result, only serves to stigmatize them when they are given grades. This suggestion, if enacted, would penalize the very children who could most benefit from some additional encouragement and tutelage. These children are as bright and energetic as children everywhere, as every educational researcher (including my own group) that has worked with them in a constructive way has confirmed. To curtail their opportunity to excel in a crucial area such as math is a cruel underestimation of their abilities, no matter how well-intentioned.

   Fortunately, this first claim has been confined mostly to fringe groups, at least as of this writing. The second claim is far more widespread: I have heard, for example, distinguished heads of women's educational institutions express it. This is the claim that female minds are structured differently from male minds, especially with regards to subjects such as mathematical logic. As a consequence, women need a different sort of math and science instruction, which ultimately may lead to a different sort of discipline with its own stream of intuitive insight. Claims like this are a reaction to test scores that show female students to be at a disadvantage to male students beginning about in the fifth grade. (For example, on high school math tests, it has been found that, in the top five percent of students, boys outnumber girls by around 13 to 1). Such test results, however, may indicate nothing more than a persistent social stereotyping of girls that begins early in childhood: in too many social circles, math and science are still considered "unfeminine." To then reify these results into the conclusion that women are truly unable to compete in "male" math and science, and thus then they require their own branch discipline, is to institutionalize the stereotype in a way that will damage the future prospects of many young girls. Schools should be working to break down the stereotype and open greater opportunities for female students rather than perpetuating harmful myths about their limited potential.

26. A. J. Neill (1960), *Summerhill: A Radical Approach to Childrearing* (New York: Hart).

27. L. A. Cremin (1961), *The Transformation of the School: Progressivism in American Education* (New York: Knopf).

28. J. Dewey (1956), *The Child and the Curriculum* (Chicago: University of Chicago Press) (original work published in 1902); and Kilpatrick, W. H. (1926), "The Project Method," *Teachers College Record, 19*: 319–335.

29. Cremin, *The Transformation of the School*; L. Cuban (1984), *How Teachers Taught: Constancy and Change in American Classrooms, 1890–1980* (New York: Longman); and P. Graham (1967), *Progressive Education from Arcady to Academe: A History of the Progressive Education Association* (New York: Teachers College Press).

30. J. S. Brown, A. Collins, and P. Duguid (1989), "Situated Cognition and the Culture of Learning," *Educational Researcher, 18* (1): 32–42; and A. Collins, J. S. Brown, and A. Holum (1991), "Cognitive Apprenticeship: Making Thinking Visible," *American Educator, 15* (3): 6–11.

31. Collins, "Epistemic forms"; D. Perkins, "The Organization of Open-ended Thinking," paper presented at the 5th International Conference on Thinking in Townsville, Australia, July 1992; and D. Perkins and R. Sim-

mons (1988), "Patterns of Misunderstanding: An Integrative Model for Science, Math and Programming," *Review of Educational Research, 58*: 303–326.

32. E. G. Cohen (1984), "Talking and Working Together: Status, Interaction, and Learning," in P. Peterson, L. C. Wilkson, and M. Hallinan (Eds.), *Instructional Groups in the Classroom: Organization and Processes* (New York: Academic Press); W. Damon (1984), "Peer Education: The Untapped Potential," *Journal of Applied Developmental Psychology, 5*: 331–343; and W. Damon and E. Phelps (1989), "Strategic Uses of Peer Learning in Children's Education," in T. Berndt and G. Ladd (Eds.), *Peer Relationships in Child Development* (New York: Wiley).

33. E. G. Cohen (1986), *Designing Groupwork: Strategies for the Heterogenous Classroom* (New York: Teachers College Press); and W. Damon and E. Phelps (1990), "Critical Distinctions Among Three Approaches to Peer Education," *International Journal of Educational Research, 13*(1): 9–19.

34. Damon and Phelps, "Critical Distinctions."

35. J. Barell (1991), *Teaching for Thoughtfulness: Classroom Strategies to Enhance Intellectual Development* (New York: Longman); J. Baron (1987), *Being Disposed to Thinking: A Typology of Attitudes and Dispositions Related to Acquiring and Using Thinking Skills* (Boston: University of Massachusetts, Critical and Creative Thinking Program); R. I. Ennis (1987), "A Taxonomy of Critical Thinking Dispositions and Abilities," in J. B. Baron and R. S. Sternberg (Eds.), *Teaching Thinking Skills: Theory and Practice* (New York: W. H. Freeman), pp. 9–26; R. H. Ennis (1989), "Critical Thinking and Subject Specificity: Clarification and Needed Research, *Educational Researcher, 18* (3): 4–10; and D. Perkins, E. Jay, and S. Tishman (in press), "Beyond Abilities: A Dispositional Theory of Thinking," *Merill-Palmer Quarterly*.

36. T. Bird (1990), "The Schoolteacher Portfolio: An Essay of Possibilities," in J. Millman and L. Darling-Hammond (Eds.), *Handbook of Teacher Evaluation: Elementary and Secondary Personnel*, 2d ed. (Beverly Hills, CA: Sage); J. Frederiksen and A. Collins (1989), "A Systems Approach to Educational Testing," *Educational Researcher, 18* (9): 27–32; Gardner, *The Unschooled Mind*; H. Gardner (1992), "Assessment in Context: The Alternative to Standardized Testing," in B. Gifford and M. O'Conner (Eds.), *Changing Assessment: Alternative Views of Aptitude, Achievement, and Instruction* (Boston: Kluwer); L. Shulman (1988), "A Union of Insufficiencies: Strategies for Teacher Assessment in a Period of Educational Reform," *Educational Leadership, 46* (33): 36–41; G. Wiggins (1989), "A True Test: Toward More Authentic and More Equitable Assessment," *Phi Delta*

Kappan: 703–713; D. Wolf (1987/1988), "Opening Up Assessment: Ideas from the Arts," *Educational Leadership, 45* (4): 24–29; and D. Wolf (1989), "Portfolio Assessment: Sampling Student Work," *Educational Leadership, 46* (7): 35–49.

37. For example, R. Gallimore, J. Boggs, and C. Jordan (1974), *Culture, Behavior, and Education: A Study of Hawaiian-Americans* (Beverly Hills, CA: Sage); and R. Tharp and R. Gallimore (1988), *Rousing Minds to Life: Teaching, Learning, and Schooling in Social Context* (New York: Cambridge University Press).

38. Such as the successful Kamehameha Early Education Program (KEEP) described in Tharp and Gallimore, *Rousing Minds to Life.*

39. J. Piaget (1932/1965), *The Moral Judgment of the Child* (New York: Free Press).

40. S. Oliner and P. Oliner (1988), *The Altruistic Personality* (New York: Free Press).

41. J. Comer (1993), *School Power* (New York: Free Press). Comer's approach is a beacon of hope for the future of schooling in our society.

Chapter 10. Community and the Spirit of Youth

1. F. Furstenberg (1993), "How Families Manage Risk and Opportunity in Dangerous Neighborhoods," in W. J. Wilson (Ed.), *Sociology and the Public Agenda* (Newbury Park, CA: Sage Publications).

2. F. Ianni (1988), *The Structure of Experience* (New York: Free Press).

3. J. Gardner (1991), *Building Community* (Washington, DC: Independent Sector), p. 5. Also quoted in A. Etzioni (1993), *The Spirit of Community: Rights, Responsibilities, and the Communitarian Agenda* (New York: Crown).

4. "Disability Grants for Children Fuel Welfare Debate," *Boston Globe*, May 12, 1994.

5. Ibid.

6. E. M. Hetherington, M. Cox, and R. Cox (1982), "Effects of Divorce on Parents and Children," in M. Lamb (Ed.), *Non-traditional Families: Parenting and Child Development* (Hillsdale, NJ: Erlbaum); and E. M. Hetherington, M. S. Stanley-Hagan, and E. R. Anderson (1989), "Marital Transition: A Child's Perpective," *American Psychologist, 44* (2): 303–312.

7. S. B. Heath and M. W. McLaughlin (Eds.), *Identity and Inner-City Youth: Beyond Ethnicity and Gender* (New York: Teachers College Press, 1993).

8. "Facing the World" interview from the Bill Moyers' PBS show.

9. "The Vision for Public Schools: Communities of Learners" (1992). Unpublished mission statement, The Border Organization, Eagle Pass, TX.

10. F. Furstenberg, "How Families Manage Risk."

11. Of course, the gist of my suggestions in Chapter 9 was to make schooling more contextualized by engaging children in instructional projects with an authentic mission. But there are limits to the authenticity of even the most well-crafted school projects. A school newspaper project in which a child reporter writes stories is a motivating way to learn literacy skills, but it cannot provide all the rich supplementary knowledge of people and the techniques that a child would get by hanging around a town newspaper for an extended period of time. Schooling provides children with necessary forms of academic understanding, but even the best versions cannot substitute for first-hand experience in the outside world.

12. It was not long ago that I believed that parents were veering on the side of overprotection when they monitored and curtailed their child's every activity outside the home. I no longer believe this. Children these days indeed are threatened by the almost unimaginable savagery of some members of our society. Our great misfortune is that parental watchfulness which in normal times—and when gauged by the true developmental needs of children—would be considered overprotective has become essential in order to safeguard children against the undeniable dangers that they face in today's society.

13. I am grateful to my colleague Tom James for informing me of these groups.

14. Etzioni, *The Spirit of Community*, p. 31.

15. Ibid., p. 35.

16. Old-fashioned but, I am grateful to see, not entirely forgotten. In an excellent practical handbook for educators entitled *Reclaiming Our Schools* (New York: Merrill, 1993), Edward A. Wynne and Kevin Ryan propose "diligence" as an "alternative to self-esteem" (p. 105).

17. See also A. Colby and W. Damon (1992), *Some Do Care: Contemporary Lives of Moral Commitment* (New York: Free Press).

18. See ibid., esp. Chapters 7 and 10.

Index